# THE LEAN THINKING HOUSE

Sustainable shortest lead time, best quality and value (to people and society), most customer delight, lowest cost, high morale, safety

### Respect for People

- don't trouble your 'customer'

- "develop people, then build products"

- no wasteful work

- teams & individuals evolve their own practices and improvements

- build partners with stable relationships, trust, and coaching in lean thinking

- develop teams

### Product Development
- long-term great engineers
- mentoring from manager-engineer-teacher
- cadence
- cross-functional
- team room + visual mgmt
- entrepreneurial chief engineer/product mgr
- set-based concurrent dev
- create more knowledge

### 14 Principles
long-term, flow, pull, less variability & overburden, Stop & Fix, master norms, simple visual mgmt, good tech, leader-teachers from within, develop exceptional people, help partners be lean, Go See, consensus, reflection & kaizen

### Continuous Improvement
- Go See

- kaizen
  - spread knowledge
  - small, relentless
  - retrospectives
  - 5 Whys
  - eyes for waste
  * variability, over-burden, NVA ... (handoff, WIP, info scatter, delay, multi-tasking, defects, wishful thinking..)

- perfection challenge

- work toward flow (lower batch size, Q size, cycle time)

Management applies and teaches lean thinking, and bases decisions on this long-term philosophy

# Experiments

## Systems Thinking

- Try...Causal loop sketching workshop to see system dynamics 16
- Try...Sketch causal loop diagrams at whiteboards with others 16
- Try...See the positive feedback loops in your system 23
- Try...See mental models and assumptions during a causal modeling workshop 25
- Try...See root causes during causal modeling and retrospective workshops, with 5 Whys and Ishikawa diagrams 29
- Try...See and hear local optimizations; these are endemic in large product groups 32

## Lean Thinking

- Avoid...Lean misconceptions 40
- Avoid...Thinking that queue management, kanban, and other tools are pillars of lean 41
- Try...Reflect on the two pillars of lean: respect for people and continuous improvement 43
- Try...Know system goals in lean thinking 46
- Try...Foundation of lean thinking manager-teachers 48
- Try...Continuous improvement with Go See, kaizen, perfection challenge, and working towards flow 52
- Try...Spread knowledge rather than force conformance to central processes 54
- Try...Study the lean meaning of value and waste; learn to see them 58
- Try...Improve by removing waste 59
- Try...Learn, see, and eliminate NVA actions including handoff, overproduction, and waiting 60
- Try...Reduce the three sources of waste: variability, overburden, NVA actions 62
- Try...Apply the 14 principles, including exceptional people, stop and fix, leveling, and pull 65
- Try...Visual management 71
- Try...Outlearn the competition 73
- Try...Long-term hands-on engineers 74
- Try...Increase the value and lower the cost of information 74
- Try...Cadence (such as timeboxing) in lean development 78
- Try...Re-use more information and knowledge through mentoring, design patterns, wikis, ... 80
- Try...Team rooms for lean development 80
- Try...Chief engineer with business acumen as chief product manager 81
- Try...Set-based concurrent engineering—several alternate designs in parallel 82

## Queueing Theory

- Try...Compete on shorter cycle times 94
- Try...Use several high-level cycle-time KPIs 95
- Try...Eradicate queues by changing the system 98
- Avoid...Fake queue reduction by increased multitasking or utilization rates 99
- Try...Small batches of equal size 100
- Try...Visual management to see the invisible queues 111
- Try...Reduce the variability in Scrum 117
- Try...Limit size of the clear-fine subset of the Release Backlog 120

## False Dichotomies

- Try...Adjust method weight empirically in Scrum 126
- Try...Identify and avoid false dichotomies 129
- Avoid...Extreme Relativism 131
- Try...Identify misconceptions and misreads 132

## *Be* Agile

- Try...*Be* agile 139
- Try...Learn and applying the four values and twelve agile principles for competitive advantage 141
- Try...Know and share the five Scrum values 141
- Try...Learn and applying nine agile management principles 144

## Feature Teams

- Avoid...Single-function teams 155
- Avoid...Component teams 155
- Try...Feature teams 174

## Teams

- Try...Self-organizing teams 194
- Avoid...Manager not taking responsibility for creating the conditions needed for teams to self-organize 194
- Try...Set challenging but realistic goals 195
- Try...Cross-functional teams 196
- Avoid...Single-function specialist teams 196
- Avoid...IBM 198
- Try...Long-lived teams 199
- Try...Team owns the process 200
- Try...Team manages external dependencies 202
- Try...Dedicated team members 204
- Try...Multi-skilled workers 204

## Large-Scale Scrum

## Scrum Primer

# Scaling Lean & Agile Development

# Scaling Lean & Agile Development

*Thinking and Organizational Tools
for Large-Scale Scrum*

Craig Larman
Bas Vodde

**♦♦Addison-Wesley**

Upper Saddle River, NJ • Boston • Indianapolis • San Francisco
New York • Toronto • Montreal • London • Munich • Paris • Madrid
Capetown • Sydney • Tokyo • Singapore • Mexico City

*Library of Congress Cataloging-in-Publication Data*

Larman, Craig.
  Scaling lean & agile development : thinking and organizational tools for large-scale Scrum / Craig Larman, Bas Vodde.
      p. cm.
  Includes bibliographical references and index.
  ISBN 978-0-321-48096-5 (pbk. : alk. paper) 1. Agile software development. 2. Scrum (Computer software development) I. Vodde, Bas. II. Title.

  QA76.76.D47L394 2008
  005.1—dc22

                                                                2008041701

ISBN-13: 978-0-321-48096-5
ISBN    0-321-48096-1
Text printed in the United States on recycled paper at Courier in Westford, Massachusetts.
Fourth printing, January 2012

*To our clients, and my friend and co-author Bas*


*To* 孙媛

# CONTENTS

# PREFACE

Thank you for reading this book! We've tried to make it useful. Some related articles and pointers are at www.craiglarman.com and www.odd-e.com. Please contact us for questions.

## Typographic Conventions

Basic *point of emphasis* or *Book Title* or *minor new term*. A **noticeable point of emphasis**. A **major new term** in a sentence. [Bob67] is a reference in the bibliography.

## About the Authors

*Craig Larman* serves as chief scientist for Valtech, a consulting and outsourcing company with divisions in Europe, Asia, and North America. He spends most of his time working as a management and product-development consultant and coach within large or offshore groups adopting agile and lean product development, usually with an embedded systems focus. He led the agile offshore adoption (with Scrum) at Valtech India and served as creator and lead coach for the lean software development initiative at Xerox, in addition to consulting and coaching on large-scale agile and Scrum adoption for long periods at Nokia, Siemens, and NSN, among many other groups. Originally from Canada, he has lived off and on in India since 1978. Craig is the author of *Agile and Iterative Development: A Manager's Guide* and *Applying UML and Patterns: An Introduction to Object-Oriented Analysis and Design & Iterative Development*, the world's best-selling books on agile methods, OOA/D and iterative development. Along with Bas, he is also co-author of the companion book *Practices for Scaling Lean & Agile Development: Large, Multisite, and Offshore Product Development with Large-Scale Scrum*.

After a failed career as a wandering street musician, he built systems in APL and 4GLs in the 1970s. Starting in the early 1980s he became interested in artificial intelligence (having little of his own). Craig has a B.S. and M.S. in computer science from beautiful Simon Fraser University in Vancouver, Canada.

*Bas Vodde* works as an independent product-development consultant and large-scale Scrum coach. For several years he led the agile and Scrum enterprise-wide adoption initiative at Nokia Networks. He has been a member of the leadership team of a very large multisite product group (in Europe and China) adopting Scrum. Bas has worked as a senior developer/architect in embedded telecommunication systems, in addition to serving as a quality manager. He has led the development of solutions and the coaching for test-driven development in embedded systems. Along with Craig, Bas is co-author of the companion book *Practices for Scaling Lean & Agile Development*. Originally from Holland, he has lived in China for years and is now based in Singapore.

### Acknowledgments

Thanks to all our clients.

Thanks to reviewers or contributors, including Peter Alfvin, Alan Atlas, Gabrielle Benefield, Bjarte Bogsnes, Mike Bria, Larry Cai, Mike Cohn, Pete Deemer, Esther Derby, Jutta Eckstein, Kenji Hiranabe, Clinton Keith, Kuroiwa-san, Diana Larsen, Timo Leppänen, Eric Lindley, Mary Poppendieck, Tom Poppendieck, Ken Schwaber, Maarten Smeets, Jeff Sutherland, Dave Thomas, and Ville Valtonen.

Current and past Flexible company team members (and reviewers), including Kati Vilki, Petri Haapio, Lasse Koskela, Paul Nagy, Joonas Reynders, Gabor Gunyho, Sami Lilja, and Ari Tikka. Current and past IPA LT members (and reviewers), especially Tero Peltola and Lü Yi.

Bas appreciates his wife Sun Yuan for all the time he had to "focus on the books" rather than on each other, and for her support when moving or traveling to different countries to work with different product groups. And he thanks Craig for the stimulating discussions and the years working together with large products and with debugging organizations—and Bas's writing.

Craig thanks Albertina for her help so that he could write.

Thanks to Louisa Adair, Raina Chrobak, Chris Guzikowski, Julie Nahil, and Mary Lou Nohr for publication support.

## Chapter

## Book

# INTRODUCTION

*The future ain't what it used to be.*
*—Yogi Berra*

We sat down in the meeting room with our hot coffee. Outside was a bitter-cold north European winter morning. In came our new client and we shook hands. "Thanks for visiting," he said. "First, you should know that our product group is not large, maybe only eighty developers."

We once met a group adopting agile development that was not sure if they could grow to *very* large-scale development: 12 people.

People have different scales in mind regarding 'large.' To some it means only 50 people or even less. To others, much more. We define a large product[1] group as *one whose members' names you could not remember if you were all together in a room.* We work typically with single-product groups in the range of 100–500 people that are adopting Scrum, lean principles, and agile development practices, usually on software-intensive embedded systems. So by this definition—at least with our limited memories—this is the realm of 'large.'

*On to our key recommendation*: After working for some years in the domains of *large*, *multisite*, and *offshore* development, we have distilled our experience and advice down to the following: *Don't do it.*

There are better ways to build large systems than with many developers in many places. Rather, build a small group of great developers and other talents that can work together in teams, pay them well, and keep them together in one place with product management or whoever acts as the voice of the customer.

---

1. Scrum (and this book) applies both to product development for an external market, and to internal applications (internal products).

But of course you are *still* going to do large, multisite, or offshore development. This is because your existing system is already structured that way, or because—in the case of large groups—there is the mindset that "big systems need lots of people." We regularly coach groups that ask, "How can we calculate how many people we will need?" Our suggestion is, "Start with a small group of great people, and only grow when it really starts to hurt." That rarely happens.

Since large, multisite, and offshore development is going to happen, we would like to share what we have tried or seen at the intersection of these domains with lean and agile product development principles and practices.[2]

## THINKING AND ORGANIZATIONAL TOOLS

When Bas was a member of the leadership team of a large product group, he frequently (in meetings) asked, "Why do we have this policy? ... What will happen to the organizational system if we do that?" Months later a member of the team told Craig, "It drove me nuts to keep hearing those questions. But later, I appreciated it." Bas wasn't trying to be annoying; he was trying to suggest and encourage *systems thinking*—a thinking tool (1) to consider the deeper dynamics of the development system as a whole, (2) to understand how a system became the way it is, and (3) to reconsider assumptions underlying the existing organization.

When people are introduced to Scrum with its short timeboxed development iterations, they first see it as a localized practice to incrementally grow a product in small manageable steps, with learning and corrective actions toward a goal. Consequently, people will say, "Oh, 'agile' doesn't affect me; that's a *development* practice." But there is a bigger picture and a potential higher-level learning

---

2. The companion book is *Practices for Scaling Lean & Agile Development: Large, Multisite, and Offshore Product Development with Large-Scale Scrum*. It covers detailed practice tips related to scaling and planning, product management, multisite, offshore development, contracts, requirements, design and architecture, coordination, legacy code, testing, and more.

loop beyond the lower-level development learning cycle: a learning organization of people that repeatedly re-examine the structures and policies that define and surround agile product development. The result of adopting Scrum or lean principles in very large product groups inevitably leads to this higher-level organizational learning challenge.

**Example**: Consider an enterprise whose R&D division tries to be more adaptive by adopting Scrum. The Sales division continues in their old mode: Maximize personal commissions and quarterly sales by promising the moon and the stars to customers, combined with almost boundless optimism for what "our great people in R&D can do." Faced with unattainable 'commitments' R&D did not them-selves design or make, R&D is then blamed for not meeting "*our* promises," and it is concluded that "Scrum doesn't really help."

If this were a book about adopting Scrum only in one small 20-per-son single-product group within a large enterprise, systems thinking and organizational tools would be interesting but non-vital topics. But they are vital to a successful adoption when Scrum is being scaled to a 400-person single-product group, probably within a larger R&D organization in the thousands that is also making the transition, with deep connections to the Sales and Delivery groups, and constrained by traditional Human Resource and Enterprise Governance policies on team structures, reporting, measurement, milestones, contracts, and rewards.

Consequently, this book suggests that one cornerstone for large-scale Scrum and agile development is people who learn and apply various *thinking tools*, including (but not limited to) systems think-ing, mental-model awareness, lean thinking, queueing theory, and recognition of false dichotomies.[3]

With those thinking tools in place, it will become increasingly clear that the existing organizational design inhibits flow of value, lead-ing to pressure for redesign. Hence, this book suggests a second cor-nerstone of *organizational tools*, including feature teams,

---

3. The term *thinking tools* was popularized in [Reinertsen97].

requirement areas, and many other changes in structure, process, task, people, and rewards.

## ACTION TOOLS

In parallel with adopting thinking and organizational tools, many *action tools*—specific development practices—help the product group get going on large, multisite, and offshore agile development. The *effective* use of these action tools—shared in the companion *Practices* book—is somewhat dependent on organization redesign. Many practices can be tried without deeper structural change, but constraints on benefit will be felt.

So the tools in this book could be seen as prerequisites for the actions tools of the companion book. Yet in reality, *practices* will be adopted first—because that is where people want to start. And that will eventually invite a look back at thinking and organizational tools.

We suggest that coaches and other change agents involved in the adoption of large-scale Scrum or lean development acquaint themselves early with thinking and organizational tools, while in parallel helping to introduce action tools. At some point the situation will be ripe—people will be ready—for a turn in the discussion from *"How do we do large-scale continuous integration?"* to *"Do existing HR policies prevent real teams?"* and *"What is flow of value and what inhibits it in our organizational design?"*

## EXPERIMENTS: TRY... AND AVOID...

Scrum emphasizes empirical process control; there is too much complexity and variability for a cookbook approach to processes for development. Therefore, the tools in both books are presented as a series of *tips* that start with *Try...* or *Avoid...* to suggest experiments, nothing more. They certainly may not work in your circumstance. The approach both in Scrum and in the lean thinking practice of *kaizen* is to first *inspect* and grasp the existing situation. Then, second, to *adapt* with new improvement experiments. The attitude of endless experimentation is vigorously encouraged in lean thinking; perhaps the only bad process-improvement experiment is the one not tried. At Toyota, Taiichi Ohno—arguably the key contributor to lean thinking—would visit an area and inspect any written standards document. If it was covered with dust or otherwise not recently changed, he would grow quite impassioned and urge people to always evolve their 'standards.'

In Scrum this inspect-and-adapt (experiment) cycle repeats every two- or four-week timeboxed iteration as long as the product exists. And in lean thinking, this continuous experimentation and improvement cycle applies both to individual products and *to the enterprise as a whole*.

## LIMITATIONS

There is still much for us to learn about these domains. What we have written here and in the companion book reflects our current (limited) experience and understanding, which we hope will evolve in the coming years. For example, although we have lived for some years in China and India, we feel we have barely scratched the surface in terms of our multicultural experience and insight in relation to offshore and multisite agile development. Nevertheless, our sincere wish is that these tips are of some value to you. We welcome further insights and stories from our readers.

Large-scale Scrum can influence almost all aspects of a product-centric enterprise. To keep the scope of this material manageable and because of our limited experience in some of these areas, we bounded or deferred subjects that are worthy of more discussion. These include:

- budgeting and finance
- sales
- marketing
- hardware development
- product development not involving any software
- deployment/delivery
- field support

Essentially, this book is relevant to general-purpose product development. Scrum and lean product development are not limited to software systems [NT86]. However, the bias is toward software-intensive systems (usually embedded) because of our background and because of the ever-growing ubiquity of software in everyday devices, from washing machines to shoes.

Especially in this book we dissect some assumptions and policies in traditional organizations that inhibit *flow of value* and *effective teams*. This analysis may come across as startling or challenging at times. We do not mean to give offense, but organizational redesign to support lean and agile development will not happen without increased scrutiny of traditional assumptions and increased transparency. Organizational change can also lead to displacement of talented people from old roles. As in Toyota, we encourage finding new areas of contribution for people within a company—both because skilled people deserve this, and because otherwise it inhibits change.

With both books combined pushing over 700 pages, we regret that we could not write or think better to make the subject of *large*...smaller.

On to thinking tools...

# Thinking Tools

## Chapter

## Book

# SYSTEMS THINKING

*I took a speed reading course and read "War and Peace"*
*in twenty minutes. It involves Russia.*
*—Woody Allen*

"No matter what we do, the number of defects in our backlog remains about the same," a manager told us; this for a 15 MSLOC C and C++ product with several hundred developers where we were working (and adopting lean principles). What's going on? Systems thinking may help. In small groups the forces at play are more quickly seen and informally understood, but in large product development—or any large system—it's tough. Gerry Weinberg highlights two decisive factors in this situation:

*Weinberg-Brooks' Law: More software projects have gone awry from management's taking action based on **incorrect system models** than for all other causes combined.*

*Causation Fallacy: Every effect has a cause... and we can tell which is which. [Weinberg92]*

These reflect the impact of our **mental models** on the system, a subject that will be revisited later in the chapter.

Problems stemming from mental models and assumptions are one issue. Another is that large-scale adoption of Scrum, lean thinking, and agile principles is not isolated to the development group. It bumps into product management, budgeting, beta-testing, launch, and governance and HR policies. Accordingly, in large-scale agile adoption it is useful to be able to get together with colleagues and *effectively reason* about the mental models, causal relations, feedback loops, and control mechanisms (or illusions of control) in a big system that is about to be seriously *perturbed*. Systems thinking is one of those reasoning tools.

## It Depends on Common Sense?

*"It depends on common sense."*—A statement sometimes heard in Scrum and common parlance. But what is this? Einstein quipped, *"Common sense is the collection of prejudices acquired by the age eighteen."*

Taiichi Ohno, the father of the Toyota Production System, said, *"[…] misconceptions easily turn into common sense. When that happens, the debate can become endless. Or, each side tried to be more outspoken than the other and things do not move ahead at all. That is why there was a time when I was constantly telling people to take a step outside of common sense and think by 'going beyond common sense.' Within common sense, there are things that we think are correct because of our misconceptions. Also, perhaps a big reason we do some of the general common sense things we do is that based on long years of experience, we see there are no big advantages to doing things a certain way but neither are there many disadvantages to it. … we are all human so we're like walking misconceptions believing that the way we do things now is the best way. Or perhaps you do not think it is the best way, but you are working within the common sense that 'We can't help it, this is how things are'"* [Ohno07].

**"Common sense" is not so reliable when trying to understanding nonlinear systems—such as large-scale product development.**

In 1958, the *Harvard Business Review* published "Industrial Dynamics: A Major Breakthrough for Decision Makers," a landmark paper by Jay Forrester, MIT Sloan School professor [Forrester58]. This paper spurred the movement of systems thinking in business education, and the MIT Sloan School of Management became known for educating people in **system dynamics**. System dynamics is sometimes treated as a synonym for **systems thinking**, though the latter is a more general term.

MIT also attracted other system-dynamics-oriented researchers such as Peter Senge.[1]

---

1. Senge wrote *The Fifth Discipline*, on systems thinking and learning organizations, named "one of the seminal management books of the last 75 years" by the *Harvard Business Review*. See [Senge94].

Consistent with *Weinberg-Brook's Law,* Forrester's research showed that decision makers who were given dynamic models of a business system and asked to improve their output performance, *usually made them run worse* [SKRRS94]. The observation was that most people have weak judgement on how to fundamentally improve systems, usually applying incorrect "common sense" and quick-fix 'solutions' that do not create long-lasting systemic improvement.

Why is the behavior of a large development group (a system) not understood or guided skillfully? The answer lies, in part, in the behavior of stochastic systems with queues and variability, as explored in the *Queueing Theory* chapter. And the same answer lies in *control theory*: Most systems of interest—such as a product development group—have complex positive and negative feedback loops and nonlinear behavior. The behavior of these systems defies our gut instinct. And then there is the minor issue of *people.*

In summary, reasons for not being skillful in fathoming or guiding a big system include (but are not limited to):

❑ lack of knowledge about the system dynamics, feedback loops, nonlinear systems behavior, and unintended consequences in workplace systems

❑ not understanding root causes of problems (and how to find)

- *causes,* not cause; in systems thinking one sees that there are multiple, indirect, and dynamic causes to problems

❑ not knowing if or why quick-fix or local-department decisions degraded overall delivery performance.

In short, not being systems thinkers.[2]

These reasons are consequential at the intersection of management and large-scale adoption of lean and agile principles. The leadership team is part of the system being perturbed; if they do not apply systems thinking, they could *really* perturb it—and not in a good way.

---

2. Another reason: Believing more control is possible than actually is. Complexity science suggests fundamental limits on predicting and controlling semi-chaotic social systems [Stacey07]. This is a rather large can of worms that will remain unopened in this book.

As a summary of systems thinking insight, we like the 'laws' described in *The Fifth Discipline*:

- Today's problems come from yesterday's 'solutions.'
- The harder you push, the harder the system pushes back.
- Behavior will grow worse before it grows better.
- The easy way out usually leads back in.
- The cure can be worse than the disease.
- Faster is slower.

- Cause and effect are not closely related in time and space.
- Small changes can produce big results...but the areas of highest leverage are often the least obvious.
- You can have your cake and eat it too—but not all at once.
- Dividing an elephant in half does not produce two small elephants.
- There is no blame.

Toyota's internal motto is "Good thinking, good products." Systems thinking is a set of *thinking* tools to help...

- ❏ **see system dynamics**—a development organization is a system of people and policies with subtle feedback loops and unintended consequences

  – we can learn to see and thus improve the system with **causal loop diagrams** created in a workshop

- ❏ **see mental models**—one reason behind suboptimal decisions is mistaken assumptions and faulty reasoning

  – causal loop diagramming and Five Whys expose these

- ❏ **see root causes**—real improvement requires learning how to find root causes of problems and see deeper relationships

  – causal loop diagrams, 5 Whys, and Ishikawa diagrams reveal these

- ❏ **see local optimization**—another source of suboptimal decisions is **local optimization**, making the 'best' decision from the viewpoint of a person or department, rather than **global optimization** for the lean systems-level goal of *deliver value fast with high quality and high morale*.

This chapter is organized around the following areas in systems thinking: Learning to see (1) *system dynamics*, (2) *mental models*, (3) *root causes*, and (4) *local optimization*.

## SEEING SYSTEM DYNAMICS

### Static versus Dynamic Complexity

Many of us, especially in engineering and finance, are educated to master **complexity of static details**—learning to analyze and manage information (requirements, financial analysis, ...), decompose complex structures into simpler ones, and so forth. That is, complexity of a static, information, or structural nature.

Why do big software systems tend to degrade, with more and more time spent on defects? What might happen if the USA invades Iraq? Seeing the dynamics behind these questions involves analysis of the **complexity of dynamics**.

In contrast to static-details education, many of us receive no *formal* education in analyzing *dynamics* complexity[3], especially workplace dynamics. Perhaps there is a belief it is sufficient to rely on common sense in the workplace. Forrester demonstrated that "common sense" is just not so in complex systems, and showed it is possible to formally educate people to become better system dynamics thinkers in the workplace using *dynamic system models* visualized in *flow diagrams* [Forrester61].

Flow diagrams encompass material, financial, and information flows, stocks (variables with a quantity, such as cash or number of defects), the impact of decisions and policies, and cause-effect relations. A popular simplification is the **causal loop diagram** that focuses on cause-effect relationships and feedback loops in a system [Sterman00]. There are a variety of similar notations; they all show stocks (variables), causal links, and delay. In [Weinberg92] this is called the *diagram of effect*.

---

3.  Macroeconomics, psychology, sociology, and biology are exceptions, among many others.

### The First Law of Diagramming: Model to Have a Conversation

A tool to learn to see system dynamics is a causal loop diagram, ideally sketched on a whiteboard in a Sprint Retrospective with colleagues. Before going further, here is the *First Law of Diagramming*

> *The primary value in diagrams is in the discussion while diagramming—we model to have a conversation.*

When a group gets together to sketch a causal loop diagram on a whiteboard (Figure 2.1), the primary value is the conversation and shared understanding they arrive at while creating the model. Its visualization as an easy-to-see diagram *is* important to make concrete and unambiguous (on the whiteboard) the ideas—the mental models people have—because words alone can be fuzzy and misunderstood. But still, the diagram is secondary to what people take away: learning and a revised understanding through a discussion.

Figure 2.1  it is the the acts of discussing and thinking that are most important when diagramming, Valtech India

### Basic Problems and Simple Enjoyable Tools

Over the years, we have learned sophisticated analysis and design skills and heuristics for engineering, management, and more. At first we were inspired and excited to apply and share all these, until we realized in the course of real-world work...

*The vast majority of problems in business (including develop-
ment) are so basic that a key solution is education in and consistent use of **simple, enjoyable** thinking and action tools.[4]*

**Simple**—For example, system dynamics and causal loop modeling
books and courses can get overly complicated, with unnecessary
overhead such as the *archetypes* idea described in the *Fifth Discipline*, computer simulation, nonlinear equations, and so forth. In
practice, this serves to intimidate ordinary people from experimenting with—and sticking with—what in essence can be applied as a
simple tool: standing around a whiteboard to sketch, discuss, and
model basic cause-effect dynamics in business.

When considering any thinking or action tools for the workplace
reality, know that

> *Le mieux est l'ennemi du bien. (The best is the enemy of the
> good.)—François-Marie Arouet (Voltaire)*

**Enjoyable**—There are many intricate thinking or action tools that
professors or methodologists bemoan are not used—or at least not
sustainably used. Why, on the other hand, are the practices in
Scrum or Extreme Programming (XP) often adopted and *remain
sticky* in practice? First, there is quick value to the hands-on worker
participants—the cost/benefit ratio is attractive and pays fast. Second, they are not painful; some will even say they are interesting or
enjoyable. It is not uncommon for people in a system dynamics
sketching workshop to say it was interesting (and useful). Humans
are humans; enjoyable practices are important for sustainable use.

 Emphasis on such tools is especially important
when scaling to large product development,
because the ability to *push* practices and processes grows very weak as group size increases.
As a bee is attracted to colorful fragrant flowers,
you want to *attract* people to simple, enjoyable
tools, including...

---

4. 'Basic' does not mean trivial or easy to solve. For example, 'motivation' and 'quality' are basic but not easy issues.

## Causal Loop Diagrams

Causal loop diagrams are presented several times in this book, to help see the dynamics of what is going on in large-scale development. It is useful to understand them for that reason alone. And more useful to you, we recommend:

### Try…Sketch causal loop diagrams at whiteboards with others

The practical aspect of this tip is more important than may first be appreciated. It is vague and low-impact to suggest "be a systems thinker." But if you and four colleagues get into the habit of standing together at a large whiteboard, sketching causal loop diagrams together, then there is a concrete and potentially high-impact practice that connects *"be* a systems thinker" with *"do* systems thinking."

The following examples seem sterile when presented in a book. But imagine you were at a whiteboard with other people and the diagrams were being sketched during a lively conversation. That's the way we suggest 'doing' systems thinking.

*Concrete modeling tip*: We start by writing on sticky notes to define *variables*. A note might read "feature velocity" or "# defects." We place these on a whiteboard. Then we sketch causal link lines between the sticky notes. There will be (or should be) lots of rewriting, erasing, and redrawing during the modeling session. The most meaningful outcome is *understanding*; in addition, some participants will want to take a digital photo of the whiteboard sketch.

### Notation and Examples

Causal loop diagrams contain many elements; the following common useful subset is explored through a scenario.

- variables
- causal links
- opposite effects
- constraints
- goals

- reactions; quick-fix reactions
- interaction effects
- extreme effects
- delays
- positive feedback loops

*The following simplified scenario is for a particular organization. It is not a generalization.*

**Variables**—Causal loop diagrams include *variables* (or stocks) such as the *velocity (rate of delivery) of software features* and *number of defects*. Variables have a measurable quantity.

**Causal links**—An element can have an effect on another, such as if feature velocity increases, then the number of defects increase; that is, more new code, more defects.

feature
velocity

# defects

Now it is time to bump into *Weinberg-Brook's Law* and the *Causation Fallacy*. It is easy to sketch a diagram; it is something else to model with insight. For example, consider the relationship between the *number of developers* and *feature velocity*.

The nature of any cause-effect relationship is actually not obvious, though it is common for people to jump to conclusions such as more developers means better velocity. Adding people late in development may *reduce* velocity (a sub-element of "Brooks' Law" [Brooks95]). Or, *more* bad programmers could really slow you down. An argument can be made that *removing* terrible developers can *improve* velocity.

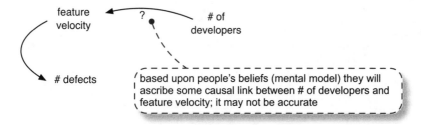

**Opposite effects**—A causal link effect may be the same or opposite direction; if A goes up then B goes up, or vice versa. Opposite effect is shown with an 'O' on the line. Suppose defects going up puts a drag on the system, lowering the velocity of new features because people spend more time fixing or working around bugs.

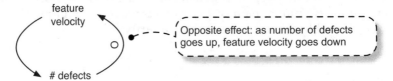

**Constraints**—Unless you can find people to work for free, there is a constraint on the number of developers, based upon cash supply.

Constraints are *not* causal links. As cash supply goes up, it is not the case that the number of developers goes up.

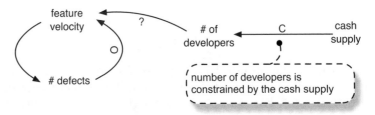

**Goals and Reactions**—People, departments, and systems have goals, such as *higher feature velocity*. Goals often generate pressure for people to react (or act), with the intent of achieving the goal. But since there is *Causation Fallacy* and *Weinberg-Brooks' Law* to contend with, people should be cautious about assuming what actions will help. Now a goal and pressure for reaction is shown:

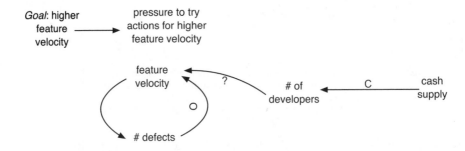

Not only does a goal with a *reward* create pressure to act, but also it creates pressure to *appear* to be acting and achieving, due to the **measurement dysfunction** generated by rewards. And the measurement dysfunction can be proportional to the perceived value of the reward because people are being motivated to get a reward, not to improve the system [Austin96]. Notice how rewards can actually degrade system performance. Visually, the system dynamics may be...

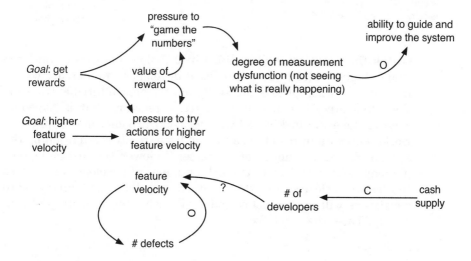

It is quite interesting that all these dynamics have been added by introduction of reward, and yet there is no necessary connection between the top part of this model and the bottom.

There is no guarantee that feature velocity has improved—or even been worked on.

Removing the reward system is a root-cause solution to the dysfunction. Another (lesser) surface countermeasure is the lean *Go See* principle and management behavior: *Go See p. 52*

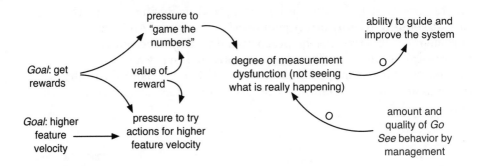

**Quick-fix reactions**—One difficult and slow solution toward the goal of higher velocity is to hire great developers, to increase coaching and education of existing staff, and to remove terrible workers. The alternative is called a *quick fix*, a reaction that is hoped to achieve the goal quickly and with less effort. Sometimes a quick fix works well both in the short and long term, really strengthening the system. Sometimes not...hence, "faster is slower." For example, people may *believe* that increasing the number of developers increases the feature velocity. And they may thereby hope that hiring more developers will most quickly and easily solve the velocity problem. 'QF' indicates the quick fix:

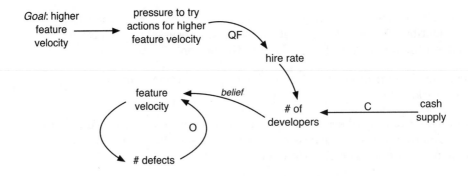

**Interaction effects**—There is the constraint of cash supply on hiring. One hard and slow solution is to get more cash. A quicker fix is to hire *much* cheaper developers. In this case, the level of cash supply now has an *interaction effect* with other causal links. Low cash tends to strengthen the hire rate of much cheaper developers when there is pressure to increase hire rates.

One could simply draw an (opposite) causal link directly from *cash supply* to *hire rate of very cheap developers*, but that merely says that less cash leads to more hiring of extremely cheap developers. That is not quite what we want to say; rather, we want to show the interaction effect—that effect A influences *effect* B. This is done by showing a causal link entering another causal link. For example, from *cash supply* to the quick-fix line going into *hire rate of very cheap developers*:

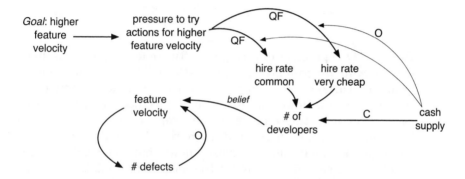

**Extreme effects**—We have worked with some very inexpensive developers with excellent skill and some very expensive developers that are terrible, but on average, you get what you pay for—when you hire from a large pool of very cheap labor, the average skill level is lower. In the model we want to show that the impact of hiring very cheap labor on the *number of low-skilled developers* is a significantly greater effect than average.

To show an *extreme effect* in the model, use a thick line:

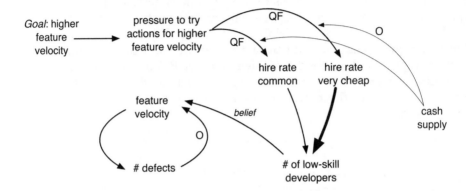

**Delays**—One problem in hiring in software development is the *fallacy of mild programmer variance*—the mistaken belief that programmer variance (in terms of productivity, code quality, etc.) is relatively small. However, programmer variance studies suggest an average of four times faster in the top versus bottom quartile [Prechelt00]. Rather significant. Also, the COCOMO model—based on large and longitudinal studies—shows that the capability of the development personnel is by far the most important factor for productivity [Boehm00]. And, on average, very weak programmers create poor-quality code (poor design) and more defects, creating another drag on the system.

But the impacts of these effects are not immediately obvious. For example, it takes a relatively long time after hiring a large pool of weak programmers before the impacts of more and more bad code/design start to be felt. Similarly, the average *decrease* in feature velocity (because of the powerful impact of programmer variance) will not show up immediately.

To show these *delayed effects* in the model, use a double-line through the effect line:

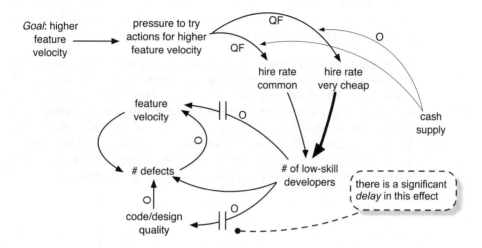

Delay has an intriguing influence on the *educational* or corrective power in a system. If an impact or unintended consequence is long delayed, one does not feel the effect (pain or gain) and so does not clearly see how A influenced B, or more subtly how *A influenced B influenced A*.

Therefore, one does not learn from or correct mistakes—in policy, management actions, tools, and so forth. Likewise, gradual improvement through the lean thinking practice of *kaizen* can take a long time; patience and insight are needed to see if and how things improve.

*kaizen p. 53*

**Positive feedback loops**—Negative or positive feedback loops[5] and delays are where things start to get more subtle in a system— and in understanding a system. For example, how does one become a better programmer? In part, by mentoring from great programmers and seeing lots of examples of great code. But an office with a lot of low-skill developers does not generate a lot of great code examples,

*Try...See the positive feedback loops in your system*

---

5. *Feedback loops* is occasionally used in this book in the colloquial sense of feedback, rather than this system dynamics sense.

nor does it attract or retain the small pool of great programmers who could act as mentors. They would rather work somewhere else.

Now the development group starts to enter a self-reinforcing downward spiral—a set of *positive feedback loops*. Fortunately, the downward trend is constrained by the supply of cash.

More great programmers—who could craft great code and mentor others—leave. So there is less and less quality code to look at and to learn from. The percentage of weak programmers grows even larger and feature velocity drops further. Code becomes more messy, awkward, and duplication-riddled, so the capacity to swiftly implement features declines. Since feature velocity is dropping further, there is more pressure to hire yet more very cheap programmers. All this leads to multiple positive reinforcement loops in the system, for example:

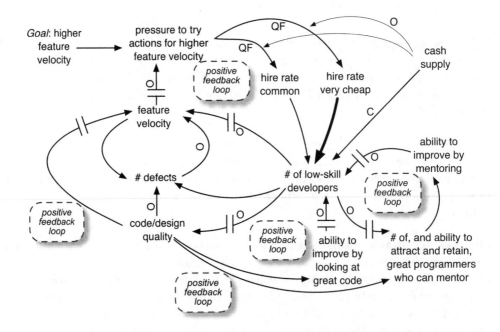

*Tip*: You can find positive feedback loops by finding cycles with an *even number* of 'Opposite' effect relationships. There are several examples in the model above.

### Conclusion

The example scenario is only that—an example. A causal loop diagram can visualize rich dynamics in a workplace system. These are best created by a group at a whiteboard.

## SEEING MENTAL MODELS

*Try…See mental models and assumptions during a causal modeling workshop*

The previous causal loop diagrams reflect people's mental models of causation, which may be wrong. It is interesting to note that people's models of causation are influenced by the timeliness (delay) and quality of feedback in the system.

The implication of "mental models" is to improve our meta-cognitive skill to see and question our own assumptions and chains of reasoning. Are we making faulty leaps of logic? It also implies when working with others to discuss (inquiring rather than abusing) the mental models of our colleagues.

*Seeing* these mental models is step one; *changing* them is the even harder part of step two. That art is beyond the scope of this introduction, though large-scale successful agile adoption must involve changes in mindset and insight among many groups.

A tip to better *see* the mental models (beliefs, chains of inference, …) playing out in the system dynamics is to ask the following question during a modeling workshop and then sketch the answers. "Let's talk about the assumptions behind this model. What do we *believe* or assume in terms of facts and effects that led us here?"

Answers are sketched on the whiteboard model, for example:

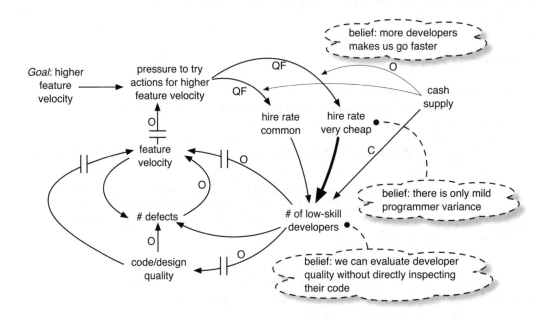

## Example: The "Faster is Slower" Dynamic

With the vocabulary of quick fixes, delays, positive feedback loops, and mental models, it is fascinating to see that there can be a short-term apparent improvement in a variable as the result of a quick fix, but a *delayed degradation* of the very same variable—the "faster is slower" dynamic. This is a recurrent dynamic in the workplace and a cause of weakness. So it is worth another illustration.

*The story of Microsoft Word and the **secret developer toolbox***: A classic example of the short-term 'improving' but long-term degrading dynamic is the story of the first release of Microsoft Word for Windows [Spolsky04]. It was released *years* later than desired. Why? *Because managers tried to follow the original schedule and pushed developers to meet it.*

The story illustrates why *wishful thinking* is identified as one of the wastes in lean thinking. In this case the wishful thinking of insisting on (apparently) following a schedule, which implies the misconception or wishful thinking that development estimates are not estimates but are commitments—a common myth that propels degradation of a system.

*lean wastes p. 58*

*misconception that estimates are commitments p. 134*

Figure 2.2 illustrates a *summary* of the dynamics of what happened when the managers pushed people to evidently keep to the original schedule, and why this quick-fix reaction to slow progress appeared to make things faster in the short term but actually even *slower* in the long term. Figure 2.2 intentionally omits some deeper dynamics that are expanded and shown in Figure 2.3.

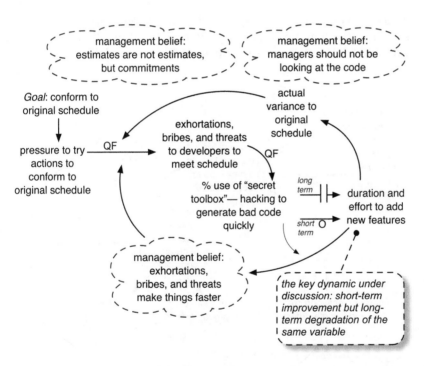

Figure 2.2 the dynamic of schedule pressure and the *secret toolbox*

As a quick fix, the Microsoft managers exhorted, bribed (with potential rewards), and threatened the Word developers to keep to the original schedule. Consequently, the developers predictably pulled out their **secret developer toolbox**—the many practices related to hacking out dirty code (no tests, no reviews, ignore known defects, copy-paste programming, poor design, ...) to apparently deliver a feature faster. You see, developers also have *quick-fix* reactions for their problems.

The tactics seemed to have worked like magic. As the managers pressured the developers, 'features' were delivered quicker as people used the secret toolbox, which reinforced the belief that pressuring developers helps. But this apparent acceleration actually had a delayed effect to make things slower, which is explored next. Since management did not quickly see the delayed effect of the secret toolbox, and because they believed managers should not be frequently looking in detail at the source code or themselves be master programmers, they did not learn from this dynamic.

A closer exploration of the system dynamics shows why things went slower in the long term and why the first Word for Windows release was years later than desired, illustrated in the model in Figure 2.3.

Figure 2.3 deeper dynamics of schedule pressure and the *secret toolbox*

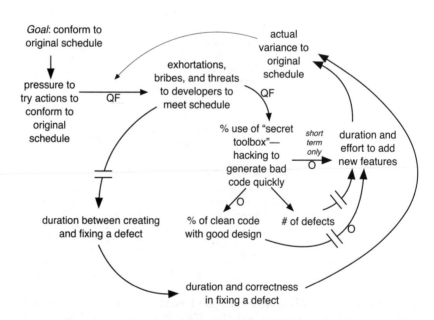

Naturally, lots of dirty code eventually slowed things down. More subtly, developers would *ignore* the bug list of ever-increasing open defects to—instead—generate new features. This led to a long delay between the creation of a defect and its correction. It turns out that this significantly increases variability and time to fix a defect because of the compounding negative effect of a long-lived bug (for example, due to workarounds and coupling) and because developers have long forgotten the detailed context of code related to the defect and therefore need to slowly rediscover that context—with more and more dirty confusing code surrounding them.

The astute reader may also notice the several positive feedback loops that reinforce the degradation cycle; this is one reason the product was years later than intended.

Solution? The lean thinking *stop and fix* and *Go See* principles. *First*, rather than trying to go faster when there are problems, manager-teachers encourage people to go *slower* and help them learn to see system dynamics and root causes, and to fix these—to improve the *system* of development. By going slower, Toyota—the masters of lean thinking—has become one of the fastest companies around. *Second*, for managers to *go see at the real place of work* to learn what is going on. The "real place" in software development is the code, which suggests that first-level managers are master programmers who are frequently evaluating the code.

*stop and fix p. 70*
*Go See p. 52*

Microsoft people did not reflect on the situation until after release. When they did finally hold a retrospective, it led to a company-wide *zero-defects* policy, meaning that the first priority was to fix known bugs in the code under development—to drive down to zero the open-defects list before writing more new-feature code.

## SEEING ROOT CAUSES

"We've been trying to adopt Scrum for the last year, but haven't seen much improvement. Why not?" Seeing root causes can help answer. Systems thinking calls upon all of us to develop thinking skills in seeing root causes and deeper forces. Unintended consequences and quick fixes can be symptoms of people not grasping the essence.

*Try...See root causes during causal modeling and retrospective workshops, with 5 Whys and Ishikawa diagrams*

Continuous improvement is one of the two pillars of lean thinking. Toyota has a "stop and fix" culture that involves:

1. people stopping when they see a problem to...

2. *do root cause analysis* to find the real issues and then...

3. introduce process-change experiments to fix and improve

Try simple tools to discuss and see root causes, such as

*Five Whys p. 57*

❑ **Five Whys**—introduced in the *Lean Thinking* chapter

❑ **Ishikawa (fishbone) diagrams**

Both are applied collaboratively in a team workshop—usually during the Scrum Retrospective.

Figure 2.4  5 Whys sketch during a Retrospective

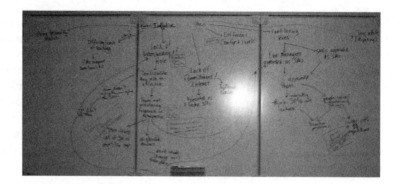

**Seeing Root Causes with Ishikawa Diagrams**

Five Whys is relatively unstructured; it can be combined with **Ishikawa diagrams** (fishbone diagrams) [Ishikawa86] to organize and relate the causes behind a problem, such as *ineffective ScrumMasters*. Step one is to brainstorm causes of the problem; we suggest *brainwriting*, in which each person writes ideas on pieces of paper, one per paper, and immediately shares them on a common table. Step two is *affinity clustering*, grouping the papers into families of related causes and giving a name to each group (Figure 2.5). Step three is to sketch the skeleton of an Ishikawa diagram with these group names as the 'bones' of the diagram. Step four is to apply 5 Whys for each group or noteworthy sub-elements under each group, to grasp and write down the deeper causes. The results are sketched onto the evolving diagram (Figure 2.6).

Figure 2.5 brainwriting and affinity clustering, Valtech India

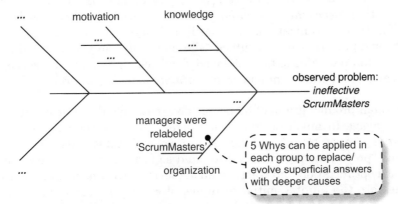

Figure 2.6 Ishikawa diagram, built from brainwriting and affinity clustering, and improved with 5 Whys

observed problem: *ineffective ScrumMasters*

motivation

knowledge

managers were relabeled 'ScrumMasters'

organization

5 Whys can be applied in each group to replace/ evolve superficial answers with deeper causes

Figure 2.7 using Ishikawa diagrams in a workshop for root cause analysis

### After Root Cause Analysis: Try a Corrective Experiment

Root-cause analysis is step two of three—it is not done just to have fun in a complaint session. Once the root causes are grasped, then the next major *action* step in the retrospective workshop is to generate an improvement experiment [Vodde07].

*Try...See and hear local optimizations; these are endemic in large product groups*

## SEEING (AND HEARING) LOCAL OPTIMIZATION

"Everyone is doing their best yet overall systems throughput is degrading. How can that be?" This is the paradox of **local optimization**—when a person or departmental decision maker optimizes for the local view or self-interest. The party making the decision frequently *believes they are making the best decision*, but because 'best' is a local optimization, in fact it sub-optimizes overall system throughput. This is a result of "silo mentality," misunderstanding, fear, limited information, delayed feedback, ignorance, careerism, avarice, and other common *organizational learning disorders*.

A small product group of 30 people does not have the time or money to engage in much nonsense or waste. But large companies, with large product groups, centralized process and tool groups, a centralized "project management office," and so forth, seem to have raised local optimization and waste to an art form. Government bureaucracies are the quintessential example, of course. As such, when you serve as a guide in large-scale agile adoption, *seeing* (or *hearing*) and dealing with local optimization is singularly vital.

For example, the legal and corporate security departments put in place a policy that seems terribly important from their perspective. In the aim of preventing loss of intellectual property (IP), the legal department decrees "no one shall put any information on the walls." Or, in response to cost-cutting pressure, the facilities management says, "It is important to ensure our walls are not dirty or damaged." And thus they shut down a practice in lean thinking, visual management (which is usually done on walls), and they inhibit a well-known innovation practice, group whiteboard work. The lawyers may succeed in reducing loss of IP (actually, that is questionable), and the facilities people will succeed in keeping the walls clean—at the cost of inhibiting the product development group from innovating and collaborating. Finally, the company falls behind with less and less IP even worth protecting because tools for innovation and delivering fast have been disallowed, but the lawyers have successfully fulfilled their mandate from the executive team to "ensure our IP is protected." And the *furniture police* have clear walls. *They have done their best.*

The following is a real e-mail quote from the furniture police in one organization that dissallowed visual management on the walls. Can you identify the local optimizations and mental models driving this?

> *Individual work cubic partition can be personalized. But things obvious higher than the partition or harming the office environment's harmony are restricted.*

We also see local optimization in centralized groups that make software tool choices for others. The common mindset is to choose a tool that is best at reducing some supposed cost (curiously, these groups seldom recommend free open source tools) or best at doing something complicated or best for the work of one specialized worker role (even though *everybody* has to use the tool), rather than maximizing the global goal of faster system throughput of value to customers.

Most examples of local optimization can be seen as variants of *following the runners rather than following the baton*.

watch the baton
p. 39

In large-scale adoption of Scrum or agile principles, most of the "Yes, but ..." issues that are raised are examples of local optimization, such as, *"Yes, but...what about management reporting?"* or more generally, *"Yes, but...what about <special case>?"* Then, policies and practices are twisted around, serving the goal of reporting or some other secondary aim rather than the primary goal of optimizing for fast value throughput. Sometimes we see *local optimization for the extreme or rare case.* For example, a person responsible for making a centralized tool choice for the enterprise presents a scenario for a complex or rare case of use, and then chooses the tool that fits that, sub-optimizing for a 5 percent case instead of optimizing for ease and speed for the 95 percent case.

Other local optimizations are due to ignorance of new ways of working. This is especially common in large-scale product groups. For example, we once helped a large networking product group in Europe adopt Scrum and the practice of *continuous integration* (CI) combined with a CI system that continually integrated, built, and automatically tested the product. After some time, an outside traditional manager inspected what was going on, and recommended the integration practices should be changed—because there was no written integration plan for how a human integration manager should manually integrate all the software, and of course, there was no integration manager. They wanted to 'optimize' around the work of an integration manager that was no longer needed. They could not see that their entire old-fashioned model of work had been eliminated with CI. This story repeats in all the departments of a large established product: local optimization around the *existing* ways of

*component teams*
*p. 155*

work, such as manual test, a separate architecture department, component teams, and so on. A coach working to introduce large-scale Scrum at the enterprise level has a *mountain* of similar local optimization thinking to deal with.

In lean thinking and agile methods, the focus is on global systems goals: Deliver value fast with high quality and morale—**global optimization**. Try to consider decisions in light of this goal. To develop an "optimize the whole" culture, challenge all decisions and policies with the question:

> *Does this decision or policy focus on delivering value to the external customer fast, or does it focus on the interests of a department, person, internal policy/practice, or rare case?*

In Scrum, the Product Owner is responsible for choosing high-value goals that could lead to potentially shippable product (at the end of the iteration) and that maximize return on investment and delight the customer, while maintaining a sustainable pace and high engineering quality. That explicit Scrum goal is meant to orient the system toward global rather than local optimization.

## CONCLUSION

In addition to becoming a systems thinker yourself, encourage others to learn more about this topic. We suggest you to try getting together at a whiteboard with colleagues to sketch a causal loop diagram, so that *being* systems thinkers and *doing* systems thinking are connected at the workplace.

## RECOMMENDED READINGS

❑ W. Edwards Deming's *Out of the Crisis* is a master work by arguably the most well-known systems thinker and quality expert. It opens with the modest goal, "The aim of this book is transformation of the style of American management... It requires a whole new structure, from foundation upward." Deming also advocates the *System of Profound Knowledge* in which managers (1) appreciate there is a *system*, (2) understand common-cause and special-cause variation (queueing theory is related to variation), (3) understand limitations of knowledge and reasoning mistakes, and (4) know credible psychology and social research results so that behavior- or motivation-related policies are *not* based on "common sense." The core of the book centers around his famous *14 Points for Management*, including (for example), "*Eliminate management by objective. Eliminate management by numbers, numerical goals. Substitute leadership.*"

❑ Jay Forrester's *Industrial Dynamics* is the classic text on system dynamics—well written and insightful. Although written in the early 1960s, it is as relevant today as when published. It goes beyond cause-effect modeling to also model the flow and inventories of information, money, and material in systems. The book includes formal mathematical modeling but this is not obligatory to appreciate system dynamics.

❑ Weinberg's *Quality Software Management: Systems Thinking* and *An Introduction to General Systems Thinking* are worthwhile. Written from the perspective of an experienced consultant in systems development.

- Senge's *The Fifth Discipline* is a classic that advocates the need for leadership to apply systems thinking (it is the *fifth* discipline) and other key disciplines for a great, sustainable enterpise. The others include leaders with (1) personal mastery and (2) reflection on their beliefs and faulty reasoning, the (3) definition and communication of a meaningful shared vision, and (4) the ability of teams to learn. We recommend ignoring—at least during the first few years of practice—the 'archetypes' notion presented in the book. It was well meant as a learning aid but has been observed to distract and intimidate people from learning and applying basic system dynamics modeling. The 'archetypes' are not part of original system dynamics.

- *The Fifth Discipline Fieldbook* is an in-depth resource, written from the viewpoint of many practitioners and consultants.

- The organizational-learning writings from Argyris, Putnam, McLain, and Schön. Important concepts include *double-loop learning* and *high-advocacy/high-inquiry dialogue*. Classic works include *Action Science* and *Organizational Learning*.

- The publications and resources available through the *Society for Organizational Learning* (www.solonline.org).

## Chapter

## Book

# LEAN THINKING

*I have enough money to last me the rest of my life,*
*unless I buy something.*
*—Jackie Mason*

Lean thinking is a proven system that scales to large development, as evidenced by Toyota and others. Later chapters explore more connections of lean, agile, and scaling; this one lays out core concepts.

 The image and metaphor we like to convey an aspect of lean thinking is the sport of relay racing.

Consider the relay racers *standing around* waiting for the baton from their running colleague. The accountant in the finance department, looking aghast at this terrible underutilization 'waste' indicated in some report, would probably mandate a policy goal of "95% utilization of resources" to ensure all the racers are busy and 'productive.' Maybe—he suggests—the waiting runners could run up a mountain while they are not busy.

Funny…but this kind of thinking lies behind much of traditional management and processes in product development.[1] Of course, in contrast, here is a central idea in lean thinking:

---

**Watch the baton, not the runners.**

---

---

1. See, for example, PRTM [McGrath96, McGrath04] for collections of very traditional—and un-lean—product development ideas.

## LEAN THINKING: THE BIG PICTURE

**Lean** (or **lean thinking**) is the English name—given by MIT researchers—to describe the system now known as the **Toyota Way** inside the company that created it.[2] Toyota is a strong, resilient company that seems to improve over time:

- In 2008 surpassed GM to become the largest vehicle company by sales, while being much more profitable.

- J.D. Power (etc.) consistently rate Toyota, Lexus, and Scion among the top in quality.

- Very profitable. In 2006 profit was $13.7 USD billion, while GM and Ford reported losses.

- Market capitalization in May 2007 was over 1.5 times that of GM, Ford, and Daimler-Chrysler **combined**.

- Innovative with social and environmental awareness—for example, creator of the Prius and hybrid technology.

- Product development at levels up to twice as fast as some competitors.

This is a sample; *Extreme Toyota* [OST08] dedicates a chapter comparing their *sustainably* robust performance compared to others in their industry. That said, Toyota is far from perfect and there are unique things to learn from agile methods and other systems that are not found in lean thinking. We are not suggesting that Toyota or lean thinking is the only model to learn from, or to simply emulate it. Nevertheless it is a long-refined meritorious system from a robust and sustainably profitable company. We suggest understanding it when scaling to large product development.

### The Pillars of Lean Are *Not* Tools and Waste Reduction

*Avoid...Lean misconceptions*

There are some common misconceptions about lean. This chapter starts with clearing these away.

What is the essence and power of lean thinking and Toyota?

---

2. The original name was *Respect for Humanity System*. Some called it *The Thinking Way*. These emphasized a Toyota culture of mentoring people to think through and resolve root causes to problems, to help society, and to humanize work [Fujimoto99, WJR90].

*When I first began learning about TPS[3], I was enamored of the power of [one-piece flow, kanban, and other lean tools]. But along the way, experienced leaders within Toyota kept telling me that these tools and techniques were not the key to TPS. Rather the power behind TPS is a company's **management commitment to continuously invest in its people** and **promote a culture of continuous improvement**. I nodded like I knew what they were talking about, and continued to study how to calculate kanban quantities and set up one-piece flow cells. After studying for almost 20 years and observing the struggles [other] companies have had applying lean, what these Toyota teachers told me is finally sinking in. [Liker04] (emphasis added)*

Wakamatsu and Kondo, Toyota experts, put it succinctly:

*The essence of [the Toyota system] is that each individual employee is given the opportunity to find problems in his own way of working, to solve them and to make improvements. [Hino06]*

### Management Tools Are *Not* a Pillar of Lean

The above quotes underscore a vital point because over the years there have been some ostensibly 'lean' promoters that reduced lean thinking to a mechanistic superficial level of management tools such as *kanban* (a visual management technique) and queue management. These derivative descriptions ignore the central message of the Toyota experts who stress that the essence of successful lean thinking is "building people, then building products" and a culture of "challenge the status quo" continuous improvement [Hino06].

*Avoid...Thinking that queue management, kanban, and other tools are pillars of lean*

*Reducing lean thinking to kanban, queue management and other tools is like reducing a working democracy to voting.* Voting is good, but democracy is far more subtle and difficult. Consider the internal Toyota motto shown in a photo we took when visiting Toyota in

---

3. Toyota Production System (TPS) is the precursor to the Toyota Way [Ohno88].

Japan some years ago; it captures the heart of lean, summarizing their focus on educating people to become skillful systems thinkers:

To simplify lean thinking to tools is to fall into a trap repeated many times before by companies superficially and unsuccessfully attempting to adopt what they thought was lean.

> ... *it was only after American carmakers had exhausted every other explanation for Toyota's success—an undervalued yen, a docile workforce, Japanese culture, superior automation—that they were finally able to admit that* **Toyota's real advantage was its ability to harness the intellect of 'ordinary' employees**. *[Hamel06]*

Consequently, **Lean Six Sigma**[4] is viewed by Toyota people to represent Six Sigma *tools* but not to represent real lean thinking. A former Toyota plant and HR manager explains:

> *Lean six sigma is a compilation of tools and training focused on isolated projects to drive down unit cost... The Toyota approach [...] is far broader and far deeper. The starting point is the Toyota Way philosophy of respect for people and continuous improvement. The principle is developing quality people who continually improve processes... The responsibility lies, not with black belt specialists, but with the leadership hierarchy that runs the operation and they are teachers and coaches. [LH08]*

### Waste Reduction Is Not a Pillar of Lean

The book *Lean Thinking* [WJ96] was justifiably popular and introduced some Toyota ideas to a much wider audience. We recommend it—while observing that it presents a *condensed* view of the Toyota

---

4. Lean Six Sigma is an amalgam of tools promoted in the Six Sigma movement [George02].

system. *Lean Thinking* draws significantly on research from the 1980s and early 1990s that focused on Toyota's production system [WJR90], and was published before Toyota's own *Toyota Way 2001* "Green Book," that summarized the priority of the broader principles from an insider's perspective. The subtitle of *Lean Thinking* is *Banish **Waste** and Create Wealth in Your Organization,* and so not surprisingly, those who have read only that one book often summarize lean as "removing waste."

Although useful, waste reduction is not a pillar of lean; it is only mentioned several levels deep within the *Toyota Way 2001*. Plus, some preeminent lean principles such as *Go See* (genchi genbutsu) that Toyota highlights are treated in *Lean Thinking* in an entertaining but anecdotal style that make it possible to miss the relative importance of some lean principles. Study *Lean Thinking*, and study more of the *Recommended Readings*.

### The Two Pillars of Lean

What *are* the pillars of lean? Toyota president Gary Convis:

> The Toyota Way can be briefly summarized through the two pillars that support it: **Continuous Improvement** and **Respect for People**. Continuous improvement, often called **kaizen**, defines Toyota's basic approach to doing business. **Challenge everything**. More important than the actual improvements that individuals contribute, the true value of continuous improvement is in creating an atmosphere of continuous learning and an environment that not only accepts, but actually **embraces change**. Such an environment can only be created where there is respect for people—hence the second pillar of the Toyota Way. (emphasis added)

*Try…Reflect on the two pillars of lean: respect for people and continuous improvement*

And from Toyota CEO Katsuaki Watanabe:

> The Toyota Way has two main pillars: continuous improvement and respect for people. Respect is necessary to work with people. By "people" we mean employees, supply partners, and customers. …We don't mean just the end customer; on the assembly line the person at the next workstation is also your customer. That leads to teamwork. **If you adopt that principle, you'll also**

*keep analyzing what you do in order to see if you're doing things perfectly, so you're not troubling your customer. That nurtures your ability to identify problems, and if you closely observe things, it will lead to kaizen—continuous improvement. The root of the Toyota Way is to be dissatisfied with the status quo; you have to ask constantly, "Why are we doing this?"* (emphasis added)

Respect for people and continuous improvement "challenge everything" "embrace change" mindset, the pillars of lean, are expanded later in this chapter. If a lean adoption program ignores the importance of these—a **cargo cult** lean adoption[5]—then the essential understanding and conditions for sustainable success with lean will be missing.

## BACKGROUND

The English term 'lean' was chosen for the Toyota system—and popularized by MIT researchers of Toyota in *The Machine That Changed the World* [WJR90]—to contrast their *lean production* with the alternative of *mass production*. The implication was a dramatic reduction in work-package or batch size, and no longer competing on economies of scale but rather competing on the ability to adapt, avoid inventory, and work in very small units—themes also found in agile methods such as Scrum. The term *lean* is now also used within Toyota; for example, in their *Toyota Way 2001* internal booklet.

Two of the authors of the *The Machine That Changed the World* went on to write *Lean Thinking*, a popular introduction that summarized five principles.

In their excellent books on *lean software development* ([Poppendieck03, Poppendieck06]), Mary—who applied lean thinking at 3M—and Tom Poppendieck raised awareness of the correspondence and complementary qualities of lean to agile software

---

5. A *cargo cult* in a tribal society performed rituals imitating the behavior of non-native visitors (often from Europe). By analogy, *cargo cult process* adoption suggests ritualism and superficiality.

development methods. And Jeff Sutherland and Ken Schwaber, co-creators of Scrum, have studied Toyota and lean thinking.

Relatively broad descriptions of the lean system are *The Toyota Way*, *The Toyota Product Development System, Inside the Mind of Toyota*, *Extreme Toyota*, and *Lean Product and Process Development*. All are based on long study of Toyota. *The Toyota Way* [Liker04] text is used by Toyota for education, in addition to their internal *Toyota Way 2001*. This introduction to lean is similar to these descriptions.

Figure 3.1 the lean-thinking house

| Sustainable shortest lead time, best quality and value (to people and society), most customer delight, lowest cost, high morale, safety |
|---|

| Respect for People | Product Development | Continuous Improvement |
|---|---|---|
| - don't trouble your 'customer'<br><br>- "develop people, then build products"<br><br>- no wasteful work<br><br>- teams & individuals evolve their own practices and improvements<br><br>- build partners with stable relationships, trust, and coaching in lean thinking<br><br>- develop teams | - long-term great engineers<br>- mentoring from manager-engineer-teacher<br>- cadence<br>- cross-functional<br>- team room + visual mgmt<br>- entrepreneurial chief engineer/product mgr<br>- set-based concurrent dev<br>- create more knowledge<br><br>**14 Principles**<br>long-term, flow, pull, less variability & overburden, Stop & Fix, master norms, simple visual mgmt, good tech, leader-teachers from within, develop exceptional people, help partners be lean, Go See, consensus, reflection & kaizen | - Go See<br><br>- kaizen<br>- spread knowledge<br>- small, relentless<br>- retrospectives<br>- 5 Whys<br>- eyes for waste<br>  * variability, over-burden, NVA ...<br>  (handoff, WIP, info scatter, delay, multi-tasking, defects, wishful thinking..)<br><br>- perfection challenge<br><br>- work toward flow (lower batch size, Q size, cycle time) |

| Management applies and teaches lean thinking, and bases decisions on this long-term philosophy |
|---|

## LEAN SUMMARY: THE LEAN THINKING HOUSE

Figure 3.1 summarizes the modern Toyota Way in a "lean thinking house" diagram, because an earlier version of the Toyota system was first summarized within Toyota by a similar house diagram. This house also defines the major sections of this chapter, such as *Respect for People* and *Continuous Improvement*. The remainder of the chapter follows the major elements of the diagram in the following order:

1. goal (roof)
2. foundation
3. pillar—respect for people
4. pillar—continuous improvement
5. 14 principles
6. lean product development

## LEAN GOAL: SUSTAINABLY DELIVER VALUE FAST

*Try…Know system goals in lean thinking*

*Sustainable shortest lead time, best quality and value (to people and society), most customer delight, lowest cost, high morale, safety.*

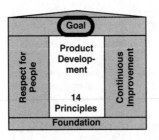

Broadly, the global or system goal of lean thinking at Toyota is to go from "concept to cash"[6] or "order to cash" as fast as possible at *a sustainable pace*—to quickly deliver things of value (to the customer *and society*) in shorter and shorter cycle times of all processes, while still achieving highest quality and morale levels. Toyota strives to reduce cycle times, but not through cutting corners, reducing quality, or at an unsustainable or unsafe pace; rather, by relentless *continuous improvement*, that requires a company culture of meaningful *respect for people* in which people feel they have the personal safety to challenge and change the status quo.

---

6. A phrase coined in [Poppendieck06].

We see echoes of this goal in the words of the creator of the Toyota Production System (TPS), Taiichi Ohno:

*All we are doing is looking at the time line, from the moment the customer gives us an order to the point where we collect the cash. And we are reducing the time line by reducing the non-value-adding wastes.[7] [Ohno88]*

So, a focus of lean is *on the baton*, not the runners—removing the bottlenecks to faster throughput of value to customers rather than locally optimizing by trying to maximize utilization of workers or machines. This is the focus of Scrum as well—delivering valuable features each short timeboxed iteration.

Not only does Toyota (and their Lexus and Scion brands) manufacture vehicles, but also successfully and efficiently *develop* new products—lean principles apply to product development. How does Toyota achieve the "global goal" in their two main processes, product development and production?

❑ **Development**—*out-learn the competition*, through generating more useful knowledge and using and remembering it effectively.

❑ **Production**—*out-improve the competition*, by a focus on short cycles, small batches and queues, stopping to find and fix the root cause of problems, relentlessly removing all wastes (waiting, handoff, …).

This chapter returns to *out-learn* and *out-improve* later on. Of course, these approaches are not mutually exclusive. Toyota Development improves and Production learns.

---

7. This allusion to *wastes* is explored later. 'Waste' has an important and specific meaning in lean thinking.

## LEAN FOUNDATION: LEAN THINKING MANAGER-TEACHERS

*Try...Foundation of lean thinking manager-teachers*

*Management applies and teaches lean thinking, and bases decisions on this long-term philosophy.*

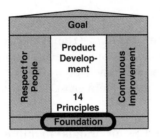

When we first visited Toyota in Japan, we interviewed people to learn more about their management culture and education system. One of the things we learned is that most new employees first go through several months of education before starting other work. During this period they learn the foundations of lean thinking, they learn to see 'waste' (a subject we will return to), and they do hands-on work in many areas of Toyota. In this way, new Toyota people...

- ❑ learn to "see the whole" [Poppendieck03]
- ❑ learn to see how lean thinking applies in different domains
- ❑ learn *kaizen* mindset (continuous improvement)
- ❑ appreciate a core principle in Toyota called *Go See* and *gemba*

*Go See* means people—especially managers—are expected to "go see with their own eyes" rather than sit behind desks or believe that the truth can be learned only from reports or numbers. It is related to appreciating the importance of *gemba*—going to the physical front-line place of value work where the hands-on value workers are.

We also learned that potential executive managers have worked their way up through years of hands-on lean thinking practice and mentoring to others. When Eiji Toyoda was president, he said to the management team, "I want you actively to train your people on how to think for themselves" [Hino06]. Note that this is *not* simply a message of *let people think for themselves*. Rather, the management culture is *managers act as **teachers** of thinking skills*. Toyota managers are educated in lean thinking, continuous improvement, root cause analysis, the statistics of variability, and systems thinking—and coach others in these thinking tools.

From this, we came especially to appreciate that for successful adoption of lean, there are management qualities needed for any meaningful, sustained success—the leadership team cannot "phone in" their lean support. Toyota is one of few companies that seems to demonstrate these qualities; to summarize [OST08]:

❑ Long-term philosophy—many in the company are educated in lean thinking through courses and mentoring from manager-teachers.

❑ Long-term philosophy—virtually all management, including the executive level, must have a solid understanding of lean principles, have lived them for years, and teach them to others.

❑ Long-term philosophy—manager-teachers have cultivated systems thinking and process-improvement problem-solving thinking skills, and they teach it to others. The culture is imbued with the mentality and behavior, "Let's stop and understand the root causes of problems."

**Manager-teachers**—the internal motto is *Good Thinking, Good Products*. How do they achieve this "good thinking" which forms the foundation of their success? It is through *a culture of mentoring*. Managers are expected to be hands-on masters of their domain of work (the saying is, "my manager can do my job better than me"), are expected to understand lean thinking, and are expected to *spend time teaching and coaching others*. We learned during an interview in Japan that Toyota HR policies include analysis of how much time a manager spends teaching. In short, managers are less directors and more teachers in the principles of lean thinking, "stop and fix right," and *kaizen* mentality. In this way, the *Toyota DNA* is propagated [LH08].

Atsushi Niimi, Toyota North America president, said that the greatest challenge in teaching the Toyota Way to foreign managers was, "They want to be managers, not teachers."

The more one learns about lean, the more one appreciates that the foundation is manager-teachers who live and teach it and have long hands-on experience. The foundation is not tools or waste reduction.

Any company executive team that wants to succeed with lean development will need to pay attention to this basic lesson—that they cannot "phone in" their support to "do lean."

## PILLAR ONE: RESPECT FOR PEOPLE

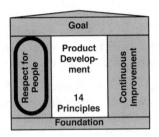

*Respect for people* sounds nebulous, but includes concrete actions and culture within Toyota. They broadly reflect respect for and sensitivity to morale, not making people do wasteful work, real *teamwork*, mentoring to develop skillful people, humanizing the work and environment, safe and clean environment (inside *and outside* of Toyota), and philosophical integrity among the management team. Figure 3.2 illustrates some implications.

The 11th agile principle and a theme in Scrum is self-organizing teams (self-directed work teams), supporting this pillar. Some of the deeper implications of the lean *Respect for People* pillar are covered in the *Teams* and *Organization* chapters.

## PILLAR TWO: CONTINUOUS IMPROVEMENT

*Continuous improvement* is based on several ideas:

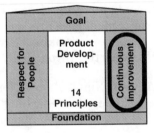

- ❑ Go See
- ❑ kaizen
- ❑ perfection challenge
- ❑ work toward flow (covered in the *14 Principles*)

*14 Principles*
*p. 65*

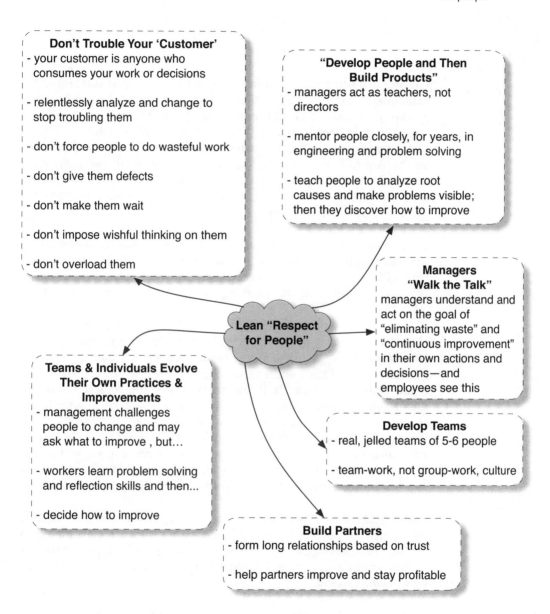

Figure 3.2 respect for people

**Don't Trouble Your 'Customer'**
- your customer is anyone who consumes your work or decisions
- relentlessly analyze and change to stop troubling them
- don't force people to do wasteful work
- don't give them defects
- don't make them wait
- don't impose wishful thinking on them
- don't overload them

**"Develop People and Then Build Products"**
- managers act as teachers, not directors
- mentor people closely, for years, in engineering and problem solving
- teach people to analyze root causes and make problems visible; then they discover how to improve

**Managers "Walk the Talk"**
managers understand and act on the goal of "eliminating waste" and "continuous improvement" in their own actions and decisions—and employees see this

Lean "Respect for People"

**Teams & Individuals Evolve Their Own Practices & Improvements**
- management challenges people to change and may ask what to improve , but...
- workers learn problem solving and reflection skills and then...
- decide how to improve

**Develop Teams**
- real, jelled teams of 5-6 people
- team-work, not group-work, culture

**Build Partners**
- form long relationships based on trust
- help partners improve and stay profitable

## Go See for Yourself (Go See)

*Try...Continuous improvement with Go See, kaizen, perfection challenge, and working towards flow*

*Go to the source [the place of real value work—gemba] to find the facts to make correct decisions, build consensus, and achieve goals at our best speed. [Toyota01]*

**Go See** is a principle not found in many management cultures. This principle is described as critical and fundamental. In the internal *Toyota Way 2001* it is highlighted as *the first factor for success* in continuous improvement. *Go See* shows up repeatedly in Toyota manager quotes, in Toyota culture and habits [LH08], in education on the Toyota Way, and in the research done by Japanese analysts of lean thinking (for example, [OST08]). All that said, it is missing from some derivative 'lean' descriptions and so—unfortunately— some are unaware of its vital role.

In a lean-thinking culture, all people, but especially managers— including senior managers—should not spend all their time in sepa- rate offices or meeting rooms, receiving information via reports, computers, management reporting tools, and status meetings.

Rather, to know what is going on and help improve (by eliminating the distortion that comes from indirect information), *management should frequently go to the place of real work and see and understand for themselves*. This "real front-line place of work" (*gemba*) does not mean proximity to the building where work happens, nor does it mean going to visit other managers. It implies to be as physically close to the real front-line work as possible—not sitting in an office nearby, but "breathing the same air." 'Work' in lean does not prima- rily mean the overhead or secondary work of accounting and so on, but the value-adding work that the customer cares about—engineer- ing, designing a car, producing things, delivering customer service.

An example of Go See is for managers to regularly visit and then sit with software developers or engineers while they are working, with the aim of understanding problems and opportunities to improve. It is similar to the unfortunately now-lost HP practice of "management by walking around."

In an interview, Toyota's chief engineer quoted Taiichi Ohno, who insisted on managers practicing Go See at *gemba*:

*Don't look with your eyes, look with your feet… people who only look at the numbers are the worst of all. [Hayashi08]*

The Japanese term for Go See, **genchi genbutsu**, has also been broadly rendered as implying *solve problems at the source instead of behind desks*. Go See not only implies *walking* to the source to find facts and decide with direct insight; it means—once you are there—to *build consensus* for goals and experiments to change. The full implication of Go See is for people—especially managers—to frequently spend time at the real place of value work, build relationships of trust with the people there, and help them fix things.

For example, Figure 3.3 shows a picture of Craig's 'office' in Bangalore, Valtech India: a little desk physically among the development teams. He has spent time sitting with developers while they program, pair programming with them, attending their Scrum Sprint Retrospectives and Sprint Planning meetings. In this way, getting a direct understanding of what's working and what's not—and how to better help.

Figure 3.3 'office'— Go See attitude

## Kaizen

*Improve for improvements' sake, endlessly.*

**Kaizen** is sometimes translated as simply "continuous improvement" but that confuses it with the broader lean *pillar* of "continuous improvement" and does not capture the full flavor. So, we will stick with the Japanese term.[8]

Kaizen is both a personal mindset and a practice. As a mindset, it suggests *"My work is to do my work and to **improve** my work"* and *"continuously improve for its own sake."* More formally as a practice, kaizen implies:

1. choose and practice techniques the team and/or product group has agreed to try, until they are well understood

2. experiment until you find a better way

3. repeat forever

***Step 1—Choose and practice techniques the team and/or product group has agreed to try, until they are well understood.*** The idea is for a group to first find (hopefully) skillful baseline practices and learn to do them well. A novice team follows the Scrum description with good coaching. The group's working agreements, such as coding standards and "definition of done"[9] are followed. People learn to do test-driven development with plenty of practice, coaching, and good education. Step one in kaizen implies having patience through the awkward learning phase and not abandoning new techniques quickly. People need a valid baseline to improve against. And in Deming's terminology, they need to be able to distinguish between common-cause and special-cause variability.

This step-one point of kaizen is that a person or team cannot accurately see if they need to improve or change a practice unless they have first mastered the basics, understood its subtle points, and can do it well. Have you ever seen, "Oh, <X> doesn't work" comments that were based on insufficient skill, practice, or education? There is no point in 'improving' or rejecting based on misunderstanding.

*Try...Spread knowledge rather than force conformance to central processes*

***Share* rather than enforce practices**—The working-agreements or norms should not be misconstrued to mean a rigid practice to follow "until notified otherwise" or a centralized top-down 'standard' from a central process group that is forced on people—ideas contrary to the lean pillar of *continuous improvement*. Toyota people promote **yokoten—spread knowledge laterally** that may evolve uniquely in different locations, like a graft from a tree. *Yokoten* means liter-

---

8. We avoid Japanese terms unless no English term works.
9. The Scrum rule of 'Definition of Done' is an important working agreement. See p. 313.

ally to *unfold* or *open out sideways*. **Spread knowledge** implies a culture that emphasizes horizontal knowledge sharing, but not being forced to conform to central processes pushed top-down.[10] Some quotes from Toyota people:

> *If we try to simply get everyone to the current standard you are missing opportunities to get better. You are not taking into account how times are changing. There has to be lots of flexibility in allowing creativity along the way... Standards are not developed and then communicated from headquarters to all the plants. Rigid standards will only kill kaizen... It is yokoten every time—share best practices. ...We must let individuals from plants decide what they will do to fix their problems and close gaps. We cannot have someone from corporate saying you need to do X, Y, Z, because this is completely contrary to Toyota problem solving. [LH08]*

**Communities of practice**—something we recommend in large-scale Scrum—are created to *spread knowledge laterally*.

*CoP p. 252*

***Steps 2 and 3—Small, incremental, relentless change of anything***. Kaizen is an on-going activity by all people (including managers) to *relentlessly* and *incrementally* change and improve practices, usually in *small* experiments, though large-scale *system kaizen* is also an option. Almost no practice, process, or existing policy is sacred—anything can go. "Challenge everything," in the words of Toyota President Convis. Also, a kaizen culture is not one where only big improvement projects by process experts are initiated. Rather, each team does it regularly themselves.

*Learn process improvement by doing*—Kaizen implies, by ceaseless repetition and mentoring, people learn by themselves how to make problems visible, analyze their root causes, and improve by experimenting. And 'failure' of experiments is OK. The only failure in kaizen is to not continuously experiment.

In *Kaizen* by Masaaki Imai, he shares:

> *The essence of Kaizen is simple and straightforward: Kaizen means improvement. Moreover, Kaizen means ongoing improve-*

---

10. There are exceptions, such as safety and accounting standards.

*ment involving everyone, including both managers and workers. The kaizen philosophy assumes that our way of life—be it our working life, our social life, or our home life—deserves to be constantly improved. [Imai86]*

Kaizen reflects the Plan-Do-Check-Act (PDCA) Shewhart improvement cycle (also known as the Deming cycle) [Deming67]. In fact many people within Toyota formally know PDCA and sometimes describe what they are doing as "endless PDCA" [LH08].

### Shu Ha Ri

*Shu Ha Ri* is a model of progressive learning discussed in martial arts; its connection to kaizen and agile methods has been noted in [Cockburn01]. In phase one, *Shu*, a person follows rules until they sink in and become automatic. In phase two, *Ha*, a person reflects on the rules, looks for exceptions, and 'breaks' the rules. In phase three, *Ri*, the rules are essentially forgotten as the person has developed mastery, and grasped the essence and underlying forces.

### Retrospectives

Kaizen most often happens during repeating team events such as retrospective workshops. Note that team kaizen is encouraged.

**Connection to Scrum**—Agile principle 12, *at regular intervals, the team reflects on how to become more effective, then tunes and adjusts its behavior accordingly,* echoes the kaizen mindset. In Scrum, each team is required to hold a maximum-three-hour kaizen event **retrospective** workshop (see Figure 3.4) at the end of each iteration, in which they inspect their practices and create new process experiments for the next short iteration. Scrum has a strong and institutionalized practice for continuous improvement.

Figure 3.4 Scrum Retrospective, a kaizen event, Valtech India

**Five Whys**

Five Whys (usually written **5 Whys**) is a simple and widely used tool used in kaizen. It helps develop problem solving and root cause analysis skills. In response to a problem or defect, a team considers "why?" at least five times.[11] For example:

Problem: *Developers are not refactoring code to be maintainable.*

1. *Why?* We feel pressured to go faster. (*first why*)
2. *Why do we feel pressured?* Because we are going slow. (*second why*)
3. *Why going slow?* Because the code is complicated and hard to work with.
4. ...

These questions may have multiple and related answers, so some teams create a "5 Whys graph" of branching answers (see Figure 3.5), or a more structured *fishbone (Ishikawa) diagram.*

*fishbone diagram p. 30*

In Scrum there is a retrospective workshop each iteration. This is an excellent time for a team to try 5 Whys.

The important point of 5 Whys is not the technique or the number 5, but that it is part of the "stop and fix" root-cause problem-solving mindset and culture pervasive at Toyota. People are taught to become deep problem solvers; to not live with problems, but to think

---

11. 'Five' is not a magic number; it is meant to imply "dig deep."

things through deeply. There is also a connection between *Go See* and 5 Whys: It is easy for people to *guess* wrong or weak answers unless they see the facts at the real place of the problem.

Figure 3.5 5 Whys graph—changing teams

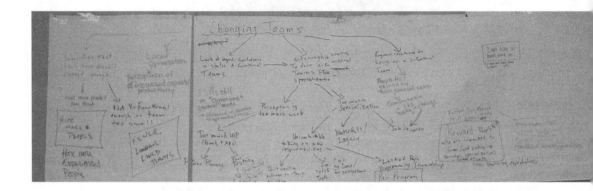

### Value and Waste

*Try…Study the lean meaning of value and waste; learn to see them*

What to improve during kaizen? In lean thinking the answer requires an understanding of value and waste.

**Value**—*The moments of action or thought creating the product that the customer*[12] *is willing to pay for.* In other words, value is defined in the eyes of the *external* customer.[13] Imagine a customer was observing the work in your office. At what moments would they be willing to reach into their pocket, pull out money, and give it to you?

**Waste**—All other moments or actions that do not add value but consume resources. Wastes come from overburdened workers, bottlenecks, waiting, handoff, wishful thinking, and information scatter, among many others.

---

12. "Value in the eyes of the customer" posits an idealized customer.
13. There are some quasi-lean descriptions that introduce the idea of *internal* business value. This is not part of lean thinking, and its application can lead to a distortion of improvement because things that are waste can be mislabeled as value.

One kind of analysis in lean thinking is to estimate all waste and value moments "from concept to cash."[14] From such a time line one can sum the value time and *lead time* (concept to cash), and then calculate

**value ratio** = total-value-time / total-lead-time

We have done many time lines with product development groups and *have not seen a value ratio in a development organization higher than 7 percent. In other words, 93 percent or more of the time in development was waste time.*[15]

**Improvement by Banishing Waste**—After having defined value and waste, we come to a noteworthy difference in lean improvement. Other systems focus on refining *existing value actions*; for example, improving skill in software design. A worthy goal no doubt.

*Try...Improve by removing waste*

However, since there are typically few value-adding moments in the time line—maybe 5 percent—then improving those does not amount to much. But with a *mountain* of waste time in the process, there are *big opportunities to improve the value ratio by eliminating waste.*

For example, a common waste in development is the waste of *over-production*—creating things not really wanted by the customer. One study estimated that on average 45 percent of features created in software products are *never* used [Johnson02]. It makes little sense to focus on measuring and improving programmer efficiency by 2 percent if there is a mountain of unused-feature waste.

As another example, one of the wastes is waiting or *delay*—customers do not pay for that. Have you ever seen the waste of waiting...

❑ for requirements or designs or clarification?

❑ for approval?

❑ for another development team to finish their part?

---

14. This is part of the lean practice *value stream mapping* [RS99].
15. This is consistent with observation by others, such as [Ward06] who estimates an average 5% value ratio in product development.

Try...Learn, see,
and eliminate
NVA actions
including
handoff,
overproduction,
and waiting

**Non-Value-Adding Action Categories**—Within Toyota people are educated to develop "eyes for waste." As a learning aid, lists of non-value-adding (NVA) actions have been created. There is not one correct list—the point is not the categories, but to learn to see and banish waste from the customer perspective. The following product-development NVA action categories are drawn from *The Toyota Way*, *Implementing Lean Software Development*, and *Lean Product and Process Development*.

| Non-Value-Adding Action | Example or Comment |
|---|---|
| 1. Overproduction of features, or of elements ahead of the next step; duplication | • features the customer doesn't really want<br>• large requirements document—more detailed requirements than can be quickly implemented<br>• duplication of data or code |
| 2. Waiting, delay | • ...for clarification, documents, approval, components, other groups to finish something |
| 3. Handoff, conveyance, moving | • giving a specification from an analyst to a developer<br>• giving code from a developer to a tester |
| 4. Extra processing (includes extra *processes*), relearning, reinvention | • forced conformance to centralized process checklists of 'quality' tasks<br>• recreating a component another developer has made |
| 5. Partially done work, work in progress (WIP) | • requirements written but not coded<br>• software coded but not tested |
| 6. Task switching, motion between tasks; interrupt-based multitasking | • interruption to handle hot defects<br>• multitasking on 3 projects<br>• partial allocation of a person to many projects |
| 7. Defects, testing and correction after creation of the product | • testing and correction at-the-end to find and remove defects is not a value action; it may be a *temporarily necessary* waste |

| Non-Value-Adding Action | Example or Comment |
|---|---|
| 8. Under-realizing people's potential and varied skill, insight, ideas, suggestions | • are people only working to their single-speciality job title, or ...?<br>• do people have the chance to change what they see is wasteful? |
| 9. Knowledge and information scatter or loss | • information in many separate documents rather than a central wiki with hypertext<br>• communication barriers such as walls between people, or people in multiple locations |
| 10. Wishful thinking (for example, that plans, estimates, and specifications are 'correct') | • "The estimate cannot increase; the effort estimate is what we want it to be, not what it is now proposed."<br>• "We're behind schedule, but we'll make it up later." |

*Improving through Removing NVAs*—The focus on delivering value through waste reduction orients a lean organization toward following the baton rather than the runners. Notice that the improvement strategy is subtractive rather than additive. Rather than (for example), "What can we get the workers to do to increase utilization?", the question is "What can we *remove* or stop doing?" In our consulting we have found this to be a mindset change for traditional quality-assurance people in large organizations who focus on conformance to checklists and *adding* activities for 'improvement.'

**Temporarily Necessary Waste versus Pure Waste**—Not every waste battle can be won given current capabilities and constraints. For example, it is wickedly hard or virtually impossible to create a software-intensive system that never had a defect to begin with. Plus there are many cases where it is cheaper to resolve defects through feedback loops with test-at-the-end in *small batches and short cycles*, especially as modern testing tools and techniques reduce the cost and cycle time of a test.[16] To be clear: This is not a recommendation to wait and only test at the end of development. However, many short and cheap iterations of small batches with automated testing may—not always—be the cheapest solution to the "build quality in" problem. Thus it is sometimes prudent or necessary, given today's capabilities, to test and correct *after* creation of a small item in a very short cycle—the waste of defects. Even Toyota does this 'waste' step, but only in short cycles with small batch sizes so that defects do not linger, replicate, or pile up.

Because of this, Toyota recognizes two types of waste:

1. **temporarily necessary waste**… a future battle; for example, testing at the end of a short cycle

2. **pure waste**… in principle can and should be eliminated now

*Is Inventory Always Pure Waste?*—A common view among those new to lean thinking is that inventory is *pure waste* and should always be eliminated. Inventories of physical things or of intangible WIP—such as requirement specifications—imply investment without profit and hidden defects. That's not good. However, a common practice in lean improvement is to create **level pull**, removing variability (one of the sources of waste) in a downstream process step by *inserting a small buffer of high-quality "equally sized" inventory items* before that downstream step.

*Product Backlog and queues p. 115*

This is one purpose of the Scrum Product Backlog. It acts as a tool for leveling or smoothing the introduction of work to feature teams. A small buffer of high-quality inventory created to support level pull is another example of useful *temporarily necessary waste*.

*Try…Reduce the three sources of waste: variability, overburden, NVA actions*

**Focus on Variability, Overburden, and NVA Actions**—In addition to NVA actions, in the Toyota Way people are taught *three sources of waste*, illustrated and commented with resolution ideas in Figure 3.6.

---

16. *Acceptance test-driven development* (see *Test* chapter in companion book), an agile practice, combines both the *value* act of defining executable tests *before* development, and the "temporarily necessary waste" act of re-executing these each development cycle.

Figure 3.6 three sources of waste

**Variability**
varying iteration lengths, varying batch sizes of features, varying size of one feature, varying team members or size, varying delivery times, defects (these introduce much variability), interruption to handle hot defects, irregular arrival of requests

**Resolution**?
- leveling the work

- cadence; for example, timeboxed iteration such as 2 weeks

- decompose a few large-effort customer features into many smaller-effort features, so that a more consistent amount of work is taken on each iteration

**Overburden**
- overtime for arbitrary deadlines

- one Product Manager having to know hundreds of features in detail

- often seen with specialist bottlenecks and over-dependence on super-specialists

**Resolution**?
- develop "eyes to see" queues & bottlenecks and those who are doing too much

- take on less work in iteration; descope

- spread the work and skill—cross-train

**3 Sources of Waste**

**NVA actions**
- for example, handoff, waiting, scattered information, partially done work, task switching

**Resolution**?
- kaizen events such as Scrum Retrospective to learn to see it and experiments to reduce

Toyota people who observe outside attempts to adopt lean note a common mis-education about waste—*the mis-education to only focus on eliminating NVA actions* [LM06a]. Within Toyota, all three weaknesses are given importance, and in fact *variability* and *overburden* are viewed as frequent root causes that give rise to NVA actions. For example, overburdened programmers create more defects.

### Perfection Challenge

This is the third element of continuous improvement in lean.

During a visit to Toyota we invited a retired engineer to dinner in Nagoya. After several rounds of *sake*, we asked, "What do you miss, no longer working at Toyota?" He replied, "No longer discussing perfection with people."

We sometimes visit an organization interested in adopting agile or lean methods and someone resists with essentially the argument, "We're shipping products, making good money, and have established processes. Why should we change our practices?" We do not think you would hear that question in Toyota. They are far from perfect and we are not suggesting simply copying them, but their culture is to have a kaizen mindset—to have high expectations and to challenge ourselves, team members, and partners to levels of skill, mastery, waste reduction, and vision beyond the status quo.

That's powerful.

### No Final Process

In 2001, Toyota created an internal *Toyota Way* booklet summarizing the lean principles. On hearing the proposed title, chairman Toyoda suggested renaming the booklet *Toyota Way 2001*. Why? To emphasize that there is no final process in Toyota (which would stifle kaizen), but rather, continuous improvement and change.

The implication of *kaizen* and *spread knowledge laterally* is that there is not a final or correct 'defined' process to follow everywhere that is communicated from a central process group. Kaizen does include learning and mastering working agreements, but they travel and evolve by the *spread knowledge laterally* model. People who have the mindset "let's define (or buy) the central process, write it down, and then we should focus on conformance to it" will not be comfortable with lean thinking. To quote the Toyota CEO, *"The root of the Toyota Way is to be dissatisfied with the status quo; you have to ask constantly, "Why are we doing this?"* Lean and agile values—and the Scrum method—are based on the idea of **empirical process**: there is no fixed or final process or cookbook that people can follow given the reality of dynamically changing systems, and given the goal of continuous improvement. Instead, in Scrum we are left with the hard work of kaizen—to relentlessly, every two-week iteration, inspect and adapt the process and create yet another "two-week process experiment." In Toyota and in Scrum, the idea is to repeat this cycle until retirement.

## 14 PRINCIPLES

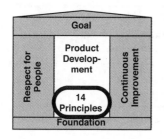

The two pillars, *respect for people* and *continuous improvement*, are not the entire picture—literally or figuratively. There are other potent lean principles that form the overall *system* of lean, some of which recapitulate elements in the two pillars.

*Try…Apply the 14 principles, including exceptional people, stop and fix, leveling, and pull*

To quote Fujio Cho, chairman of Toyota:

*Many good American companies have respect for individuals, and practice kaizen and other [Toyota] tools. But what is important is having all the elements together as **a system**. It must be practiced every day in a very consistent manner. [Liker04]*

Part of this broader *system* is covered in the 14 principles described in the *Toyota Way* book that comes out of decades of direct observation and interviews with Toyota people. Table 3.1 summarizes the principles, some of which are further discussed after the table.

Table 3.1  14 principles

| Principle | Comment/Reference |
|---|---|
| 1. Base management decisions on a **long-term philosophy**, even at the expense of short-term financial goals. | see local optimization p. 32 |
| 2. Move toward **flow**; move to ever-smaller batch sizes and cycle times to deliver value fast & expose weakness. | see p. 67 |

| Principle | Comment/Reference |
|---|---|
| 3. Use **pull systems**; **decide as late as possible**. | see p. 68 |
| 4. **Level the work**—reduce variability and overburden to remove unevenness. | see p. 117 (in *Queuing Theory*); see also p. 62 |
| 5. Build a culture of **stopping and fixing problems**; teach everyone to methodically study problems. | not only fix, but apply **5 Whys** analysis to understand the root causes, and *really* fix it; see p. 57 |
| 6. **Master norms** (practices) to enable kaizen and employee empowerment. | these are changeable working agreements, not rigid organization standards; see p. 53 |
| 7. Use **simple visual management** to reveal problems and coordinate. | see p. 71 |
| 8. Use only **well-tested technology** that serves your people and process. | open-source software tools often help |
| 9. Grow **leaders from within** who thoroughly understand the work, live the philosophy, and **teach it to others**. | *leaders from within* may *not* be a good idea if your existing culture is not lean—the point is *educated* lean-thinking leaders; see p. 48 |
| 10. Develop **exceptional people** and teams who **follow your company's philosophy**. | this reflects the Toyota "build (lean thinking) people, then products" message; it includes "towering technical competence" |
| 11. Respect your extended network of **partners** by challenging them to grow and **helping them improve**. | bring partners into lean thinking as well; there is an emphasis on sharing knowledge and openness |
| 12. **Go see for yourself at the real place work** to thoroughly understand the situation and help. | see p. 52 |
| 13. Make **decisions slowly by consensus**, thoroughly considering all options; **implement rapidly**. | activities such as the Scrum Retrospective support this |

| Principle | Comment/Reference |
|---|---|
| 14. Become and sustain a learning organization through *relentless reflection* and *kaizen*. | see p. 53 |

### Flow

**Flow** suggests making value flow without delay to the customer. As a counter example, a customer request waits in a queue waiting to be approved, analyzed, implemented, reworked, or tested. That is *not* flow. Rather, as value is created—in products, software, information, decisions, service—it flows immediately to the customer. It is related to the *follow the baton* metaphor and to the goal of faster "concept to cash." Flow is a *perfection challenge*; zero waste in the system and immediate continuous flowing delivery of value are profound challenges, probably never achieved. The journey is usually *moving toward* flow.

In the lean 'house' diagram (Figure 3.1), flow is included in both the 14 principles and in the key elements of continuous improvement. Why? Because to move toward flow it is necessary to reduce batch size, cycle time, delay, WIP, and other wastes. And this has the beneficial side effect of revealing more weaknesses and waste, providing new opportunities for continuous improvement. *This is an important but subtle point*, expanded in the "Indirect Benefits of Reducing Batch Size and Cycle Time" section on page 112.

Moving toward flow is associated with applied queueing theory, pull systems, and more. By understanding these, people can move the system toward flow by smaller work package sizes, smaller queue sizes, and reduction in variability. This is explored in the *Queueing Theory* chapter.

### Pull Systems

**Pull versus push**. Consider a process for manufacturing and storing laptop computers. In a pure **pull system**[17] no laptop is built or stored in inventory until there is a customer order. Zero inventory[18] is a goal, and work is done only in response to a 'pull' signal from the customer. That is the key meaning of pull: Build in response to a signal from the 'customer,' and otherwise rest or improve. Pull examples? Printing just the twenty-book order or preparing just one restaurant dish.

*But a pull system goes deeper than that*—the 'customer' is not just the final customer. Rather, in a multi-stage process with an upstream team doing partial work before a downstream team, *a downstream team is the customer to their upstream team*. In a pure pull system the upstream team does not create anything unless pulled from downstream request.

On the other hand, in a **push system**, one speculatively builds and stores laptops in the hope of orders, and then tries to push them to customers. In a multi-stage process, upstream teams create an inventory of partially done work for downstream teams. Any kind of speculative inventory—pizzas, big detailed plans, books, specifications for many features whose value is uncertain—are related to push systems.

Resource management strategies that focus on high utilization of workers—a focus on *watch the runners* rather than *watch the baton*—create an environment in which people will create a large inventory of things (requirements, designs, code) in a push model.

**Expose defects**—If you only create *one* thing in response to *pull* from a 'customer' request (in this context, your customer is anyone

---

17. Pull is related to a **Just-in-Time** system—JIT implements pull.
18. In pull systems for development, low or zero inventory means less inventory of detailed specifications, plans, untested code, and so on.

downstream) and the customer consumes it quickly, any *defects* in that one thing—created either by accident or design—are quickly discovered. That can lead to further systemic improvement if people have "stop and fix" mindset. On the other hand, in push systems, defects are hidden in an unconsumed inventory (of requirements, code, ...). For example, pushing a large batch of requirements will delay the discovery of misunderstandings or problems, because it is a long time before they are implemented and evaluated (as running software) by a customer.

**Decide as late as possible**—In pull systems, you do not decide early, quite the opposite—you **"decide as late as possible"** and **"commit at the last responsible moment"** [Poppendieck03, Smith07]. In this way, you have the most information to make an informed decisions. You do not waste resources making unnecessary inventory or early decisions that will have to—or at least should—change in response to discovery.

**Small batches can lead to radical improvement**—A pull system implies smaller batches in frequent short cycles. Using the old large-batch push-based processes (based on economies-of-scale thinking that avoided change), more short cycles may increase overall over-head or *transaction cost*, and hence be viewed as inefficient. The way out of that conundrum is an out-of-the-box radical improvement in processes that can embrace change and small batches efficiently. This is a secret behind Toyota's efficiency—pull systems with small batches combined with kaizen drive new ways of working that lower the transaction cost of a process cycle. This improvement dynamic is explored in the "Indirect Benefits of Reducing Batch Size and Cycle Time" section on page 112.

Thus, in several ways, pull systems support moving towards flow.

**Avoid a false dichotomy**—To categorically state that pull is good and push is bad would be a *false dichotomy*. Usually because of hard constraints (for example, the speed of transportation), some inventory and some push may be useful—a *temporarily necessary waste*. Toyota speculatively creates vehicles for overseas shipment—sometimes to their advantage, sometimes not. In Scrum, the group pushes a small inventory of well-analyzed and small equally-sized requirements to the top of the Product Backlog to reduce variability.

*false dichotomy*
*p. 125*

*waste p. 58*

How do pull systems apply to product development? For example, compare **pull planning** with **push planning**:

❑ In *push planning*, a large, upfront, detailed plan is created of what requirements will be done and when, and all tasks for these are estimated, sequenced, and assigned to people or teams—from the beginning until delivery. Then the tasks are pushed to the workers and there is an attempt to control toward the original speculative plan. Note that push planning requires that all requirements are therefore elaborately analyzed and detailed before planning (at least if done rationally), and it assumes low or no change, and no surprises.

❑ In **pull planning**, or **adaptive iterative planning**, a **Product Backlog** of high-level requirements or goals is created. At "the last responsible moment"—the first day of a short time-boxed iteration—the Product Owner selects a list of small goals for the iteration, from a slightly larger set that was analyzed and estimated in the last one or two iterations. In response to this *pull signal*, the team builds and delivers what they can. Note that since the decision was made as late as possible, with *fresh insight and maximum information in a variable world*, more informed choices are made. Pull planning is related to what is also known as *rolling wave planning*.

### Stop and Fix

Toyota people are coached by manager-teachers to take the time to pause when defects or problems arise. Rather than creating only a *quick fix* response (or no response), a team will hold a kaizen event to grasp the root causes, and then initiate steps toward a deep solution—one that ideally prevents the defect or weakness from being possible and thus building quality in.

For example, Toyota is famous for their "stop the line" practice in which anyone can pull a cord when they see a defect, to stop all work on the line. This is step one in a systematic response toward building quality in. Another example: Toyota encourages human-friendly manufacturing devices that themselves detect a failure, automatically stop, and alert people to the problem. This was inspired by Sakichi Toyoda who made his original fortune by designing a weaving loom that automatically detected a failure and then stopped [Hino06]. This is the lean practice of **jidoka**.[19]

Similarly, agile software development recommends a "stop the line" mentality as part of *continuous integration*: If the build breaks (due to compile, link, or test failure), it is considered a minor crisis and those responsible for the failure should relatively quickly work to bring the build back to health. Perhaps at the next Sprint Retrospective they will explore the root causes of why the build is breaking and experiment with ways to improve.

### Simple Visual Management

Toyota emphasizes simple and BIG visual tools to signal problems, communicate, and coordinate a pull system. There are big displays on walls, bright and big physical color-coded cards that people can touch and move, and so forth. Key themes are *ease of viewing from a distance, physical tokens* (such as cards), *color,* and *simplicity.* This is the opposite of displaying many little or detailed elements of information on small computer displays from software-based systems; however, a computer display that is simply filled with a blob of red color to show a broken build is in the spirit of visual management.

*Try...Visual management*

These **information radiators** for **visual management** are applicable to product development, to show tasks, software build status, and so on; they were first widely promoted in software development in the XP agile method and its Big Visible Charts practice [JAH00].

The *Queueing Theory* chapter explores queues in more detail, and the value in making visible the normally *invisible* queues of product development through physical tokens.

*visual management and queues p. 111*

Visual management implies *physical* tokens (not tokens in a computer program[20]) for queues of stuff. For example, in Scrum and other agile methods, it is common to represent all the tasks for the iteration on paper cards (task cards) that are placed on the wall and

---

19. Jidoka is difficult to rename in English; it is sometimes described as "automation with a human touch."
20. *Physical* tokens are an aspect of lean visual management that is not always appreciated.

moved around as tasks are completed (Figure 3.7)—a task board. Physical tokens. Putting these tasks into a computer program defeats the purpose of lean visual management and the way *humans*—with countless eons of evolutionary instinct working with concrete things—need to *see and feel tangible queues*.

Figure 3.7 lean visual management creates *physical* tokens, such as task cards on a task board and paper charts on a wall, so that invisible queues can become tangible—really *seen and felt*

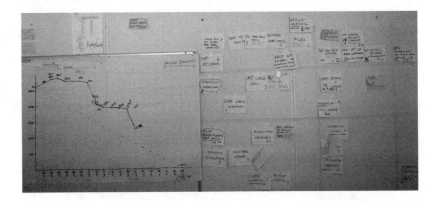

An error display (*andon*) is a common visual aid in Toyota to signal defects in things. In agile software development, a common error display is a light or webpage that turns red when the automated build (compile and tests) fails, so that people can *see* the failure.

**Kanban** is one type of visual management to signal a pull event (a replenishment request) in a *pull system*. The classic example is a store with something for sale on a shelf, such as one pie. Behind the pie on the shelf is an orange card labeled "one pie"—the **withdraw kanban**. When the pie is eventually taken off the shelf by a customer, the withdraw kanban is revealed and taken to the bakery to get another pie to refill the shelf. This is possible because there is one finished pie in inventory in the bakery waiting for this event.

Also at this time, a **creation kanban** is sent to the baker to starting baking one more pie. A single pie is *pulled* onto the shelf by the withdraw kanban, rather than pies being pushed.

Of course, product development is not a manufacturing process like baking pies, and concurrent engineering with cross-functional teams (with virtually no handoff between processes) does not require this production use of kanban and pull. However, the *terms* kanban card (or **agile kanban** card) and **kanban board** have been co-opted by product development people with somewhat different meaning [Poppendieck03, Hirinabe08]. **Agile kanban** means a task or requirement card that someone may volunteer to fulfill. The cards are shown on a task board also known as the **kanban board** (Figure 3.7). This visual management practice was popularized in XP [Beck99], but it has been overlaid more recently with lean terminology.

**Self-directed work**—This is a theme found in effective-team research. Notice that visual management supports self-directed work because people can easily see what is going on, to coordinate. Also, the work of a kanban card is self-explanatory, such as "one pie" or "change style of webpage."

*self-organizing teams p. 194*

# LEAN PRODUCT DEVELOPMENT

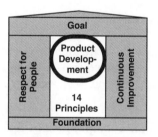

The two pillars and 14 principles are core to lean thinking. However, there are other principles and practices to *outlearn the competition*, specific to lean product development.

*Try...Outlearn the competition*

Toyota people execute two key processes well, (1) product development and (2) production. University of Michigan researchers did a three-year study of Toyota and North American companies product development effectiveness [LM06b]. Results? ...

For example, the average die[21] design-to-complete duration was five months for Toyota engineers and twelve months for the competition. All this, while maintaining the lowest R&D-to-sales ratio of any

---

21. A *die* is a template for stamping or molding metal or plastic parts.

major automotive company in the world, due to the effectiveness of their development practices.

How do they do it? What is a focus of lean product development? Answer:

*"Outlearn the competition"* [22]

When Toyota developed the hybrid Prius, what did they create?

- ❑ the *design* of the car (and implementation of embedded software); in development they have a *knowledge* value stream to create a profitable *production* value stream

- ❑ *knowledge* or *information*—about customers, alternatives, ...

*Try...Long-term hands-on engineers*

Lean product development (LPD) focuses on creating *more useful knowledge* and *learning better* than the competition.

Also, leveraging that knowledge and not wasting the fruits of the effort by forgetting what has been learned. Figure 3.8 and Figure 3.9 illustrate some of the lean practices to outlearn the competition in LPD; follow-up sections elaborate a few items.

### More-Valuable, Lower-Cost Learning

Not all new knowledge or information is valuable; the ideal is to create economically useful new information [Reinertsen97]. This is challenging because it is a discovery process—you win some, you lose some.

*Try...Increase the value and lower the cost of information*

A general lean (and agile) strategy, based on a simple insight from information theory, is to *increase the value of information created* and *lower the cost of creating knowledge*.

---

22. Coined by Toyota product development researcher Dr. Allen Ward.

Figure 3.8  how to outlearn the competition

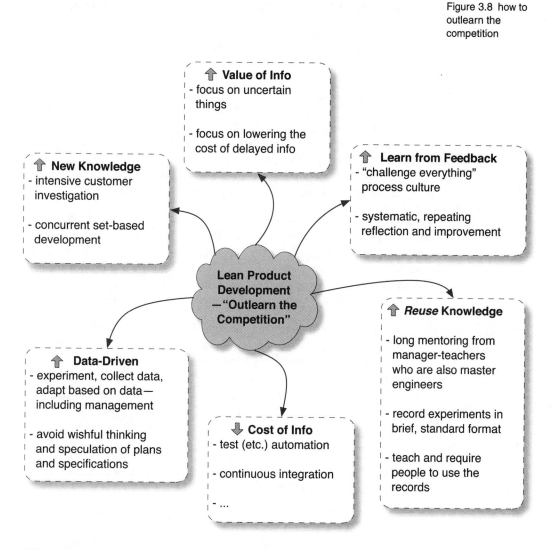

**Higher-value information**—Several ideas in lean and agile development help. For example:

❑ *Focus on uncertain things*—In Scrum, one prioritization guideline is to choose to implement and test *unclear* or *risky* things early. The value of the feedback is high precisely because the outcomes are less predictable—predictable things do not teach us much.

❑ *Focus on early testing and feedback*—Information has a real *cost of delay*, which is one reason why testing only once at the end of a long sequential cycle—motivated by the misguided local optimization of believing that it will lower testing costs—is almost always unskillful. It can be very costly to discover during stress performance testing, after 18 months of development, that a key architectural decision was flawed. In lean (and in Scrum), short cycles with early feedback loops are critical; by implementing less predictable things early and in short cycles that include testing, the cost of delay is reduced.[23]

**Lower-cost information**—The "Indirect Benefits of Reducing Batch Size and Cycle Time" section on page 112 examines how adopting lean and agile principles ends up reducing the overhead cost of processes. In fact, one can broadly look at these methods as succeeding by *lowering the cost of change*—competing on agility. And that includes lowering the cost of learning. For example:

*see Test in companion book*

❑ *Focus on large-scale test automation*—to learn about defects and behavior. The setup costs are non-trivial (if you are currently doing manual testing) but the re-execution costs are almost zero.

*see Continuous Integration in companion*

❑ *Focus on continuous integration*—to learn about defects and lack of synchronization. By integrating frequently in small batches, teams reduce the average overhead cost due to the nonlinear effort-impact of integrating larger sets of code.

❑ *Focus on mentoring from experts and spreading knowledge*—to reduce the cost of rediscovery.

---

23. Note that reducing the cost of delay of information in product development almost always requires building and testing something.

Figure 3.9 LPD practices

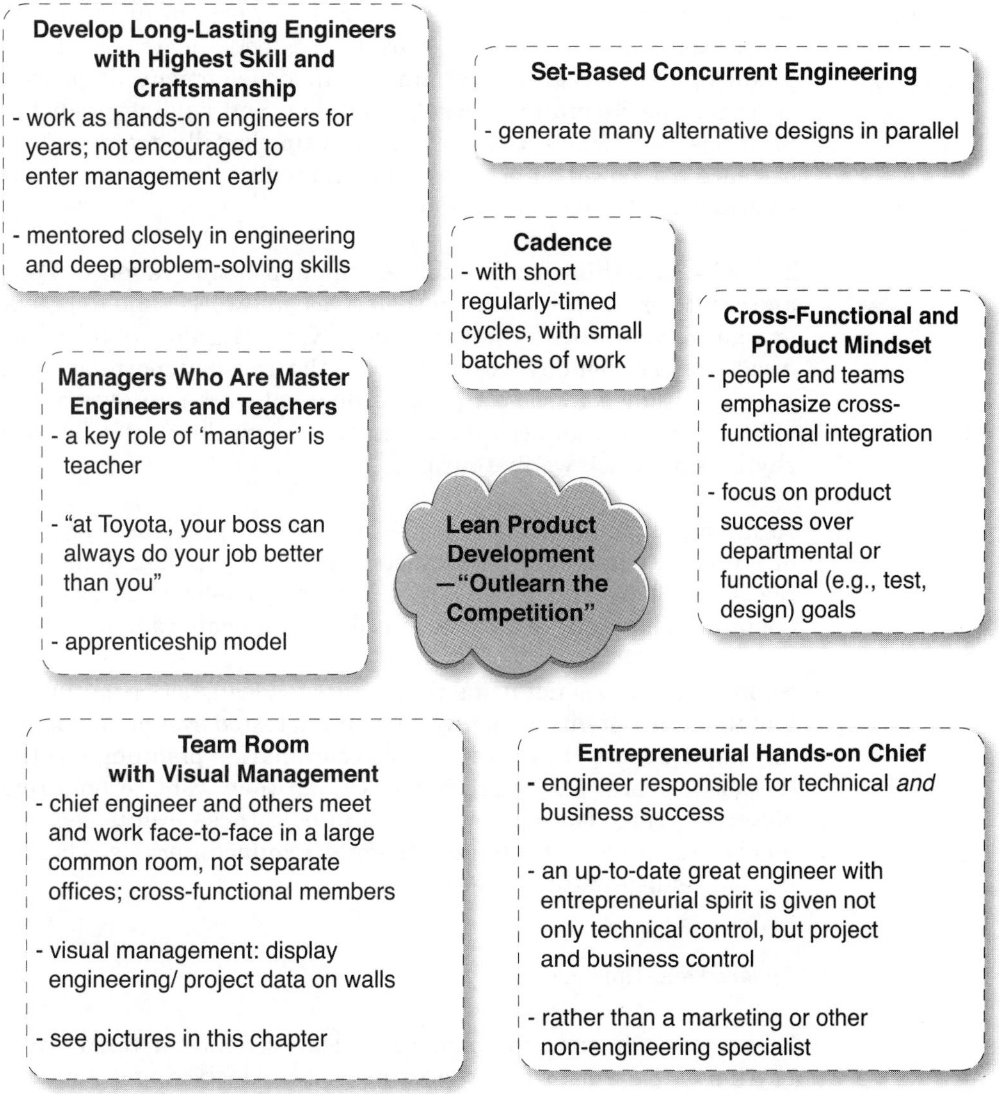

**Develop Long-Lasting Engineers with Highest Skill and Craftsmanship**
- work as hands-on engineers for years; not encouraged to enter management early

- mentored closely in engineering and deep problem-solving skills

**Set-Based Concurrent Engineering**

- generate many alternative designs in parallel

**Cadence**
- with short regularly-timed cycles, with small batches of work

**Managers Who Are Master Engineers and Teachers**
- a key role of 'manager' is teacher

- "at Toyota, your boss can always do your job better than you"

- apprenticeship model

**Lean Product Development —"Outlearn the Competition"**

**Cross-Functional and Product Mindset**
- people and teams emphasize cross-functional integration

- focus on product success over departmental or functional (e.g., test, design) goals

**Team Room with Visual Management**
- chief engineer and others meet and work face-to-face in a large common room, not separate offices; cross-functional members

- visual management: display engineering/ project data on walls

- see pictures in this chapter

**Entrepreneurial Hands-on Chief**
- engineer responsible for technical *and* business success

- an up-to-date great engineer with entrepreneurial spirit is given not only technical control, but project and business control

- rather than a marketing or other non-engineering specialist

## Cadence

Working in regular rhythms or **cadence** is a lean principle, both in production and development [Ward06]. A steady heart beat. In lean production, it is called *takt* time.[24] In development, it is called cadence. The Scrum practice of delivering (and holding predictable meetings) in a regular two- or four-week timebox illustrates cadence. Cadence is a powerful principle in lean product development, so the subject is examined in some detail...

There is something basic and very human about cadence: People appreciate or want *rhythms* in their lives and work—and appreciate or want *rituals* within these rhythms [Kerth01]. Most of us work in a cadence of seven-day weeks. There is the Tuesday-morning weekly meeting ritual. And so on. Simply, cadence at work improves predictability, planning, and coordinating. At a deeper level, it reflects the rhythms by which we live our lives.

In large groups adopting Scrum—groups that previously had little or no cadence and long unbounded work—it is common to hear people say, "Short timeboxes are the most beneficial things we've adopted." This reflects how much people appreciate cadence.

Suppose a group is not using Scrum (not following a Scrum timebox) and they can potentially deliver a running tested system any hour of any day. Suppose they want to hold coordination planning meetings (because several teams are involved) and they want to hold retrospectives. Their two options are (1) to hold these events semi-randomly over time, or (2) to hold them at regular intervals. This lean principle suggests the latter choice.

### Cadence and Timeboxing

Scrum creates an unambiguously clear cadence defined by the rhythm of the two- or four-week timeboxes. Timeboxing is not a panacea for all product development problems, but it has advantages:

❑ Timeboxing enforces cadence.

---

24. *takt*—rhythmic beat (German)

❏ In small-group products with naturally tiny requirements (such as many Web applications), a two- or four-week timebox can sound like a step backwards... *"You want us to deliver a working system every four weeks? We already do that every week!"* But consider a 300-person group that is accustomed to a 'single' requirement taking 18 months, and a release every three years for an embedded-system product with sites in São Paolo, Oxford, and Warsaw. A suggestion such as, *"Start to continuously develop micro-requirements with a continuously integrated and tested system so that you can always ship the product"* is *light years* away from their capacity. In this context, "deliver a working system *exactly* every four weeks" provides a compelling and unambiguous attainable improvement goal, and starts to introduce cadence into a system that had little.

❏ Research and development work is often *fuzzy unbounded (or weakly bounded)* work. When the team knows that the Sprint Review will be in two weeks on March 15, it bounds the fuzzy work and increases focus. One game company doing Scrum observed that timeboxing the art work provided an immediate benefit [Keith08]. In short:

- Timeboxing limits scope creep, limits *gold-plating*, and increases focus—one of the Scrum values.

*Scrum values p. 141*

❏ Timeboxing reduces *analysis paralysis*.

❏ Suppose you are in university and have an assignment due on Monday. When do you start? For many, the answer is, "Close to Monday." This is called *Student Syndrome* [Goldratt97] and timeboxing is a counterbalance.

❏ If teams must deliver something well done in exactly two weeks, the waste and ineffectiveness in current ways of working become painfully clear. For example, parallel development (rather than serial development) leads to faster delivery of value, shorter feedback loops, and other benefits; therefore, timeboxing creates a change-force to improve toward parallel development with cross-functional feature teams.

❏ In large multiteam development, a planning meeting is sometimes needed *between* several teams. Sprint Planning on the first day of each timebox simplifies their coordination.

❏ Timeboxing simplifies scheduling—you know when to show up for planning and reviews. This is especially useful for a meeting-challenged busy Product Owner; she can schedule long into the future when to attend predictable events.

❏ Humans are probably more sensitive to time variation than to scope variation—"It was late" is remembered more strongly than, "It had less than I wanted." Timeboxing avoids the erosion of confidence that happens for business stakeholders when product development people say, yet again, "… maybe in *one* more week it will *all* be done."

## Re-use Information or Knowledge

*Try…Re-use more information and knowledge through mentoring, design patterns, wikis, …*

In addition to the long-term shift toward a culture of *mentoring* by master engineers and manager-teachers to re-use information, a *simple sharing tool* can help. In our coaching we have seen a pattern that the most 'sticky' or successful tool is a wiki. Simplicity and a "Web 2.0"-centric hypertext model seems to win out over older document-centric tools.

*Design patterns* in both hardware and software leverage the use of existing design insight; learn and communicate patterns.

## Team Room with Visual Management

*Try…Team rooms for lean development*

Lean product development encourages a **team room** (or "big room"—big enough for a team) without internal partitions or walls, where a cross-functional team works and meets, and the entrepreneurial chief engineer sits.[25] Walls are covered with large physical displays of project and engineering information, to support visual management. The team room is in contrast to people working in sep-

---

25. In *Peopleware* [DL99] the authors recommended separate offices for programmers; that was in the context of non-team work. The authors have revised that advice and now recommend a *War Room* (team room): "I'm beginning to think that a project not worth a war room may be a project not worth doing" [DeMarco08]. Why? Research shows that team co-location in a team room is correlated with higher productivity [TCKO00].

arate offices or cubicles with communication barriers such as partitions between the team members. See Figure 3.10.

Figure 3.10 team room with rolling whiteboards to support visual management, Valtech India

### Entrepreneurial Chief Engineer with Business Control

In most product development organizations that we visit, a *product management* group is responsible for the business goals and feature selection, and typically the members are not master engineers with up-to-date and profound technical depth. Toyota does things differently. Their product development is led by one great chief engineer with "towering technical excellence" who is also attuned to and responsible for the business success of the new product. In Toyota, product and engineering leadership is combined in one entrepreneurial chief engineer who understands the market, product management, the profit, and the engineering.[26]

*Try...Chief engineer with business acumen as chief product manager*

---

26. We have seen successful products with product managers who are not master engineers—though they *do* need to be great product managers with detailed knowledge of the market, product, and existing customers.

## Set-Based Concurrent Engineering

*Try...Set-based concurrent engineering— several alternate designs in parallel*

Have you seen development as follows?

1. pick or prototype *one* solution or design (one user interface, one architecture, ...)
2. evolve it
3. deliver

**Set-based concurrent engineering** is also called **set-based design**, and is different. For example, rather than one engineer or team creating one cooling system design, several alternatives may be explored at Toyota in parallel by different teams—and so too for other components. These sets of alternatives are explored and combined, and gradually filtered in cycles, converging on a solution from what was at first a large set of alternatives, then a smaller set, and so on. They *outlearn the competition* by *increasing alternatives and combinations*.

In software, a step in this direction is to explore at least *two* alternative for non-trivial design elements. For example, some years ago we worked with a team that had to build a handler for a printing protocol called JDF. Rather than all getting around one wall of whiteboards and doing one design as one team, we split into two groups and worked at two giant whiteboards (sketching UML-ish diagrams[27]) at opposite ends of the team room. Every 45 minutes or so we visited each other's wall designs and did "show and tell"—collecting ideas from each other. Toward the end of the day, we got together, looked at the two design ideas (that covered large whiteboards), and decided which of the two was more appealing. Then the team implemented it, taking inspiration from this design idea sketched on the wall.

---

27. UML, Unified Modeling Language, is a diagramming notation.

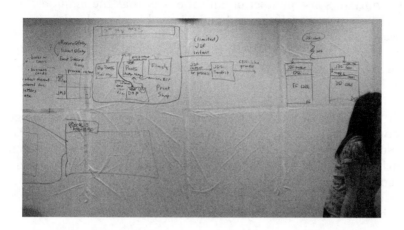

Figure 3.11 design workshop that explored competing designs

The spirit of set-based design, if not as elaborate as at Toyota, can be applied to many design problems. You can prototype, in parallel:

❑ two or three user interface alternatives

❑ two alternatives for a performance-critical component, ...

### Can Lean Production Lessons Help Development?

New product development (NPD) or research and development (R&D) is not predictable repetitive production (manufacturing), and the assumption they are similar is one cause of the misuse of early-1900s manufacturing "economies of scale" management practices in R&D; for example, sequential development and big batch transfers of requirements.

Yet, some of the principles and ideas applied in lean production—including short cycles, small batches, stop-and-fix, visual management, and queueing theory—*are* successfully applied in lean product development. Why? Modern lean production is different, the small batches, queues, and cycle times in part reflect *queueing theory* insight (among other sources of insight)—a discipline that was created for the variable behavior in networks that is much more like product development than traditional manufacturing.

An irony in some product organizations is that the *manufacturing* engineers have revolutionized and adopted lean production, moving away from "economies of scale" toward flow and flexibility in small batches without waste. But these lessons—which fit well to NPD— remain unused by R&D management, who continue to apply practices found in older economies-of-scale manufacturing management.

All that said, a caution: NPD is not manufacturing, and analogies between these two domains are fragile. Unlike production, NPD is (and must be) filled with discovery, change, and uncertainty. Some variability is both normal and desirable in new product development; otherwise, nothing *new* is done. Therefore, lean thinking includes unique practices for NPD, which can be further enhanced with agile development in Scrum.

## EXAMPLE: "KANBAN SYSTEM" ANALYSIS

As in the *Systems Thinking* chapter, a concluding example may be useful to make the chapter subject more concrete. This case study is minor and detailed, and may easily be skipped.

This section will analyze an example practice from a lean perspective, to help develop evaluation skills. This particular practice, called "*kanban* system," had the appearance of being lean because a Japanese name was used, but it will be seen that it had weaknesses.

> One problem in lean adoptions is to assume a practice labeled from the Japanese lean lexicon is *a priori* lean.

This problem is additional motivation for the analysis, as any lean-sounding practices may attract people new to lean thinking.

The practice was promoted some years ago in software development under the name "kanban system"—using a visual management board with a limited number of cards representing software change requests [Anderson07]. Note this is a specific practice, different than the general notion of kanban visual management for pull systems.

## Queue Management is Not Lean Thinking

To quote a summary of the practice under analysis:

> *The kanban limit for the system is 20 cards [on a wall], divided in to different stages in the process—systems analysis, development, test, build / merge, deployment. [Anderson07]*

A limited number of work-request cards on a wall limits the work queue size; the practice is an example of queue management. As explored earlier, queue management is not lean thinking, but a tool—and secondary to key lean elements such as lean-thinking manager-teachers and continuous improvement with Go See and kaizen. Likewise with cards on a wall (visual management).

Limiting a queue size of requests combined with cards is useful, though not new. It has been practiced in the agile method Extreme Programming [BF00], discussed in lean development [Poppendieck03], and its use surveyed in [Hirinabe07, Hirinabe08].

## Serial versus Parallel Development: Eradicating Queues

In this particular variation of the practice, note that the cards on the wall identify and affirm separate development stages, promoting or sustaining a sequential development model—micro-waterfall stages of "*systems analysis, development, test, ...*" and so forth. So what?

This example applies queue management to improve (by limiting the queue size and WIP) an existing *serial* perspective on development. But is queue management the best way to improve a development method? It demonstrates the traditional belief that several serial development stages—even if small and close together—are inevitable and that queues must exist.[28]

Related to lean concepts, this "kanban system" practice illustrates an inside-the-box improvement perspective that in Toyota is called **point kaizen**, improvement (usually not dramatic) within the existing system or paradigm. In this case, within the paradigm "develop-

---

28. This point of "no stages" could be overstated. There are no doubt usually at least two stages—*develop* and *deploy*.

ment is serial, has stages, and queues must exist." But queue management may in fact be *Plan B*.

In contrast, many (entertaining) stories from battle-hardened Toyota lean coaches demonstrate **system kaizen**—not merely improving the system with WIP reduction and so forth, but *replacing* the system by challenging fundamental assumptions and paradigm.

*eradicate queues*
*p. 98*

In this case, a powerful system kaizen alternative is *Plan A—fundamentally change the system from serial to parallel*. The most powerful form of "queue management" is to utterly eradicate a queue by changing the system. For example, move to more *concurrent engineering* and parallel development with *cross-functional Scrum feature teams, acceptance test-driven development*, and *continuous integration* so that there are fewer serial stages (and thus no need to identify stages with cards on a wall). But this would require more—and deeper—mindset and organizational changes, as system kaizen usually does. If that is not possible in the short run, a point kaizen solution such as the practice under analysis is a reasonable "Plan B."

By affirming serial stages (systems analysis, development, ...) the system may also increase handoff (and hence delay) and single-function workers "only working to job title," wastes in lean thinking.

Thus, the practice under analysis has weaknesses: It is a *point kaizen* solution that makes some improvements but still supports serial queues, handoff (and so, delay), and under-realized talent.

### Variability and Large Work Packages

The practice also allows work of variable size to enter the front-end queue (as though this were desirable). To quote:

> *Even though we are making a release every two weeks, items in the system can take up to 60 days to move through depending on their size and complexity. Items that would be too big for a single two-week iteration can still be fed in to the system...*

*reducing*
*variability with*
*Scrum p. 117*

Is this a good idea?

In lean thinking *leveling* (smoothing) variability of incoming elements and reducing batch size are principles related to flow.[29]

Queueing theory shows that allowing entry of items with variation at the front of a system with several stages is undesirable because the *Law of Variability Placement* [HS08] identifies variability at the front end (the incoming requests) as the worst place in terms of average cycle-time impact. Theory also shows a big work package is not good. From this perspective, the practice has a weakness.

A powerful alternative is to split the incoming requests into *user stories* of small and equal size—to level the work packages and reduce the batch size. This is automatically done in timeboxed agile methods with cadence (such as Scrum) because items must fit within the small timebox. Short timeboxes tend to reduce *common-cause variation* in work requests, and non-timeboxing systems (such as the practice under analysis) may increase the variation. Note that this user-story-leveling strategy can—and should—be applied whether timeboxing is or is not used.

**Kaizen and Learning**

The example system is also complimented for removing 'overhead':

> ...*the kanban system has freed us from the management overhead of running each iteration like a mini-project.*

Is that desirable or an improvement?

Removing pure-waste overhead is obviously good. However, is there any *value* in the regular meetings of self-managing teams in a timeboxed method, or are they just waste?

Recall that in lean product development what is being created of value is not only a product, but new *knowledge*. And proactive *continuous improvement* is a pillar of lean thinking.

For example, the Scrum Sprint Review and Sprint Retrospective are frequent, formal, and focused opportunities to *learn* from all parties and to do *kaizen*. They are not overhead, but events to learn and improve, performed in a rhythm. Recurring kaizen events are a com-

---

29. A 'single' requirement in software development is usually a hidden batch that can be split or reduced in size to increase leveling.

mon lean practice and ubiquitous in Toyota. They do kaizen not only reactively in response to the appearance of visible problems, but regularly and proactively to reflect and improve.

Further, Sprint Planning is a time for teams to *learn* what product management wants (and for product management to learn what is possible), enhanced by eliminating the lean waste of handoff through increased face-to-face conversation. The part-two workshop is a chance for the team to collaborate and *design* in the team room—a creative learning act promoted in lean product development. These are not wasteful events from a lean perspective.

### Cadence of Improvement and Learning

Related to the above points, there is no *cadence* of learning, improving, and proactive retrospecting in the practice under analysis. There is only the two-week delivery cycle.

*timeboxing benefits p. 78*

There are non-trivial reasons why cadence (which applies to more than delivery) is identified in lean product development as a key principle, and why the short timeboxes—that create it—used in Scrum, XP, and DSDM have been a popular, 'sticky' practice for many years. It is true that timeboxing is not without weaknesses, but it also has strengths; careful appreciation of the deeper dynamics at play is useful. These include the subtle factors mentioned previously, such as reducing *Student Syndrome,* reducing gold-plating, driving to parallel development, reducing analysis paralysis, bounding fuzzy work, reducing variability (in work requests and other elements), creating a cadence of learning, and driving out-of-the-box thinking for deep improvement.

### Workers from Resource Pool versus Stable Long-Lived Teams

The practice draws on people from a resource pool (as though this were desirable). To quote:

> *Our sustaining process is driven from a floating pool of regular software engineering resources, there is no dedicated sustaining or maintenance team.*

However, Toyota emphasizes stable teams over resource-pool management [LM07]. Plus, research [Katz82] shows that long-lived stable R&D teams are correlated with higher productivity than
temporary project groups of people drawn from a resource pool.

*long-lived teams*
*p. 199*

The practice does not use a permanent maintenance group, but
instead uses rotating contributors. This rotation has advantages,
but can alternatively be achieved by rotating entire long-lived teams
in and out of a defect-handling role. Most of our large-scale lean and
agile development clients use a cadence of rotation into the role of
"bug team" based on the Scrum timebox—a stable Scrum feature
team may serve as a bug team for one or two iterations before
returning to new feature work.

### Summary

The practice under analysis helps by limiting queue size and WIP,
but should not *a priori* be considered a strong example of lean thinking only because a Japanese lean term is used or because queue or
visual management is used. This evaluation applies to any practice.

The case study was also used to illustrate that

❏ eradicating queues through system kaizen with parallel development is more powerful than managing queues

❏ variability in request size, and large requests, are undesirable

❏ a cadence of kaizen and learning has value

❏ timeboxes with learning and kaizen events can be useful

❏ Toyota uses stable teams

### CONCLUSION

As you investigate lean thinking, it is easy to see that it is a broad
system that intersects with agile principles, and spans all groups
and functions of the enterprise, including product development,
sales, production, service, and HR. Lean thinking applies to large-
scale product development—indeed, it *applies to the enterprise.*

That realization started for us several years ago...Xerox develops large digital presses, printing full color at over 110 pages per minute. One of these products requires many hundreds of engineers and scientists, and involves tens of millions of lines of code. Big systems, big groups. Some years ago Craig was invited to lead the coaching of lean development for software-intensive embedded systems at Xerox. That initiative has lasted years and furthered our appreciation that lean thinking applies to large-scale product development—and fits well with Scrum. Xerox also applies lean development practices within electro-mechanical-optical engineering. Thus, lean provides some common vocabulary and framework for different engineering groups—and that turns out to be useful.

Lean thinking is much more than *tools* such as kanban, visual management or queue management, or merely elimination of waste. As can been seen at Toyota, it is an enterprise system resting on the foundation of manager-teachers in lean thinking, with the pillars of respect for people and continuous improvement. Its successful introduction will take years and requires widespread education and coaching. To re-quote Fujio Cho, chairman of Toyota:

> *Many good American companies have respect for individuals, and practice kaizen and other [lean] tools. But what is important is having all the elements together as a system. It must be practiced every day in a very consistent manner...*

## RECOMMENDED READINGS

- ❏ Dr. Jeffrey Liker's *The Toyota Way* is a thorough cogent summary from a researcher who has spent decades studying Toyota and their principles and practices.

- ❏ *Inside the Mind of Toyota* by Professor Satoshi Hino. Hino spent many years working in product development, followed by an academic career. Hino has "spent more than 20 years researching the subject of this book." This is a data-driven book that looks at the evolution and principles of the original lean thinking management system.

- ❏ *Extreme Toyota* by Osono, Shimizu, and Takeuchi is a well-researched analysis of the Toyota Way values, contradictions, and culture, based on six years of research and 220 interviews. It includes an in-depth analysis of Toyota's strong business performance. Hirotaka Takeuchi was also co-author of the famous 1986 *Harvard Business Review* article "The New New Product Development Game" that introduced key ideas of Scrum.

❑ *Lean Product and Process Development* by Allen Ward and *The Toyota Product Development System* by Liker and Morgan are useful for insights into development from a lean perspective.

❑ *Toyota Culture* by Liker and Michael Hoseus. Hoseus has worked both as a plant manager and HR manager at Toyota, bringing an insider's in-depth understanding to this book on the heart of what makes a lean enterprise work.

❑ *Lean Thinking* by Drs. Womack and Jones is an entertaining and well-written summary of some lean principles by authors who know their subject well. As cautioned earlier in this chapter it presents an anecdotal and condensed view that may give the casual reader the wrong impression that the essential key of lean is waste reduction rather than a culture of manager-teachers who understand lean thinking and help build the pillars of respect for people and continuous improvement with Go See and other behaviors.

❑ *The Machine That Changed the World: The Story of Lean Production* by Womack, Jones, and Roos was based on a five-year study at MIT into lean and the Toyota system.

❑ *Workplace Management* by Taichii Ohno is a short book by the creator of the Toyota Production System. It was out-of-print but has been recently re-translated by Jon Miller and is now available. The book does not talk much about TPS but it contains a series of short chapters that show well how Taichii Ohno thought about management and lean systems.

❑ Mary and Tom Poppendieck's books *Lean Software Development* and *Implementing Lean Software Development* are well-written books that make important connections between lean thinking, systems thinking, and agile development.

## Chapter

## Book

# QUEUEING THEORY

*The joy of engineering is to find a straight
line on a double logarithmic diagram.*
—*Thomas Koenig*

*We notice that queueing theory garners polar reactions; some
find it inconsequential (for development) while others find it
useful to motivate or apply lean product development.*

Queueing theory offers insight into why traditional product development is unnecessarily slow—and what to do about it. We very occasionally coach web-application groups where—really—the *maximum* effort for a feature is half of *one* person-day. They do not have a major large-batch problem. But in large products one feature (before splitting) may be *"add support for HSDPA protocol"* or *"add support for PDF version 1.7."* In such domains, it is particularly helpful to see that large batches and long queues exist, and that something can be done to improve. This thinking tool is relevant for large products because big variable batches of work have a *nonlinear impact* on cycle time—they can *really* mess things up.

An interesting incongruity: Queueing theory—the mathematical analysis of how *stuff* moves through a system with queues—was developed to understand and improve throughput in telecommunication systems—systems with lots of variability and randomness similar to product development. As a consequence, telecommunication engineers understand the basic insights. And yet, telecom infrastructure development people (telecom is a domain of large products) do not always see that *it applies to them* to reduce the average cycle time in their development system.

> **Lotus 1-2-3?**—Some readers may not have even heard of Lotus 1-2-3, but it once *owned* the spreadsheet market. Borland and Microsoft came out with competing products with better graphics. Lotus was slow to respond (long cycle times), and three years later the competitors held 52% of the market share, about $500 million USD in sales. Lotus 1-2-3 RIP. [Meyer93]

*leveling p. 65*

Toyota people understand statistical variation and the implications of queueing theory; this is reflected in the lean *leveling* principle to reduce variability and more generally in the lean focus on smaller batches and cycle times to move toward *flow*. As will be evident, Scrum supports the management implications of queueing theory.

Before diving directly into the subject, note that lean is sometimes described as focusing on *smaller batch (work package) size, shorter queues,* and *faster cycle time*. Delivering value quickly. Lean is much more than this—the pillars are *respect for people* and *continuous improvement* resting on a foundation of *manager-teachers in lean thinking*. Queue management is a mere tool far removed from the essence of lean thinking. That said, faster cycle time is part of the "global goal" in lean: *Sustainable shortest lead time, best quality, most customer delight, lowest cost, high morale, safety*. So, on to cycle time…

## TRY…COMPETE ON SHORTER CYCLE TIMES

A lean product development organization is focused on *value throughput in the shortest possible sustainable cycle times,* focused on the *baton* rather than runners. Toyota people, the progenitors of lean thinking, are masters of faster and faster (shorter) cycle times without overburdening people.

What are some process cycles or cycle times in product development?

- "concept to cash" for one release
- "concept to done" for one feature
- potentially shippable time—how frequently *could* you ship?
- integration time (to integrate and fully test the product)
- compile time (of all the software)
- "ready to pilot" to delivery time
- deployment time for testing (into embedded hardware)
- analysis and design times

Key performance indicators (KPIs) in lean are *not* focused on the utilization of workers doing these processes. Rather, *lean KPIs focus more on throughput cycle times*—the baton rather than the runners.

*Try…Use several high-level cycle-time KPIs*

That said, a caution: Measurement usually generates dysfunction or 'gaming' of the system by sub-optimizing to appear to achieve a good score [Austin96]. This is especially true on 'lower' process cycles. Higher-level cycle times such as potentially shippable cycle time and "order to cash" or "order to delivery" (the quintessential cycle times) are most relevant.

What would it mean if you could deliver in *half or a quarter of the time* at a *sustainable pace* without overburdening people? And on the other hand, what is the cost of delay?

Consider the benefits of delivering fast in terms of life cycle profits, opportunities gained, response to competition, and innovation. For most companies—not all—it would be an *extraordinary* advantage.

**Half the time is not half the cost**—When people hear "half the time" they may think, "Twice as many products, features, or releases—twice the old efficiency." But there could be more **transaction cost**, the overhead for each cycle. Shipping more frequently might increase testing or deployment costs—or not, as will be seen.

> **Economic model includes cycle time**—How to consider the trade-off of shorter cycles versus transaction costs? Use an economic model of your product that *includes cycle time factors* [SR98]. Suppose you could ship six months sooner. What are the estimated total life cycle profit impact and the increased testing costs (transaction cost)? If you could gain $20 million at a 40 percent increase in testing costs ($1.3 million), it is money well spent. The flip side of this is the

*cost of delay.* One product study showed a 33 percent loss of total profit due to a six-month delay [Reinertsen83]. Unfortunately, many product groups we work with do not seriously analyze cycle time factors in their life cycle profit economic model.

**Half the time is not twice the cost**—Before you put away your spreadsheet on the transaction cost analysis, hold on. There is a subtle connection between cycle time, transaction cost, and efficiency that will soon be explored—a secret behind the impressive efficiency of Toyota and other lean thinking enterprises...

**Queue management**—There are plenty of strategies to reduce cycle time; both lean and agile practices offer a cornucopia of skillful means. One tool is the subject of this chapter—queue management.

## QUEUE MANAGEMENT TO REDUCE CYCLE TIME

*"Queues only exist in manufacturing, so queueing theory and queue management don't apply to product development."* This is a common misconception. As mentioned, queueing theory did not arise in manufacturing but in operations research to improve throughput in telecom systems with high variability. Furthermore, many development groups—especially those adopting lean or agile practices—have adopted queue management based on queueing theory insight for both *product development* and *portfolio management.* One study from MIT and Stanford researchers concluded:

> *Business units that embraced this approach [queue management for portfolio and product management] reduced their average development times by 30% to 50%. [AMNS96]*

## Queues in Product Development and Portfolio Management

Example queues in development and portfolio management?

- products or projects in a portfolio
- new features for one product
- detailed requirements specifications waiting for design
- design documents waiting to be coded
- code waiting to be tested
- the code of a single developer waiting to be integrated with other developers
- large components waiting to be integrated
- large components and systems waiting to be tested

In traditional sequential development there are many queues of partially done work, known as work-in-progress or **WIP queues**; for example, specification documents waiting to be programmed and code waiting to be tested.

In addition to *WIP queues*, there are **constrained-resource** or **shared-resource queues**, such as a backlog of requests to use an expensive testing lab or piece of testing equipment.

## Queues Are a Problem

First, if there are no queues—and no multitasking that artificially makes it appear a queue has been removed—then the system will move toward flow, the lean principle and perfection challenge that value is delivered without delay. Every queue creates a delay that inhibits flows. More specifically, why are queues a problem?

**WIP queues**—WIP queues in product development are seldom seen as queues for several reasons; perhaps chief among these is that they tend to be *invisible*—bits on a computer disk. But they are there—and more importantly they create problems. Why?[1]

❏ WIP queues (as most queues) *increase average cycle time* and reduce value delivery, and thus may lower lifetime profit.

---

1. See also the *Recommended Readings* for a cogent analysis of queues in product development and what to do about them.

❏ In lean thinking, WIP queues are identified as *waste*—and hence to be removed or reduced—because:

  – WIP queues have the aforementioned impact on cycle time.

  – WIP queues are *inventory* (of specifications, code, documentation, …) with an investment of time and money for which there has been no return on investment.

  – As with all inventory, WIP queues hide—and allow replication of—defects because the pile of inventory has not been consumed or tested by a downstream process to reveal hidden problems; for example, a pile of un-integrated code.

  – We saw a traditional product group that spent about one year working on a "deal breaker" feature. Then product management decided to remove it because it threatened the overall release and the market had changed. Replanning took many weeks. In general, WIP queues *affect the cost and ability to respond to change* (deletions and additions) because (1) time and money were spent on unfinished deleted work that will not be realized, or (2) the WIP of the deleted item may be tangled up with other features, or (3) a feature to add can experience a delayed start due to current high WIP levels.

*benefits of reducing cycle and batch p. 112*

As will be explored, there is a subtle but potentially powerful systems-improvement side effect that can occur through the process of eliminating WIP queues.

**Shared resource queues**—In contrast to WIP queues, these are more often seen as queues—and seen as a problem. They clearly and painfully slow people down, delay feedback, and stretch out cycle times. *"We need to test our stuff on that printer. When will it be free?"*

### Try...Eradicate queues by changing the system

The bottom line is that (usually) *queues are a problem*. Given that, you may jump to the conclusion that the first line of defense against this problem is to *reduce the batch and queue size*, because these are classic queue-management strategies. Yet, there is a *Gordian Knot* solution that should be considered first…

The remainder of this chapter will indeed explore reducing cycle time through batch- and queue-size management. But that entire management strategy should be *Plan B*. Rather, start with *Plan A*:

> Plan A in queue management is to *completely eradicate the queue, forever, by changing the system—of development, tools, ...*

Think outside the current box and shorten cycle times by changing the *system* so that queues no longer exist—by removing bottlenecks and other forces that create the queues. These constraints and the queues they spawn may be created or eradicated by the very nature of a development system and its tools.

Suppose the existing system is based on sequential or serial development with single-specialist workers or groups. There will be WIP queues: The analyst group hands off specification work packages to the programming group that hands off code work packages to the testing group. The *inside-the-box* response to improving cycle time with queue management is to reduce batch size, reduce variability, and limit the WIP queue sizes between these groups.

But there is a deeper alternative that will more dramatically improve cycle time: Discard that system and the bottlenecks and WIP queues it spawns. If you adopt cross-functional feature teams that do complete features (analysis, programming, and testing) without handing off work to other groups, and that apply automated acceptance test-driven development (TDD), the above WIP queues *vanish* by moving from serial to parallel development.

*feature teams*
*p. 149*

### Avoid...Fake queue reduction by increased multitasking or utilization rates

Suppose you are busy working on item A, and items B, C, D, and E are in your queue. Fake queue reduction is to work on *all* these items at more or less the same time—a high level of multitasking and utilization. Multitasking is one of the lean wastes because as will be soon seen, queueing theory shows that this would *increase* average cycle time, not reduce it. Bad idea.

Do not increase multitasking[2] or utilization rates to create the *illusion* that queues have been reduced and the system has improved; rather, improve the system so that the bottlenecks and other forces that create queues are removed.

### After Plan A, What Queues May Remain?

Traditional WIP queues can be eliminated by the move to Scrum with cross-functional feature teams and the use of acceptance TDD. Banished and vanished via Plan A—change the system. Still, queues can and do remain:

❑ shared-resource queues, such as a testing lab

*Product Backlog and queues p. 115*

❑ the queue of feature requests in the Product Backlog

❑ WIP queues because (1) Plan A is not yet possible (deep change in large product groups takes time), or (2) tools and techniques, such as moving from manual to fully automated testing, are weak and slow to improve

Whatever queues remain—and at the very least, the Scrum Product Backlog will remain—you can improve average cycle time by Plan B in queue management…

### Try…Small batches of equal size

For queues that cannot be eradicated, improve average cycle time by reducing the batch size in the queues, and by making each batch equally sized.

In Scrum, a smaller batch means a smaller work package of items or features to develop in an iteration. Equally sized batches imply that each is estimated to be roughly equal in effort.

---

2. Naturally, taking on two tasks in parallel (multitasking) is appropriate if it is possible to be blocked from working on one of the tasks and it is not possible to improve the system to remove the block.

Concretely, how to apply this in Scrum? That will be explored later in the chapter, but first, on to the field of queueing theory...

## QUEUEING THEORY

It might take hard work or a new perspective, but it doesn't take much theory to "manage queues" by *eradicating* them. On the other hand, when they must still exist, it is helpful to know how to deal with them with the thinking tool of queueing theory.

### A Formal Model for Evaluating Processes

You may accept at face value that queues with smaller feature-batches of equal size improve average cycle time. Or not. In any event, it is useful to know that this suggestion is not based on opinion but is grounded in a formal mathematical model that can be demonstrated. It *is* possible to reason about some aspects of a development process, using a formal model. For example:

- ❏ *Hypothesis*: It is fastest to do sequential ('waterfall' or V-model) development with large-batch transfers between groups.

- ❏ *Hypothesis*: It is fastest for people or groups to have high utilization rates and multitask on many projects at the same time.

An understanding of queueing theory, independent of opinion, can reveal if these hypotheses help reduce average cycle time.

The topic is relatively simple; a scenario captures key elements...

### Qualities of a Stochastic System with Queues

Consider Los Angeles or Bangalore at rush hour. By some miracle there are no accidents and all lanes are open. Traffic is tight and slow, but moving. Over a short period of time, there are accidents on three different major four-lane highways (twelve lanes), and three lanes are closed—only nine lanes are still

open. Boom! Before you can say, "Why didn't I buy a helicopter?" much of the city does a *phase shift* into *gridlock*. When the accidents are finally cleared (ranging from thirty to sixty minutes later), the massive queue buildup takes *forever* to clear. Observations:

- ❑ **Nonlinear**—When the highway is from zero to fifty percent loaded, it is smooth sailing—virtually no queues or delays. But between fifty and one-hundred percent, slowdown becomes noticeable, queues build up. The relation of utilization to queue size is nonlinear, not a smooth linear increase from zero.

- ❑ **Delay and overload does not start at 99.99% utilization**— It is *not* the case that everything goes fast and smooth on the highway until just before 100 percent capacity of cars on the road. Rather, things slow down and gridlock happens well before capacity is reached.

- ❑ **Clearing the queue takes longer than making it**—Forty-five minutes of blockage in Los Angeles at rush hour creates queues that take more than forty-five minutes to clear.

- ❑ **Stochastic, not deterministic**—There is variation and randomness with probabilities (it is a **stochastic** system): arrival rates of cars, time to remove blocks, exit rate of cars.

This is worth spelling out if you wish to grasp how systems behave, because it seems all us humans do *not* have an intuitive sense of the stochastic and nonlinear quality of systems with queues. Gut instinct may be that they are deterministic and behave linearly. This incorrect "common sense" leads to *thinking mistakes* in analyzing problems and managing product development. These observations— and thinking mistakes—apply to WIP queues in traditional product development and to virtually all other queues.

One common thinking mistake in product development is that the queues, delay, and the people that serve them behave as in Figure 4.1—the misunderstanding of *"delay only starts when the highway is 100 percent full."* But slowdown starts happening on the highway long before it is 100 percent full. Perhaps at 60 percent capacity, you start to notice slowdown—a longer average cycle time.

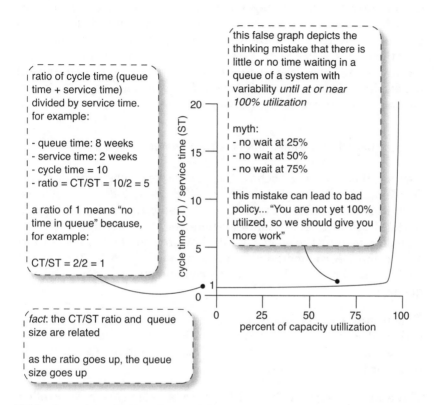

Figure 4.1 a common myth or thinking mistake regarding queues in systems with variability

ratio of cycle time (queue time + service time) divided by service time. for example:

- queue time: 8 weeks
- service time: 2 weeks
- cycle time = 10
- ratio = CT/ST = 10/2 = 5

a ratio of 1 means "no time in queue" because, for example:

CT/ST = 2/2 = 1

this false graph depicts the thinking mistake that there is little or no time waiting in a queue of a system with variability *until at or near 100% utilization*

myth:
- no wait at 25%
- no wait at 50%
- no wait at 75%

this mistake can lead to bad policy... "You are not yet 100% utilized, so we should give you more work"

*fact*: the CT/ST ratio and queue size are related

as the ratio goes up, the queue size goes up

*(Graph axes: vertical axis labeled "cycle time (CT) / service time (ST)" with values 0, 1, 5, 10, 15, 20; horizontal axis labeled "percent of capacity utillization" with values 0, 25, 50, 75, 100)*

With the misunderstanding *"delay only starts when the highway is 100 percent full,"* there is a misguided focus on trying to improve cycle time by *increasing* resource utilization—getting the people in product development to be more busy, usually by more multitasking. *This is the mistake of watching the runner rather than the baton.*

*multitasking p. 60*

What really happens to average cycle time when one increases the utilization level of things or people in a system with variability?

At Xerox they have expensive, large digital print presses in a test lab. There is often a shared-resource queue of testing requests for one of these devices. Without understanding how queues really work (that is, believing they work as in Figure 4.1), the management approach would be to encourage that these expensive systems are reserved and utilized close to 100 percent of the time. But the reality is that there is *variability* all over the place—a stochastic system. Tests arrive randomly, some fail quickly, some take forever to complete, sometimes the equipment breaks, and so forth. *This same variability of behavior applies to people and the queues of work that they work on.*

### Modeling a Basic Single-Arrival System with Queues

How do these systems behave—in traffic, test labs, or traditional development with people working on WIP queues? You have a sense of it from the traffic story. Mathematically, the behavior may be modeled as variations of M/M systems. M/M means that the inter-arrival rate into the queue is Markovian and the service rate is Markovian.[3] A common, basic queueing model is M/M/1/∞—it has one server (for example, one test printer or team) and an infinite queue.[4]

Now it starts to get interesting... In a M/M/1/∞ system, how does cycle and service time relate to utilization of the server—be it a test printer or people working on WIP queues? Figure 4.2 shows the behavior [Smith07].

These are *averages* in Figure 4.2, because elements have random variability, such as:

❑ requests arrive at different times with different effort

❑ tests or programming effort take variable time

❑ people work faster or slower, get sick, or work longer or shorter

---

3. Markovian: A simple concept—a random process with probabilities (stochastic) in which the future state cannot be deterministically known from the present state; that is, similar to "messy reality."
4. Development queues are not normally infinite, but this simplification does not impact the basic pattern of how the systems behave.

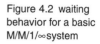

Figure 4.2 waiting behavior for a basic M/M/1/∞ system

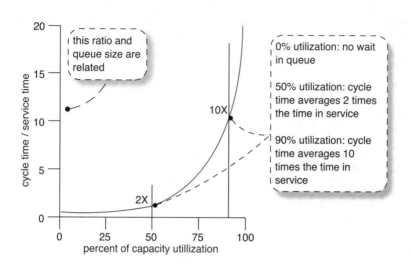

The essential point to grasp is that an item (such as a requirement request) starts sitting in a queue waiting for service long before people are 100 percent utilized. It is also fascinating to see the impact of increased utilization of people on cycle time: *As utilization goes up in a system with lots of variability, average cycle time gets worse, not better.* This is counterintuitive to an average accountant or management consultant who has been taught to "improve productivity by increasing utilization of resources." Most have not been exposed to queueing theory—how to understand stochastic systems with queues (people doing work with variability)—and so demonstrate a thinking mistake.

It is this real-world variability that creates, on average, this increased queue size and waiting time in product development.

### Modeling a Batch System with Queues (Traditional Development)

It gets *even more* interesting (if you could believe that)... The basic M/M/1/∞ system assumes that a *single* item (for testing, analysis, programming, ...) arrives in isolation—that arriving items are never clumped (or batched). Yet in traditional product development, work packages *do* arrive in big clumpy batches, such as sets of requirements or testing work or code to be integrated. Or an apparent 'single' requirement is received such as "provide HSDPA support" that is in fact itself a batch of sub-requirements.[5]

Figure 4.3 waiting behavior in a $M^{[x]}/M/1/\infty$ system, analogous to traditional development with variable batches

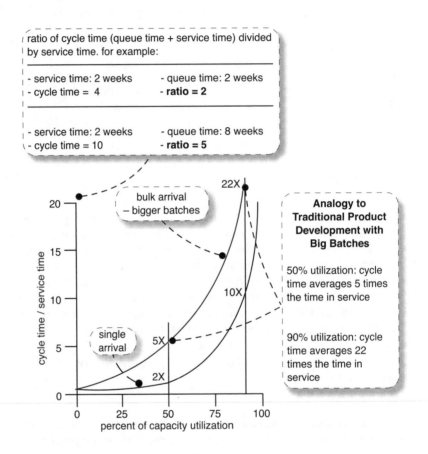

Probably obvious, but it needs to be said:

*As work-item size or batch size increases, variability increases.*

---

5. "One big requirement is itself a batch" is a critical point that will be revisited later in this chapter.

One mega-requirement, more variability. A big batch of requirements, more variability. Big pile of code to integrate or test, more
variability. And if you are involved in budgeting or finance... A big
pile of budgets, more variability.

What effect does this increased size variability have on queues and
waiting time? Now, instead of the simpler single-arrival M/M/1/∞
model (a single work item arrives), we have a $M^{[x]}$/M/1/∞ system (a
batch of items arrive). This model is a better analogy to traditional
product development. Example behavior is shown in Figure 4.3.

At first glance, people may not grasp the startling and counterintuitive implication of what just happened to their cycle time.

A scenario may help: Suppose a person or team is currently 50 percent utilized and you usually give them single small-sized requirements now and then that arrive with some randomness and some
variability in size. Assume it will take them *two weeks* of hands-on
work to complete a particular requirement-X. And assume it is the
simple single-arrival system modeled in Figure 4.2 (and repeated in
the lower curve of Figure 4.3).

As a table, here is an approximation of the average situation:

| arrival | util. | queue time | service time | cycle time | ratio CT/ST |
|---|---|---|---|---|---|
| single arrival | 50% | 2 wk | 2 wk | 4 wk | 2 |

Next, instead, suppose that you are typically giving the 50-percent-
utilized team significantly bigger *batches* of requirements, or 'one'
giant requirement that actually encompasses a big batch of sub-
requirements; these arrive with some randomness and size differences. Assume it will take *twenty weeks* of hands-on service time to
complete some particular batch-X or 'single' big requirement.

Knowing the prior table, this is what some people will predict:

| arrival | util. | queue time | service time | cycle time | ratio CT/ST |
|---------|-------|------------|--------------|------------|-------------|
| single arrival | 50% | 2 wk | 2 wk | 4 wk | 2 |
| *prediction if big batch / requirement arrivals* | *50%* | *20 wk* | *20 wk* | *40 wk* | *2* |

A gut instinct prediction is a *linear* increase in the cycle-time impact. Ten times as much work on average being pushed through the system, so ten times the cycle time. Four weeks versus 40 weeks.

But it does not work that way, because more variability is introduced into the system. A much bigger batch or much bigger 'single' requirement that encompasses many sub-requirements means more variability within the batch, and of course batches can arrive of different sizes. So what happens?

At 50 percent utilization, the cycle-to-service-time ratio is '5' in the $M^{[x]}/M/1/\infty$ example. This approximates the contrasting situations:

| arrival | util. | queue time | service time | cycle time | ratio CT/ST |
|---------|-------|------------|--------------|------------|-------------|
| single arrival | 50% | 2 wk | 2 wk | 4 wk | 2 |
| big batch/ requirement arrivals | 50% | 80 wk | 20 wk | 100 wk | 5 |

Things just got a *lot* worse. Of course, these are averages and cannot be assumed for any one real case, and this model is a simplified abstraction of development. But this is why understanding—and acting on the insight—of queueing theory is vital for large-scale development, because large systems are often associated with big requirements, and big work (requirements, testing, integration, ...)

in big batches arriving at variable times. That can have an astonishing impact on average cycle time.

And as explored earlier, pushing for high utilization rates of your workers in this situation with big batches of work is a recipe for... blackstrap molasses in Alaska.

The reality is a nonlinear increase in cycle time. This impact on delay and queue size defies our instinct because people are not used to analyzing stochastic systems with queues. One might think, "If I make the work package ten times bigger, it will take ten times as long to exit the system." Do not count on it.

*Series of WIP Queues Aggravate Delays*—These delays are further aggravated in traditional sequential development because there are a *series* of processes with WIP queues in front of them; this compounds the variability and adds more negative impact to the overall average cycle time. The *Law of Variability Placement* [HS08] reveals that the worst place for variability (in terms of negative cycle-time impact) is at the front end of a multi-stage system with queues. This is what happens in phase-one requirements analysis with large batches of specifications.

### Conclusion

So, what has been learned?

- ❑ product development is a stochastic system with queues; it is nonlinear and non-deterministic

- ❑ behavior of a stochastic system with queues defies our instincts

- ❑ batch size, size of requirements, and utilization levels affect queue size and cycle time in nonlinear random ways that are not obvious—throughput can get *slow* if not understood

- ❑ queue size affects cycle time

- ❑ in a variable system, high utilization *increases* cycle time and lowers throughput—it does not help; a traditional resource management approach [for example, McGrath04] can make things worse by focusing on the runner rather than the baton

- ❏ a system with variability and a series of processes and WIP queues further aggravates the delay; this situation describes traditional sequential development

- ❏ variability at the front end of multi-step system with queues has the worst impact

## HIDDEN BATCHES: EYES FOR BATCHES

If you bake three cherry pies at the same time, then it is clear that there is a batch of three items. Things are not so clear in product development: What exactly is 'one' requirement? At one level, "a 600 DPI 12 PPM color printer" is one requirement, but it is also a *composite requirement* or a batch of sub-requirements that can be split; for example, into "a 600 DPI color printer." Decomposition of a 'single' large composite requirement is especially relevant (and easy) in software systems. This topic, and its connection to representing very large requirements as *user stories* that can be split, is considered in the *Requirements* chapter of the companion book. For now, the key point to appreciate is that 'one' requirement—especially in large software-intensive embedded systems—is almost always itself a batch of sub-requirements. These hidden batches need to be seen.

Large variable-sized batches are bad for cycle time. *Single* large items with variability are bad for cycle time. Variation in size of batches or items is bad for cycle time. So, the implication for queue management in Scrum is this:

To reduce average cycle time, all apparently 'single' large items (requirements) in the Product Backlog need to be (eventually) split into many small and roughly equal-sized items. This is easily achieved by representing backlog items as user stories.

## HIDDEN QUEUES: EYES FOR QUEUES

When people join Toyota, they learn "Eyes for Waste." They learn to see things as waste that they had not considered, such as *inventory*—queues of stuff. Now, queues of *physical* things are easy for people to perceive, and to perceive as a problem... My goodness, there's a *gigantic* pile of *Stuff* queuing up over there! Making any money from the pile? Are there defects in there? Does it need to be combined with other stuff before we can ship it? Do we need—and will we make money with—*each and every item* in the pile?

**Invisible queues**—In traditional development there are also all kinds of queues, but because they are *invisible* they are not seen as queues or *keenly felt* as problems. If you are a business person who has invested ten million euros to create a gigantic pile of partially done *Stuff* sitting on the floor, not making any money, you walk by it and *see it* and you feel the pain and urgency to get it moving. And you think about no longer making big piles of partially done stuff. But product development people do not really see and feel the pain of their queues.

Yet, they *are* there. Queues of WIP—information, documents, and bits on a disk. Invisible queues. Product development people need a lesson in "Eyes for Queues" so that they can start to perceive what is going on, and develop a sense of urgency about reducing queue sizes.

**Visual management for tangible queues**[6]—To develop "eyes for queues" and a sense of attention, one lean practice is *visual management*, making *physical* tokens (not tokens in a computer program[7]) for these queues. For example, in Scrum and other agile methods, it is common to represent all the tasks for the iteration on paper cards that are placed on the wall and moved around as tasks are completed (Figure 4.4). Physical tokens. Putting these tasks into today's computers[8] defeats the purpose of lean visual management and the

*Try...Visual management to see the invisible queues*

---

6. This section intentionally repeats part of the *Lean* chapter.
7. *Physical* tokens are a critical aspect of lean visual management that is not always appreciated. Some people create software systems for "visual management" and defeat the purpose.
8. Someday, displays will be wall size and one will move computer objects with physical gestures; that will negate this point.

way *humans*—with countless eons of evolutionary instinct working with concrete things—need to *see and feel tangible queues.*

Figure 4.4 lean visual management creates *physical* tokens, such as task cards and paper charts on a wall, so that invisible queues can become tangible—really *seen and felt*

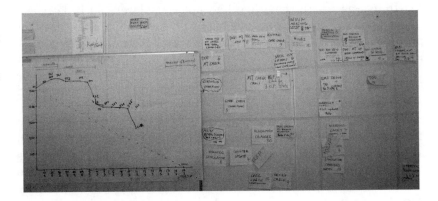

## INDIRECT BENEFITS OF REDUCING BATCH SIZE AND CYCLE TIME

**"Why bother? Our customers don't want a release every two weeks, nor do they want just a sub-requirement."**

We get this question regularly from product groups and business people. They do not yet appreciate the advantages of small batches in short cycles:

- ❑ The *overall* larger release-cycle-time reduction that can come by eradicating queues and by applying queue management so that many development cycles are shorter.

- ❑ The elimination of **batch delay**, where one feature is unnecessarily held back because it is moving through the system attached to a larger batch of other requirements. Eliminating this provides another degree of freedom for the business to ship a smaller product earlier with the highest-priority features.

- ❑ And last but not least, there are *indirect* benefits due to the *"lake and rocks"* effect described next.

## Indirect Benefits: The Lake and Rocks Metaphor

A metaphor shared in lean education: **lake and rocks**. The depth of the water may represent the inventory level, batch size, iteration length, or cycle time. When the water is high (large batch or inventory size, or iteration length), many rocks are hidden. These rocks represent weaknesses. For example, consider an eighteen- month sequential release cycle with a massive batch transfer; inefficient testing, integration, and poor collaboration are all hidden below the surface of such a long cycle and such a large batch. But if we work with that group and ask, "Please deliver a small set of small features that is potentially shippable in two weeks, every two weeks," then suddenly all the ineffective practices become painfully obvious.

Said another way, the *transaction cost* (overhead cost) of the old process cycle becomes unacceptable. That pain then becomes a force for improvement, because people cannot stand re-experiencing it each short cycle, and indeed it may simply be impossible to the iteration goals with the old inefficient system of development.

*Tip*: Not all 'rocks' are big or immediately visible. The lean journey—and the journey of Scrum—is to *start with the big rocks* that are most painfully obvious yet movable, and over time work on smaller impediments.

The causal loop diagram in Figure 4.5 illustrates this lake and rocks effect in terms of a system dynamics model.

Figure 4.5 indirect
and delayed
benefits of reducing
batch and cycle size

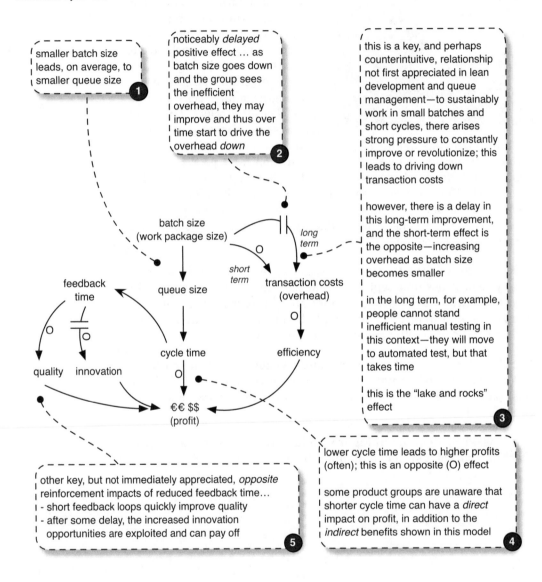

## APPLYING QUEUE MANAGEMENT IN SCRUM

There are dozens of strategies to manage queues. *Managing the Design Factory* by Don Reinertsen explains many. However, we want to focus on a few key steps in a Scrum context:

1. change the system to utterly eradicate queues

2. learn to see remaining queues with visual management

3. reduce variability

4. limit queue size

*Change the system*—(see p. 98). Must you manage *existing* queues? Step outside the box. For example, Scrum feature teams and acceptance TDD eliminate many queues in traditional development.

*Reduce variability*—(see p. 117). Some people first try to reduce work queues by increasing utilization or multitasking (with negative results), or by adding more developers. True, adding people—if they are talented—can help (there are exceptions), but it is expensive and takes time. People who have grasped queue management recognize a simpler place to start in Scrum: Reduce variability, which includes reduction in batch size.

### A Closer Look at the Product Backlog as a *Set* of Queues

It is possible to view the Product Backlog as one big near-infinite priority queue[9], but we suggest a more fine-grained view. It has distinct subsets. One view is that it contains two backlogs: (1) the Release Backlog for the current release, and (2) the "future backlog." A second perspective is that the Product Backlog contains the following two subsets:

❑ the *clear-fine* subset[10] of user stories that are clearly analyzed, well estimated, and fine grained enough to do in one iteration (or less)

---

9. The term *priority queue* is used in the formal sense—a queue of items whose priority in the queue may change according to a potentially complex sorting algorithm.

❏ the *vague-coarse* subset of coarse-grained user stories needing more analysis, estimation, and splitting before entering the clear-fine subset

The Release and future backlogs may both contain clear-fine and vague-coarse user stories. At the start of a release cycle, the Release Backlog typically contains mostly vague-coarse user stories, and iteration by iteration they are refined into clear-fine stories, and then implemented.

This leads to some key points (illustrated in Figure 4.6):

❏ It is common—and advisable—in Scrum to prioritize only the clear-fine subset of the Release Backlog.

❏ In Scrum, this "clear-fine priority queue" is the critical queue of implementation work before the teams.

❏ The vague-coarse subset of the backlog is a feeding queue of user stories into a backlog refinement process that adds high-quality small stories to the clear-fine subset.

Figure 4.6 Product Backlog contains several queues

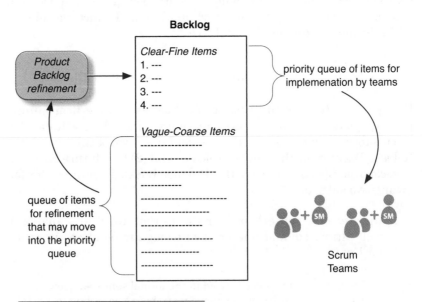

---

10. Scrum has no official name for these subsets.

### Try…Reduce the variability in Scrum

Before getting carried away with the idea of variability reduction—new development is not manufacturing; without variation nothing *new* happens or is discovered. It is both appropriate and inevitable that there is variability in research and development. However, there are indeed varieties of variability than can be diminished—the topic of this section. In the terminology of Edwards Deming, there is **common-cause variation** and **special-cause variation**. The first category is *common noise* variation in the process, and not easy to assign a specific cause. On the other hand, special-cause variation—also known as **assignable variation**—can be identified. For example, *variation in feature-request size* is special-cause variation. By reducing identifiable special-cause variation—in Scrum or work processes—a system with queues has improved average throughput.

*Variability* is one of the three sources of waste in lean thinking (the other two are *overburden* and *non-value-add actions*). With an understanding of queueing theory, it may be clearer why variability is considered a source of waste.

*lean sources of waste p. 58*

What are some sources or kinds of variability in Scrum?

- big batches and big user stories
- ambiguity of *what* a user story means
- ambiguity of *how* to implement a story
- different (estimated) efforts for different stories
- number of stories in the Release Backlog clear-fine priority queue

- estimate-versus-actual effort variance, which can reflect what/how ambiguity, unskillful estimation, learning, and much more
- the arrival rate of user stories into the clear-fine priority queue of the Release Backlog
- team and individual variability
- overloading or failure of shared resources, such as a testing lab

… and more. In queueing-model terminology, they usually boil down to variability in the *service* and *arrival rate*.

In lean thinking, *flow* is a key principle—and flow requires reduction or elimination of variability. That is why *leveling* is also a lean principle; it is an antidote to variability and helps move toward flow.

*flow p. 67*
*leveling p. 65*

This leads to some variability-reduction suggestions in Scrum:

*leveling in the*
*Product Backlog*
*p. 62*

**Reduce variability by a small queue (buffer) of clear-fine, similar-sized user stories in the Release Backlog**—In the *Lean Thinking* chapter, it was explained that a small buffer of high-quality inventory is used in lean systems to smooth or level the introduction of work to a downstream process. This inventory (a temporarily necessary waste) positively supports *level pull* because the Scrum feature teams now have a queue of similar-sized stories to work on; no waiting and fewer surprises. Stories in the vague-coarse subset of the Release Backlog have high *what/how ambiguity* and are large; so choosing those for implementation is unskillful because it increases variability.

*Product Backlog*
*Refinement*
*p. 318*

*see Requirements*
*in companion*
*book*

**Reduce variability by holding a "five percent" Product Backlog Refinement Workshop each iteration**—One of the less-known guidelines in Scrum is to dedicate at least five percent of duration of each iteration to requirements analysis, user story splitting, and estimation or re-estimation. This is done for user stories for *future* iterations, not the current iteration, and may be done in a *Product Backlog (PB) Refinement Workshop*. This reduces what/how ambiguity or variability, plus reduces estimation variability because re-estimation may improve as people learn.

During this workshop, split items *into small and equally sized user stories*. A big 'single' requirement is actually a hidden batch. For example, the 'one' story "...HSDPA protocol support..." can be split into smaller customer-centric user stories. This reduces batch size and its attendant variability. It also reduces *batch delay*—the artificial holding back of an important sub-feature because it was stuck to a larger batch of features, some of which are less important.

This repeating workshop also creates a *regular cadence* of adding clear-fine stories to the queue, reducing variability in arrival rate.

**Reduce variability by stable feature teams**—Use stable long-lived feature teams in Scrum to reduce the variability in the 'servers'—the teams. Also, the cross-functional, cross-component feature teams increase parallelism and flow because a user story can flow to any one of several available teams.

**Reduce variability by timeboxed effort-boxed learning goals**—This tip is most useful in domains with large *research-oriented* requirements. It reduces *what/how ambiguity* and variability.

Sometimes non-trivial investigation is needed just to *start* to understand a feature. For example, we were once consulting at a site in Budapest; the mobile-telecom product group wanted to provide "push to talk over cellular." The international standards document for this is *thousands* of pages. Just to vaguely grasp the topic is a formidable effort. One approach is to ask a team to "study the subject." Yet, that is fuzzy unbounded work that will introduce more service variability and may expand into the lean waste of over-processing. An alternate approach—our suggestion—is to offer the team a timeboxed and effort-boxed goal to learn. Perhaps the concrete goal is to present a research report at the end of the iteration, in addition to their work implementing user stories. For example, *"introductory report on push to talk, maximum 30 person hours."* A leveled amount of effort is put into the research and learning, balanced with the team also implementing user stories. The Product Owner Team may then decide to invest more bounded effort into another cycle of research in a future iteration (probably more focused as the subject clarifies), until finally the subject is clear enough for people to start writing, splitting, and estimating user stories.

### Other Benefits of Reduction in Variability

Another benefit of all this variability reduction is *improved prediction* (estimation) of the duration of the release.

Finally, it allows *higher utilization of teams*. Queuing theory predicts that irregularly loading large high-variability batches of big requirements onto groups and then pushing for high levels of utilization or multitasking *increases* cycle time. Avoid that.

On the other hand, queueing theory predicts that utilization *can be higher without negative cycle-time impact* if there was leveling or removal of variability in all elements.

Imagine a highway that only allows small, equally sized motorcycles all going the same speed. Bikes only enter the highway one at a time at an even pace controlled by a pacing light on the ramp entrance. This idealized highway—on average—can be more fully utilized while still maintaining good flow than can a typical high-variability highway.

### How Small?

 If a one-week requirement is better than a one-*year* requirement, is a one-*minute* requirement even better?

The way to look at this is the transaction cost or overhead of each batch of work. At some point, the cost or effort of user-story splitting becomes too high or difficult. And the overhead of doing each small story eats away the advantages. That said, it is worthwhile recalling that moving to smaller batch sizes has a subtle indirect benefit to drive down overhead costs over time, as explored on p. 113. And yet, at some point splitting is no longer worth it—though that point will change over time.

> For large-product development, our guideline is to split (the typically large) user stories until *one user story is small enough for one Scrum feature team to do it in one-quarter of an iteration*.

### Try...Limit size of the clear-fine subset of the Release Backlog

Another queue management technique is to limit queue size. This does not necessarily reduce variability, but it has other virtues. In a traditional development first-in first-out (FIFO) WIP queue, a *long* queue is a problem because it will take forever for an item to move forward through the queue and eventually be finished—a straightforward reason to limit FIFO WIP queue size.

That problem is less pernicious in a Scrum Release Backlog *priority queue*, since it can be re-sorted—something just added can move to the head of the list. Still, there are good reasons to limit the number of items in the clear-fine priority queue of the Release Backlog:

❑ A long list of fine-grained complex features is hard to understand and prioritize. In large-product development, we regularly hear complaints from the Product Owner Team that the backlog is too big for them to "get their head around."

❑ A big backlog of clearly analyzed, finely split and well-estimated user stories has usually had some investment in it, proportional to its size. It is inventory with no return on that investment. As always with inventory, that is a financial risk.

❑ People forget details over time. All the user stories in the clear-fine subset have been through in-depth analysis in PB Refinement Workshops. If that list is short, there is a good chance that the Scrum Team implementing the story has *recently* analyzed it in a workshop, perhaps within the last two months. If the queue is very long and growing, there is a greater chance the team will take on a story analyzed long ago. Even though there will probably be written documentation that was generated long ago in the workshop, it will of course be imperfect, and their grasp of the details will be hazy and stale.

## THEORY OF CONSTRAINTS

*Theory of Constraints* (TOC) is a management system originally created for manufacturing [Goldratt84]. It is mentioned here because TOC also deals with bottlenecks, cycle time, batch size, and queues.

A key idea of TOC is that there is always at least one—usually just one—primary constraint (or bottleneck) that limits throughput or performance of a system. The constraint may be in a physical form, in some knowledge work, or in a policy—and there will usually be a queue building up behind it. Broadly—and at risk of gross oversimplification—the journey of applying "basic TOC" is to find that one dominant constraint or bottleneck, reduce it so it is no longer dominant, and then look for the new primary constraint. Repeat forever. There is much more, but space prevents a thorough treatment.

Basic TOC has appealing logic to it, such as focusing on the major bottleneck and reducing it. Try that.

Some people who write about TOC primarily focus on the simple idea of "remove the dominant constraint" and a few other straightforward tools. No problem.

But... the story gets messy. Some promote TOC for project management without having seen the full picture in action. In the 1990s Goldratt extended TOC to project management for product development work [Goldratt97]. Here is a key point: *Official* "project management TOC" is more than what is described in the books, and involves specialized courses, tools, and coaching from the Goldratt Institute or authorized providers. It includes a relatively complex and detailed plan-and-control centralized management system with detailed task assignment to people, intensive upfront estimation and scheduling in detailed Gantt charts, and several other traditional management practices. Bottom line: We have seen two very large *official* "project management TOC" adoption attempts (and heard of one more) in companies developing software-intensive embedded systems. Big companies with large product groups. The management was educated formally in the method, tools were purchased, TOC consultants tried to help. The practice was clearly heavy, not agile, and not lean. In all three cases, the approach was eventually found cumbersome and not very effective, and was dropped.

## CONCLUSION

Queue management can become a *hammer* so that you go looking for queue *nails*. Resist the temptation to manage existing queues—that is an inside-the-box response to the problem. Rather, consider doing *system kaizen* so that the underlying system is changed in some way so that queues can no longer form or exist. Parallelizing with cross-functional teams and acceptance test-driven development are common examples, but there are more. Only apply queue management—a *point kaizen* tactic—when you cannot eradicate a queue.

## RECOMMENDED READINGS

There are dozens, if not hundreds, of general texts on queueing theory. More specifically, we suggest readings that make the connection between this subject and product development:

❏ *Managing the Design Factory* by Don Reinertsen is a classic introduction on queueing theory and development. Reinertsen has a broad and deep grasp of both product development and business economics and weaves these insights together into one of our favorite books on product development. This is the book that popularized the model of *thinking tools* for process improvement and organizational change.

❏ *Flexible Product Development* by Preston Smith was the first widely-popular general product development book that introduced agile software development concepts—including Scrum and Extreme Programming—to a broader audience. This text includes an analysis of queueing theory and variability, and their relationship to development.

## Chapter

## Book

# FALSE DICHOTOMIES

*2B ∨ ¬2B, that is the question*
*—Hamlet, early hexadecimal programmer*

In 1999, Craig visited a client in Houston to help with an agile adoption.[1] At the beginning of the first-day kickoff, someone said, "We're trying XP but we hate it!" I asked, "How long are your timeboxed iterations?" "What's that?" she replied. I queried, "What about your continuous integration practices?" She didn't know. I asked, "What is your experience with test-driven development and refactoring?" She said, "I don't think we do that." "So," I asked, "what are you doing in XP?" "Well," she said, "programming without any documentation, of course!"

*disciplined*          *agile*               *agile*          *disciplined*

"Gymnasts are very agile, but they do not have discipline. Navy Seals are very disciplined but they do not have agility." Obviously not true—this is a simplistic, *binary* view.

---

1. I shared this story at one of the earliest Extreme Programming (XP) courses; it has since been attributed to several people.

Some years ago, the oddly named book *Balancing Agility and Discipline* was published [BT03]. The title frames the subject of agile methods in contrast to 'discipline,' as though these were at opposite ends of a scale that needs to be balanced. In other words, a **false dichotomy**—an artificial argument or framing of a situation set up with two and only two binary alternatives.

The irony of this false dichotomy is rich when one considers the practices and principles in a typical two-week timeboxed Scrum Sprint (which is usually combined with XP engineering practices):

- Sprint Planning Part One: Timebox of two-hour meeting with team and Product Owner to clarify Sprint goals and Definition of Done.
- Sprint Planning Part Two: Timebox of two hours for team to design, break down and estimate all tasks for the iteration.
- Sprint execution: Build well-done fully integrated and tested software, never deviating from quality levels defined in Definition of Done.
- Create automated unit tests for all code.
- Continuously integrate all code across the product.
- Continuously review code with others to aid quality and learning.

- Product Backlog Refinement workshop to refine requirements and re-estimate for future iterations.
- Sprint Review: Timebox of two hours to demo the running product and discuss with Product Owner.
- Sprint Retrospective: Timebox of 1.5 hours for kaizen event to analyze process situation and create process improvement actions. Goal: Continuously improve.
- Create automated acceptance tests for all features.
- Continuously refactor the code so it is of high quality.
- Immediately fix a broken build.

How is this *not* disciplined? In fact, the reality is that when we start coaching a group, they are not able to do all the Scrum and XP practices because agile methods demand a level of planning, estimating, engineering, and process-improvement discipline, rigor, and structure well beyond what they are used to or capable of. The reality is that…

> Scrum and XP use and require a high level of discipline; otherwise, agility is not easily attained or maintained.

*Try…Adjust method weight empirically in Scrum*

## METHOD WEIGHT AND EMPIRICAL PROCESS WITH SCRUM

Scrum is an **empirical process** or **adaptive process** in which the process complexity (roughly, the **method weight**) is based on context, and adjusted each iteration at the Sprint Retrospective—a *cadence* of process improvement. Rather than a false dichotomy of "heavily documented work" versus "no documented work" and so on, in Scrum, people adjust the method weight adaptively each iteration according to the *principle of barely sufficient methodology* [Highsmith02]. *Barely sufficient* is high when creating nuclear power plant systems.[2]

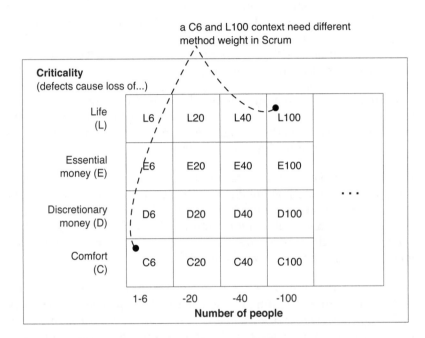

a C6 and L100 context need different method weight in Scrum

Figure 5.1 example partial context for Scrum; this 2-dimensional view is merely an example—the context is an N-dimensional issue and cannot be trivially reduced to this simple case

In *Agile Software Development* [Cockburn04] Alistair Cockburn frames this contextual adaptation in terms of appropriate **method weight**, the method size and formality in terms of defined steps, documents, working agreements, reviews, degree of compliance, and so on. Method weight in Scrum depends on context: *criticality*

---

2. Some years ago, I (Craig here) introduced Scrum and XP—and agile modeling and documentation practices described in my book *Applying UML and Patterns*—on a nuclear-related system. Our team and project was audited by NUPIC because it was the first 'agile' project in the nuclear industry that they knew of. The auditor had "no findings" (somewhat rare in a nuclear audit) and sent information to another project on our agile practices and agile documentation, as an example of real, useful discipline and "how it should be done."

(impact of failure), *distribution* (co-located versus distributed), *staff size*, and more.

A *Cockburn scale* of two aspects of context (size and criticality) is shown in Figure 5.1 to visualize the concept. Note however that the full context is N-dimensional, it is not two-dimensional. In this example, C6 means a product group of 1–6 people, where the worst that can happen from a system failure is loss of comfort. L100 is a product group of 41–100 people where lives may be lost, such as a failure in aircraft control software.

Skillful behavior is to adjust the method weight in Scrum according to context. That is why in Scrum there is no cookbook, prescription, or rule of the exact method weight. A C6 product group doing Scrum needs different weight than an L100 group.

Further, there is too much variability and local context to delegate the appropriate method weight decision to a cookbook—that would trivialize and make deterministic what is in fact a subtle, complex problem requiring local insight. That is why in Scrum the self-organizing teams themselves decide—based on their judgement—the method weight of Scrum for a product group.

Finally, skillful behavior is to adjust the weight *over time* as the context changes, and according to the nature of the people. That is why in Scrum there is only ever a *one-iteration process experiment*. Each iteration the teams inspect and adapt Scrum. Empirical, adaptive process evolution.

*large-scale Scrum p. 289*

This book discusses *large-scale Scrum*, but that should not be interpreted as a special method or special Scrum. Rather, regular Scrum—an empirical process framework that can realize and adapt any method weight and work in any size of group[3]—is what is being described. Large-scale Scrum is just Scrum; it is shorthand for "regular Scrum in the context of a relatively large multiteam product group."

On this note, people sometimes ask if there will be an 'improved' version of Scrum—Scrum 2.0. Ken Schwaber, the co-creator of Scrum, put it well:

---

3. We have seen Scrum adoption on a thousand-person product group.

*There will be no Scrum Release 2.0…Why not? Because the point of Scrum is not to solve [specific problems of development]… The underlying premise of Scrum is that the people, technology, and requirements of most development is too complex for single solutions. Scrum unearths the problems caused by the complexity and lets the organization solve them, one by one, over and over again. Traditional methodologies provide answers to all problems, and this is why they don't work—they assume a simplistic rather than a complex problem [Schwaber07]*

## FALSE DICHOTOMIES

*Try…Identify and avoid false dichotomies*

Variations of the following can be heard or read:

*You are disciplined or agile.*

*We need detailed documentation of all requirements in phase one, or we can't know goals or effort.*

*Will it be all finished on May 1?*

*Are the estimates correct or not?*

*We need to define all release goals at the start, or we don't have a release plan.*

*We need to schedule all tasks to people, or we aren't planning.*

*We need to invest all money at the start, or we can't invest.*

*A Gantt chart means we have a good plan and are planning; otherwise, we aren't planning.*

*All steps are predicted, or we can't predict.*

*Acceptance TDD good, unit TDD bad.*

*Self-organizing teams are anarchy.*

*We need to do the 'architecture' or design before programming, or we aren't doing design and won't have a good architecture.*

*We're doing TDD, so we won't do any modeling.*

*We're doing modeling, so we don't do TDD.*

*The UI interaction design must be finished before development, or there is no disciplined UI design.*

*We need to define the process details for all tasks and workers, or we have no process.*

*We're doing TDD, so we only do unit tests, not integration tests.*

*Modeling bad; programming good.*

*Database design must be finished before implementation, or we won't have skillful database design.*

*You can use either Scrum or XP.*

*We have to do everything.*

*Re-use must be planned; otherwise, there won't be any re-use.*

*We can only have feature teams and no component teams.*

...ad nauseam. Computer people are so *binary* and *discrete*. (We don't know why, we'll have to think about that for a while...). People set up false dichotomies. Of course, these are thinking mistakes. Simply, strive to identify these when you hear or see them, avoid them, and help others see them. And you will not only hear these dichotomies from co-workers; many writers, speakers, and traditional or agile 'gurus' cast "X versus agile" topics as false dichotomies.

A better way to frame all these issues is along *continuums*:

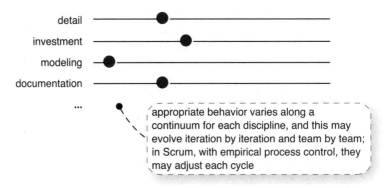

This is the view in Scrum: Practices adjust along continuums according to context.

Tips on alternatives to false dichotomies in any one of these areas—such as design or investment—can easily consume its own book. Many of the chapters in the companion book, *Practices for Scaling Lean & Agile Development*, have pointers.

False dichotomy thinking is, perhaps, common to human nature. We do it too. This book surely contains some false dichotomies that we can't see because of our ignorance or myopia.

**False Dichotomies and Agile Values**

The four values of the agile manifesto are sometimes misread and framed as false dichotomies. For example, the first value is

*Individuals and interactions **over** processes and tools.*

This does not mean processes and tools are wrong. The conclusion that follows the four values provides perspective.

*That is, while there is value in the items on the right, we value the items on the left more.*

For example, try to effectively introduce a new process if the people are not educated or willing. You will quickly see the dominant force.

Some have incorrectly described agile methods as not having documentation—another a false dichotomy. The value is

*Working software **over** comprehensive documentation.*

Most people understand that's a reasonable perspective.

## AVOID…EXTREME RELATIVISM

Seeing and avoiding false dichotomies does not mean everything is good or acceptable—an *extreme relativism* mistake. Slavery is *bad*. Period. Closer to home, there is a mass of statistics in product development identifying poor practices—poor in the sense of correlated with more failure, lower productivity, more delay, and so forth. For example, the COCOMO data shows that the capability of development people is the single most important factor for productivity, and low complexity the second most important [Boehm00]. So, hiring lots of weak developers is not good for productivity. Executing a long sequential life cycle with a massive batch transfer of requirements (higher complexity) is not good for productivity. Research shows that iterative and incremental life cycles (for example, as used in Scrum) are correlated with less cost and schedule overrun than sequential development (for example, [MJ05]); therefore a large batch and long sequential life cycle case is not good for cost and schedule goals.

## MISCONCEPTIONS

There are misconceptions regarding lean, Scrum, and agile principles. It is useful to spot these, and to help others understand them. To start, there is one special misconception worth highlighting...

### Misconception: There Is No Possible Formal Theory to Evaluate Development Process; It Is All Opinion or 'Religion'

This is a misconception at the root of many conflicts regarding approaches to development processes and improvement. From this view one will logically claim that lean or agile principles (or indeed, any process) are only opinion-based or someone's definition of "best practices." However, there are formal models that can be applied to understand and evaluate a process or work system with people:

- ❑ queueing theory[4]

- ❑ control theory

- ❑ information theory

- ❑ game theory

These developed in the late 1800s through mid-1900s in physics, economics, and communications to understand and improve the behavior of *systems*—with variability, nonlinearity, information and request flows, autonomous actors, and other complex or chaotic behaviors. Knowledge work, such as the non-repetitive discovery work of product development, is variable and involves information flows and people making decisions. It may be modeled, understood, and improved with insights from these theories. They provide a set of mathematically grounded models to understand if a particular system is likely to improve or degrade long-term value throughput.

*Queueing theory*—Deals with systems with variability, workers, and queues with requests. Useful to evaluate product development options in work package size, cycle time, and worker utilization; cov-

---

4. 'Theory' in the sense of a validated system rather than supposition; e.g., number theory (proven) versus string theory (supposition).

ered in the *Queueing Theory* chapter. See also *Fundamentals of Queueing Theory* [GH98].

*Control theory*—Deals with dynamic systems with feedback (*cybernetics*) and their control. Useful to evaluate the impact of open-loop versus double-loop feedback management strategies, such as defining the requirements at the start of development and controlling toward that goal, versus other options. The *Systems Thinking* chapter explores how to visualize existing or future causal loops and feedback in your system. See *Feedback Control of Dynamic Systems* [FPE05] for a general overview, and *Quality Software Management: Systems Thinking* [Weinberg92] for management perspective.

*Information theory*—This was originally developed in the context of communication systems, but the insights are more broadly applicable to general data analysis and information feedback. The topic is broad and deep, but as explored in *Managing the Design Factory* [Reinertsen97] at a simple level it provides a formal way to look at the value and cost of information in a product development process. This can be useful to evaluate the cost of delayed information, priorities of implementation, and testing in product development.

*Game theory*—This deals with the decisions people make in the context of cooperation and competition with others; organized into *cooperative* and *noncooperative games*. Cockburn has framed product development as a *cooperative game* [Cockburn01]. It can be used to evaluate possible decisions and behavior of people working together in the context of some development process and work policies. See *Game Theory* [Davis97].

Over the years, evidence (for example, [MJ05]) has grown correlating long sequential development life cycle with big-batch transfer ('waterfall', V-Model) with poor results in terms of cost, schedule, and other factors compared with small-batch short-cycle iterative and evolutionary systems such as Scrum. Without underlying theory, these alternatives can only be considered in terms of opinion or empiricism—not that data is a bad thing. Queueing, control, information, and game theories provide formal models to understand *why* a system of people working with lean or agile principles is correlated with good performance, and to evaluate new process ideas.

## Other Misconceptions

**Estimates are not estimates; estimates are commitments—**
*Not so*. This tragicomic confusion drives all kinds of dysfunction in
organizations… "Why is the estimate wrong?" The Merriam-Webster
dictionary defines *estimate* as "a rough or approximate calculation."
In Scrum *estimates are estimates*; each iteration there is a re-estimation activity as part of the *Product Backlog Refinement* workshop
(five to ten percent of each iteration) as new information arrives and
estimates can evolve and ideally improve.

**Agile means a practice—***Not so*. As the chapter *Be Agile* considers, 'agile' is a set of values and principles aiming toward the ability
to be adaptive and responsive for business competitive success. It is
a quality of the organization (including, of course, its people) rather
than a technique or practice. Many practices support agility and
hence can be called *agile practices*.

**Agile means XP—***Not so*. Several methods support agile values,
including Scrum, XP, DSDM, and others—Scrum being the most
popular [VersionOne08]. These methods have some very different
practices. For example, pair programming is an XP practice, but is
not mentioned in Scrum or DSDM. This misconception arose
because XP was the first agile method to become widely known in
the mid-1990s, although both Scrum and DSDM predate it. Scrum is
flexible with respect to practices and is often combined with XP
engineering practices such as continuous integration.

**Agile means pair programming—***Not so*. This is a variation of
the *Agile means XP* misconception (since pair programming is an XP
practice).

**Agile means iterative—***Not so*. Iterative, incremental, timeboxed,
and evolutionary software-intensive development *is an agile practice*
that has been around since at the least the 1960s, and applied on
many large systems—with good results [LB03]. Timeboxed iterative
and evolutionary development is one old, well-established agile
practice, among many others. *Agile means **agile**—adaptive, embrac-
ing change, and learning.

**Agile is for small development—***Not so*. Scrum has been used in
large product development involving hundreds of developers, for

many years [Larman03]. This is another side effect of the *Agile means XP* misconception, because XP was originally focused on small-group development. Note that 'XP2' [Beck04] was shown to be applicable to large-group product development, but journalists did not follow this development, and repeated early old stories.

**Agile is ugly hacking, no design or architecture, and no modeling**—*Not so*. The ninth agile principle is *Continuous attention to technical excellence and good design enhances agility*. It is hard to be fast and adaptive in development if the code is a mess. This misconception arises due to false dichotomy thinking, such as *if not all design is decided before programming, there is no design*. Also, this is a side effect of the *Agile means XP* misconception, because XP promoted little modeling (which does not mean hacking, nor does it mean *no* modeling). Scrum is neutral on the subject; teams can do as much modeling or upfront 'architecture' work as they find useful. Some elaboration on the XP model: It is noteworthy that Kent Beck, the prime creator of XP, is also a founder of the field of *design patterns* for better software design [BC88]. XP emphasizes high-quality design/code, achieved primarily through constant code review and mentoring between programmers, and continual improvement of the design through refactoring; short modeling sessions are also accepted in XP.

**Agile has no estimates, end date, release plan, or release content definition**—*Not so*. This comes from false dichotomy thinking or ignorance of the practices of various agile methods. For example, the false dichotomy *if not every requirement is completely analyzed, frozen, and estimated with a detailed work breakdown structure, it is impossible to estimate an end date or release content*. Scrum adoption starts with an *initial Product Backlog creation* step, before the first iteration, in which the first release goals are identified and estimated, and an end date and release content is defined. And, there is improved estimation each iteration as more information accumulates. Of course, the reality of variable discovery-oriented product development is that it is… well, *variable*. Scrum works *with* (rather than against) this inherent change and variability; it has mechanisms for adapting and improving the release goal and better predicting the future, iteration by iteration, as the "cone of uncertainty" slowly collapses.

**Agile means no requirements analysis**—*Not so*. Again, a false dichotomy such as *if not all requirements are written in long detail, there is no requirements analysis*. In Scrum, requirements analysis usually starts with an *Initial Product Backlog Creation* workshop before the first iteration if no Product Backlog or analysis has been created. Plus, this analysis continues each iteration—Scrum includes the *Product Backlog Refinement* rule—that between five and ten percent of each iteration is dedicated by the Scrum team to more requirements analysis, splitting, and re-estimation.

**Agile means no documentation**—*Not so*. False dichotomy... *One must document in detail and freeze requirement specifications and design before implementation or there is no documentation*. In Scrum, teams can document as much as they find useful, when they find useful.

**Agile means no contracts, or no fixed-time fixed-scope contracts**—*Not so*. This derives from the *Agile has no estimates or release plan* misconception. In Scrum there is a release plan—the *Release Backlog*—created before the first iteration, in which all release elements are identified and estimated. Of course, this should be separated from the misconception that *estimates are not estimates*. Contracts have been written for decades in outsourced software development recognizing that estimates are estimates, so this is nothing new. The common response is to include a margin in the contract pricing model. This misunderstanding also derives from the *Agile means the requirements **must** change* misconception. Valtech India does fixed-time fixed-scope contracted projects using Scrum. In those cases, more upfront analysis and estimation is done before the first iteration—perfectly acceptable in Scrum. That said, some agile outsourcing companies also encourage a "replaceability clause" in their fixed-scope contracts so that the client can replace an existing element with a new one of (estimated) equal size. See the *Contracts* chapter in the companion book for more.

**Agile means the requirements *must* change**—*Not so*. There is no mandate in Scrum that the requirements must change. It is, in theory, possible that all the original (before the first iteration) identified requirements in the *Release Backlog* will be done without adaptation. Scrum *works with* changing requirements, it does not *demand* change.

**Agile is only for highly innovative and variable exploratory development; 'other' development is best done with sequential life cycle ('waterfall')**—*Not so. First*, data on successful results with agile development spans all kinds of development, small to large, legacy to greenfield, low change to high change [VersionOne08]. *Second*, with the insight of queueing theory and information theory, it can be shown that large-batch transfer, delayed integration, delayed testing, and delayed feedback are not good practices in any development—innovative or mundane. *Third*, variability does not only exist in requirements; there is all kinds of variability in development related to people, practices, tools, and much more. *Fourth*, a story: We have been closely involved in a pure rewrite project for a large product moving from one technology (PowerBuilder) to another (Java). Essentially no innovation and zero requirements change or variability; and also very clear requirements—as the old application was running and available to us to check. The project was done in Scrum, with the client doing manual user-acceptance testing (UAT) each iteration. Key point: All kinds of problems were uncovered—thankfully—by the advantage of working with adaptive iterative planning in short iterations and small batches. For example, it turned out that our predictions of what would be technically difficult and that therefore should be done early were wrong. We adjusted our priority each iteration as we learned. Further, of course, the original estimates were not reliable. As we learned the group's average velocity we made adjustments to improve overall velocity. Also, there were subtle weaknesses in the new frameworks and there were subtle defects introduced, because humans are imperfect and the work is complex. Integrating early and testing early revealed those defects quickly, which led to their architectural resolution early, so that the subtle problems did not propagate or linger. The client UAT that was done each iteration gave the client new ideas about priority which were different from their original ideas. Also, the client (product experts) uncovered subtle bugs through exploratory testing that were not caught by the official test cases, and this early feedback prevented propagation of some misunderstanding. In other words, ***the last simple project was done in 1962***. Do not believe that there is any project that does not involve learning or complexity or some variability, and that will not benefit from agile development.

## Chapter

• **The Agile Manifesto: Four Values** 141

• **Scrum: Five Values** 141

• **The Twelve Agile Principles** 143

• **Agile Management Principles** 144

## Book

# *Be* Agile

*The sooner you get behind schedule,*
*the more time you have to make it up.*
*—anonymous*

Broad introductions to agile methods are covered elsewhere
[Larman03]. In this thinking-tool chapter, there is essentially one
suggestion:

*Try...**Be** agile*

> *Be* agile rather than *do* agile.

'Agile' is not a practice. It is a quality of the organization and its people to be adaptive, responsive, continually learning and evolving—to
be *agile*, with the goal of competitive business success and rapid
delivery of economically valuable products and knowledge. One cannot *do agile*, although it is a common misconception that one can.
Such miscommunication is related to the *Agile means iterative* or
*Agile means XP* misconceptions. From this, we see (in our consulting) incongruities such as

> *"Our product group is going to do agile; we are bringing in*
> *teachers over the next few months to teach 70 new ScrumMas-*
> *ters in some Scrum courses. By the way, when will the require-*
> *ments be finished and the release-content contract be signed?"*
> *... "You are supposed to be doing agile now, so how come it isn't*
> *all finished on time?"*

A product group can *do* Scrum or XP—concrete methods. And they
can *do* practices that encourage agility—**agile practices**. But they
can only really *be* agile, or not.

The term *agile* was not chosen at random; at the Utah workshop in 2001 where a group of modern methodology leaders convened, two alternative names were considered: *adaptive* or *agile*. Both emphasize flexibility. The Merriam-Webster dictionary defines *agile* as *ready ability to move with quick easy grace*. This is more than a lesson in lexicon; if you are a thought leader introducing agility into an organization, it is useful to open the discussion with colleagues by reflecting on the word *agile...*

*Agile* does not mean delivering faster. Agile does not mean fewer defects or higher quality. Agile does not mean higher productivity. *Agile means agile*—the ability to move with quick easy grace, to be nimble and adaptable. To embrace change and become masters of change—to compete through adaptability by being able to *change faster* than your competition can. This agility is supported by both lean and agile practices.

*Perhaps* faster delivery and higher quality will be achieved with an agile method such as Scrum, but it is vital for business and engineering leaders to appreciate that the *raison d'être* of agile methods is...agility. Furthermore, it is vital to appreciate that organizational agility cannot be achieved by a development team in isolation—it is a *system* challenge for organizational redesign. Especially when you are interested in large-scale Scrum within an R&D department of thousands, where each product group may have 200 or 700 people distributed in two or five sites around the world. If an engineering team has the technical capacity to adapt or change quickly, but requirements management, legal practices, product management, HR policies, site strategies, and deployment processes all emphasize rigidity, conformance to original plans, conformance to the status quo, and slow practices, then how can there be real agility?

We suggest the foundation of enterprise agility is to apply the thinking tools offered in this book, including *systems thinking, lean thinking,* and *queueing theory.* And ideally to understand the economics of information from an *information theory* perspective: Why and how to get higher-value, lower-cost information? What is the cost of delayed feedback?

Further, that foundation also rests on applying the organizational tools, including *feature teams, real teams, large-scale Scrum,* and a *new organizational model* in which products are structured around *requirement areas*, and there is a change in task, process, and reward systems to support competing and winning through agility.

## THE AGILE MANIFESTO: FOUR VALUES

Agile development is based on sets of values—not practices—that support and encourage *being* agile. It is useful to know, contemplate, and share these values in any organization that wants to succeed with enterprise agility and large-scale Scrum. The four values of the agile manifesto:

*Try...Learn and applying the four values and twelve agile principles for competitive advantage*

| | |
|---|---|
| *Individuals and interactions* | *over processes and tools* |
| *Working software* | *over comprehensive documentation* |
| *Customer collaboration* | *over contract negotiation* |
| *Responding to change* | *over following a plan* |

*That is, while there is value in the items on the right, we value the items on the left more.*

The *False Dichotomies* chapter discusses some ways that these values are misinterpreted.

## SCRUM: FIVE VALUES

Although many people are aware of the Scrum practices, few are aware of its five values [SB01]. As with the agile values, learn and teach these values within a group that wants to succeed with being agile through large-scale Scrum.

*Try...Know and share the five Scrum values*

**Commitment**—*Be willing to commit to a goal. Scrum provides people all the authority they need to meet their commitments.* This does not refer to fake commitments. For example, someone in sales promises the moon to a customer "to be delivered in six months." Then, the Sales division asks the R&D organization to commit to *our* promise, although R&D had no role or control in the decision. Assigning a target—a fake commitment. Or, a project manager gives work to a group and then plans and schedules the tasks and assigns them to people. Controlling how the work is done—a fake commitment. In contrast, Scrum is based on self-organizing teams that decide what and how much to take on from the wish list offered by the Product Owner during Sprint Planning. No work is pushed to teams, and no team is told how to do the work. This provides the foundation and opportunity for real commitment. When you are in control of deciding what you can realistically take on for a two- or four-week iteration, and you are in control of how you will do it, then the willingness to commit—and the ability follow through on that commitment—is enhanced.

**Focus**—*Do your job. Focus all your efforts and skills on doing the work that you've committed to doing. Don't worry about anything else.* In Scrum, work is not arbitrarily forced on people, and work cannot be added during the iteration. Nor is there any multitasking or distraction, because each team is 100 percent committed to the set of small achievable items chosen for the short iteration. There is no partial allocation on different projects; partial allocation means partial results. Each person's time is 100 percent allocated to the goals of the iteration for the product. This provides the foundation for the focus and reduction in multitasking that leads to quick delivery and productivity.

**Openness**—*Scrum keeps everything about a project visible to everyone.* The foundation of inspect and adapt—empirical process control—is to be able to see what is really going on. The backlogs and burndown charts are open to all—and made even more open with the lean practice of visual management (for example, posting the backlogs on walls). The Daily Scrum of each team is an open event in which team members share with each other what is going on; and it is an open event in that everyone is invited, although only the 'pigs' (Scrum Team members) can talk since only they have "skin in the game." Higher-level coordination meetings in Scrum, such as a Scrum of Scrum or Town Hall Meeting, are also open to everyone. There are no closed door meetings or hidden project management information.

**Respect**—*Individuals are shaped by their background and their experiences. It is important to respect the different people who make up a team.* Squabbles and difference are normal in any group; they are aggravated when the group is composed of isolated people who are essentially in competition with each other. This aggravation and lack of respect increases when the organizational culture emphasizes individual goals and individual rewards. In Scrum, a small *team* has a common and clear goal (the features for the iteration); the focus is not individual heroics and rewards, but team accomplishment. This provides the fertile ground for team members to want to understand how to make their *team* succeed and thus, to work with members' strengths and weaknesses. And that inevitably supports more insight and respect for this diversity.

**Courage**—*Have the courage to commit, to act, to be open, and to expect respect.* Courage in Scrum is not the courage of heroic effort; it is the courage to follow the Scrum rules, to change the organization, and the courage for a self-organizing team to take initiative. For example, the iteration is underway and someone from management asks a team member or the entire team to do an additional task. It is the courage to say, "Sorry, no. If you want something else, the Product Owner must first agree to abnormally terminate the iteration." It is the courage to be utterly transparent when things are going down the drain—individually and as a team. And it is the courage, when confronted with a challenging goal, for the team to explore, learn, decide, and act, rather than wait for someone else to decide or solve the problems.

## THE TWELVE AGILE PRINCIPLES

More specifically, beyond the four agile values are the twelve agile principles that support *being* agile...

1. Our highest priority is to satisfy the customer through early and continuous delivery of valuable software.

2. Welcome changing requirements, even late in development. Agile processes harness change for the customer's competitive advantage.

3. Deliver working software frequently, from a couple of weeks to a couple of months, with a preference to the shorter time scale.

7. Working software is the primary measure of progress.

8. Agile processes promote sustainable development. The sponsors, developers, and users should be able to maintain a constant pace indefinitely.

9. Continuous attention to technical excellence and good design enhances agility.

4. Business people and developers must work together daily throughout the project.

5. Build projects around motivated individuals. Give them the environment and support they need, and trust them to get the job done.

6. The most efficient and effective method of conveying information to and within a development team is face-to-face conversation.

10. Simplicity—the art of maximizing the amount of work not done—is essential.

11. The best architectures, requirements, and designs emerge from self-organizing teams.

12. At regular intervals, the team reflects on how to become more effective, then tunes and adjusts its behavior accordingly.

## AGILE MANAGEMENT PRINCIPLES

*Try...Learn and applying nine agile management principles*

The nine principles for agile management [Highsmith04] recapitulate basic agile and lean principles. However, they are worth distinctly highlighting—and learning and sharing—because they summarize key principles to be agile in a "short and sweet" list.

1. Deliver something useful to the client; check what they value.

2. Cultivate committed stakeholders.

3. Employ a leadership-collaboration style.

4. Build competent, collaborative teams.

5. Enable team decision making.

6. Use short timeboxed iterations to quickly deliver features.

7. Encourage adaptability.

8. Champion technical excellence.

9. Focus on delivery activities, not process-compliance activities.

## CONCLUSION

*cargo cults p. 44*

Especially in large-scale development, it seems common that a product group will demonstrate superficial agile *cargo cult process adoption* by doing agile practices such as holding a Daily Scrum, working in team rooms, applying timeboxed iterative development, fraudulently relabeling project managers as *ScrumMasters*, and more. The fake ScrumMasters may post big visible burndown charts on the walls and declare a new era of empowered teams while simultaneously collecting the teams' "productivity data" each week. It is a mirage, and a sham of what real agility implies. Such fake Scrum-Masters gradually create "the death of agile" by resisting rather than driving deep organizational change.

More important from a business perspective, the ability to compete and make money with the potential power of lean and agile principles has been squandered by *doing agile* rather than *being agile*.

We encourage those that want to realize enterprise agility to take the time to learn the implications of values such as *responding to change over following a plan*, and to take the time to discuss and share these insights with others.

## RECOMMENDED READINGS

❑ *Agile Software Development* by Alistair Cockburn. Emphasizes the principles and theory underlying agile methods, with a special focus on communication.

❑ *Agile Software Development with Scrum* (Schwaber and Beedle) and *Agile Project Management with Scrum* (Schwaber) both explore how to *be* agile.

❑ *Agile & Iterative Development: A Manager's Guide* (Larman) summarizes the key ideas and introduces Scrum, Extreme Programming, and older iterative methods such as Evo.

❑ *Extreme Programming Explained: Embrace Change* (2E) by Kent Beck with Cynthia Andres. Although both Scrum and the DSDM agile methods predate XP, this is the book and Beck is the person that really kicked off the widespread popularity of agile development. Beck credits his 1980s co-worker Ward Cunningham with making seminal agile contributions. Beck and Cunningham are also noteworthy for having introduced the idea of *design patterns* to the software community [BC88], and Cunningham created the widely popular *wiki* concept and technology that is used for Wikipedia (www.wikipedia.org) and within many companies applying agile methods.

# Organizational Tools

## Chapter

## Book

# FEATURE TEAMS

*Better to teach people and risk they leave, than not and risk they stay*
*—anonymous*

## INTRODUCTION TO FEATURE TEAMS

Figure 7.1 shows a **feature team**—a long-lived,[1] cross-functional team that completes many end-to-end customer features, one by one.

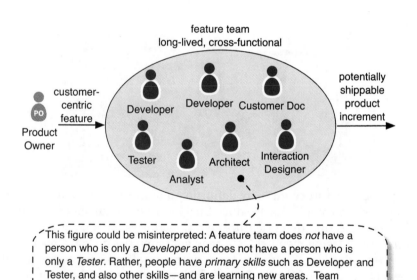

Figure 7.1 feature team—long-lived, cross-functional, learning-oriented, multi-skilled people

feature team
long-lived, cross-functional

Product Owner

customer-centric feature

Developer   Developer   Customer Doc

Tester   Analyst   Architect   Interaction Designer

potentially shippable product increment

This figure could be misinterpreted: A feature team does *not* have a person who is only a *Developer* and does not have a person who is only a *Tester*. Rather, people have *primary skills* such as Developer and Tester, and also other skills—and are learning new areas. Team members may help in several areas to complete the feature. An 'architect' may write automated tests; a 'tester' may do analysis.

---

1. A misunderstanding is that new teams re-form for each feature. Not true. A great feature team may stay together for years.

In Scrum and other agile methods the recommended team structure is to *organize teams by customer-centric features.* Jim Highsmith, in *Agile Project Management [Highsmith04],* explains:

> *Feature-based delivery means that the engineering team builds [customer-centric] features of the final product.*

*lean thinking*
*wastes p. 58*

In lean thinking, minimizing the wastes of handoff, waiting, WIP, information scatter, and underutilized people is critical; cross-functional, cross-component feature teams are a powerful lean solution to reduce these wastes.

Why study the following in-depth analysis? Because feature teams are a key to accelerating time-to-market and to scaling agile development, but a *major* organizational change for most—changing team structure is slow work, involving learning, many stakeholders, and policy and mindset issues. If you're a change agent for large-scale agility, you need to really grasp the issues.

Figure 7.2  a long-lived feature team; developers, testers, and others create a complete customer feature

*Scrum team*
*p. 309*

A proper **Scrum team** is by definition a feature team, able to do all the work to complete a Product Backlog item (a customer feature). Note that Scrum team (feature team) members have no special title other than "team member." There is not emphasis on 'developer' versus 'tester' titles. The goal is to encourage multi-skilled workers and "whole team does whole feature." Naturally people have primary specialities, yet may sometimes be able to help in less familiar areas to get the job done, such as an 'analyst' helping out with automated testing. The titles in Figure 7.1 should not be misinterpreted as promoting working-to-job-title, one of the wastes in lean thinking.

Feature teams are not a new or 'agile' idea; they have been applied to large software development for decades. They are a refinement of **cross-functional teams**, a well-researched proven practice to speed and improve development. The term and practice was popularized at Microsoft in the 1980s and discussed in *Microsoft Secrets* [CS95]. Jim McCarthy [McCarthy95], the former development lead of Visual C++, described feature teams:

*cross-functional team p. 196*

> *Feature teams are about empowerment, accountability, identity, consensus and balance...*
>
> ***Empowerment***—*While it would be difficult to entrust one functional group or a single functional hierarchy, such as Development, for instance, with virtually absolute control over a particular technology area, it's a good idea to do that with a balanced multi-disciplinary team. The frontline experts are the people who know more than anyone else about their area, and it seems dumb not to find a way to let them have control over their area.*
>
> ***Accountability***—*... If a balanced group of people are mutually accountable for all the aspects of design, development, debugging, QA, shipping, and so on, they will devise ways to share critical observations with one another. Because they are accountable, if they perceive it, they own it. They must pass the perception to the rest of the team.*
>
> ***Identity***—*... With cross-functional feature teams, individuals gradually begin to identify with a part of the product rather than with a narrow specialized skill.*
>
> ***Consensus***—*Consensus is the atmosphere of a feature team. Since the point of identification is the feature rather than the function, and since the accountability for the feature is mutual, a certain degree of openness is safe, even necessary. I have observed teams reorganizing themselves, creating visions, reallocating resources, changing schedules, all without sticky conflict.*
>
> ***Balance***—*Balance on a feature team is about diverse skill sets, diverse assignments, and diverse points of view.*

Feature teams are common in organizations learning to deliver faster and broaden their skills. Examples include Microsoft, Valtech (applied in their India center for agile offshore development), the Swedish software industry [OK99], Planon [Smeets07], and telecom industry giant Ericsson [KAL00]. The report on Ericsson's feature teams clarifies:

> *The feature is the natural unit of functionality that we develop and deliver to our customers, and thus it is the ideal task for a team. The feature team is responsible for getting the feature to the customer within a given time, quality and budget. A feature team needs to be cross functional as it needs to cover all phases of the development process from customer contact to system test, as well as all areas [cross component] of the system which is impacted by the feature.*

To improve development on large products (one sub-project may be one million person hours) in their GSM radio networks division, Ericsson applies several practices supporting agility, including feature teams and daily builds. It's no coincidence that *both* these practices were popularized by Microsoft in the 1990s; Ericsson also understands the synergy between them [KA01]:

> *Daily build can only be fully implemented in an organization with predominantly customer feature design responsibility.*

> *... The reasons why feature responsibility is a prerequisite for taking advantage of daily build is the amount of coordination and planning needed between those responsible for delivering consistent parts of each module that can be built. ... In a feature team this coordination is handled within the team.*

In another book describing the successful practices needed for scaling agile development, Jutta Eckstein similarly recommends *"vertical teams, which are focused around business functionality"* [Eckstein04]. Feature teams do 'vertical' end-to-end customer features (GUI, application logic, database, ...) rather than 'horizontal' components or layers. In her more recent scaling book she again emphasizes *"In order to always keep the business value of your customer in mind, there is only one solution: having feature teams in place"* [Eckstein09].

A common misunderstanding is that each feature team member must know everything about the code base, or be a generalist. Not so. Rather, the team is composed of specialists in various software component areas and disciplines (such as database or testing). Only collectively do they have—or can learn—sufficient knowledge to complete an end-to-end customer feature. Through close collaboration they coordinate all feature tasks, while also—important point—learning new skills from each other, and from extra-team experts. In this way, the members are **generalizing specialists**, a theme in agile methods [KS93, Ambler03], and we reduce the waste of underutilized people (working only in one narrow speciality), a theme in lean thinking.

*multi-skilled workers p. 204*

To summarize the ideal **feature team**[2]:

| Feature Team |
|---|
| ❏ long-lived—the team stays together so they can 'jell' for higher performance; they take on new features over time |
| ❏ cross-functional and cross-component |
| ❏ co-located |
| ❏ work on a complete customer-centric feature, across all components and disciplines (analysis, programming, testing, …) |
| ❏ composed of generalizing specialists |
| ❏ in Scrum, typically 7 ± 2 people |

*long-lived teams p. 199*

Feature teams work independently by being empowered and given the responsibility for a whole feature. Advantages include:

*work redesign p. 234*

---

2. A Scrum feature team is typically stable, long-lived. The name "feature team" was first popularized by Microsoft, but is also used in the (relatively rare) method **Feature-Driven Development** (FDD). However, in FDD a "feature team" is only a short-term group brought together for one feature and then disbanded. Such groups have the productivity disadvantage of not being 'jelled'—a rather slow social process—and the disadvantage of not providing stable work relationships for people.

❑ **increased value throughput**—focus on delivering what the customer or market values most

❑ **increased learning**—individual and team learning increases because of broader responsibility and because of co-location with colleagues who are specialists in a *variety* of areas

- critical for long-term improvement and acceleration; reduces the waste of underutilized people

❑ **simplified planning**—by giving a whole feature to the team, organizing and planning become easier

- for example, it is no longer necessary to coordinate between single-specialist functional and component teams

❑ **reduced waste of handoff**—since the entire co-located feature team does all work (analysis, design, code, test), handoff is *dramatically* reduced

❑ **less waiting; faster cycle time**—the waste of waiting is reduced because handoff is eliminated and because completing a customer feature does not have to wait on multiple parties each doing part of the work serially

❑ **self-managing; improved cost and efficiency**—feature teams (and Scrum) do not require a project manager or matrix management for feature delivery, because coordination is trivial. The team has responsibility for end-to-end completion and for coordinating their work with others. Data shows an inverse relationship between the number of managers and development productivity, and also that teams with both an internal and external focus are more likely to be successful [AB07]. Feature teams are less expensive—there isn't the need for extra overhead such as project managers.

- For example [Jones01]: *"The matrix structure tends to raise the management head count for larger projects. Because software productivity declines as the management count goes up, this form of organization can be hazardous for software."*

❑ **better code/design quality**—multiple feature teams working on shared components creates pressure to keep the code clean, formatted to standards, constantly refactored, and surrounded by many unit tests—as otherwise it won't be possible to work with. On the other hand, due to long familiarity, component teams live with obfuscated code only they can understand.

❏ **better motivation**—research [HO80, Hackman02] shows that if a team feels they have complete end-to-end responsibility for a work item, and when the goal is customer-directed, then there is higher motivation and job satisfaction—important factors in productivity and success.

❏ **simple interface and module coordination**—one person or team updates both sides of an interface (caller and called) and updates code in all modules; because the feature team works across all components; no need for inter-team coordination.

❏ **change is easier**—changes in requirements or design (*we know it's rare, but we heard it happened somewhere once*) are absorbed by one team; multi-team re-coordination and re-planning are not necessary.

## AVOID...SINGLE-FUNCTION TEAMS

A Scrum feature team is cross-functional (cross-discipline), composed of testers, developers, analysts, and so on; they do all work to complete features. One person will contribute primary skills (for example, interaction design or GUI programming) *and* also secondary skills. There is no separate specification team, architecture team, programming team, or testing team, and hence, much less waiting and handoff waste, plus increased multiskill learning.

*cross-functional teams p. 196*

## AVOID...COMPONENT TEAMS

An old approach to organizing developers in a large product group is **component teams**—programmer groups formed around the architectural modules or components of the system, such as a single-speciality GUI team and component-X team. A customer-centric feature is decomposed so that each team does only the *partial* programming work for their component. The team owns and maintains their component—single points of specialization success or failure.

In contrast, feature teams are not organized around specific components; the goal is a cross-component team that can work in all modules to complete a feature.

> Components (layer, class, ...) still exist, and we strive to create good components, but we do not organize teams by these.

### What About Conway's Law?

Long ago, Mel Conway [Conway68] observed that

> [...] there is a very close relationship between the structure of a system and the structure of the organization which designed it.

> ... Any organization that designs a system [...] will inevitably produce a design whose structure is a copy of the organization's communication structure.[3]

That is, once we define an organization of people to design something, that structure *strongly* influences the subsequent design—typically in a one-to-one homomorphism. A striking example Conway gave was

> [An] organization had eight people who were to produce a COBOL and an ALGOL compiler. After some initial estimates of difficulty and time, five people were assigned to the COBOL job and three to the ALGOL job. The resulting COBOL compiler ran in five phases, the ALGOL compiler ran in three.

Why raise this topic? Because "Conway's Law" has—strangely—been incorrectly used by some to promote component teams, as if Conway were recommending them. But his point was very different: It was an *observation of how team structure limits design, not a recommendation*. Cognizant of the negative impact, he cautioned:

---

3. In [Brooks75] this was coined **Conway's Law.**

*To the extent that an organization is not completely flexible in its communication structure, that organization will stamp out an image of itself in every design it produces.*

*... Because the design that occurs first is almost never the best possible, the prevailing system concept [the design] may need to change. Therefore, flexibility of organization is important to effective design. Ways must be found to reward design managers for keeping their organizations lean and flexible.*

In this way, Conway underlines a motivation for feature teams.

In *Microsoft Secrets* [CS95], Brad Silverberg, senior VP for Windows and Office, explained their emphasis on feature teams, motivated by the desire to avoid the effects of "Conway's Law":

*The software tends to mirror the structure of the organization that built it. If you have a big, slow organization, you tend to build big, slow software.*

### Disadvantages

It is extraordinary the amount of delay, overhead, unnecessary management, handoff, bad code, duplication, and coordination complexity that is introduced in large groups who organize into component teams, primarily driven by two assumptions or fears: 1) people can't or shouldn't learn new skills (other components, testing, ...); and 2) code can't be effectively shared and integrated between people. The first assumption is fortunately not so, and the second, more true in the 1970s, has been resolved with agile engineering practices such as continuous integration and test-driven development (TDD).

Component teams seemed a logical structure for 1960s or 1970s sequential life cycle development with its fragile version control, delayed integration, and weak testing tools and practices because the *apparent* advantages included:

- ❏ people developed narrow specialized skill, leading to apparently faster work when viewed locally rather than in terms of overall systems throughput of customer-valued features, and when viewed short-term rather than long-term

❑ those specialists were less likely to break their code

❑ there were no conflicting code changes from other teams

Fortunately, there has been much innovation since the 1960s. New life cycle and team structures have been discovered, as have powerful new version-control, integration, and testing practices.

Systems and lean thinking invite us to ask, "Does a practice globally optimize value throughput with ever-faster concept-to-cash cycle time, or locally optimize for a secondary goal?" From that perspective, let's examine the disadvantages of a component team...

### Promotes Sequential Life Cycle Development and Mindset

Customer features don't usually map to a single component nor, therefore, to a single component team; they typically span many modules. This influences organization of work.

*Who is going to do requirements analysis?* If several component teams will be involved, it is not clear that any particular one of them should be responsible for analysis. So, a separate analyst or analyst team does specification in a first step.

*Who is going to do high-level design and planning?* Again, someone *before* the component teams will have to do high-level design and plan a decomposition of the feature to component-level tasks. She is usually titled an architect or systems engineer; in [Leffingwell07] this role is called requirements architect. In this case, one usually sees a planning spreadsheet similar to the following:

| Feature | Component A | B | C | D | E | ... |
|---------|-------------|---|---|---|---|-----|
| Feature 1 | x | x | | | x | |
| Feature 2 | x | x | x | | | |
| ... | | | | | | |

*Who is going to test the end-to-end feature?* This responsibility doesn't belong to any one component team, who only do part of the work. So testing is assigned to a separate system-test team, and they start high-level testing *after* development has finished—sometimes long after, as they need the work of multiple component teams and these teams seldom finish their work at the same time. Plus, they have a backlog of other features to test.

Now what do we have?

1. (before development) requirements analysis by a separate analyst
2. (before) high-level design and component-level task planning by a separate designer
3. (during) implementation by multiple interdependent component teams that have to coordinate partially completed work
4. (after) system testing of the feature

Back to a waterfall! There is massive handoff waste in the system and plenty of delay. This is traditional sequential life cycle development and mindset, even though—ironically—people may incorrectly think they are doing Scrum or agile development simply because they are doing mini-waterfalls in a shorter and iterative cycle (Figure 7.3). *But mini-waterfalls are not lean and agile development*; rather, we want real concurrent engineering.

Completing one non-trivial feature now typically takes *at least* five or six iterations instead of one.[4] And it gets worse: For very large systems the organization adds a subsystem layer with a subsystem architect and subsystem testing—each specialized and each adding another phase delay before delivering customer functionality.

---

Component team structures and
sequential life cycle development are directly linked.

---

4. Five or six iterations is optimistic. With multiple component teams, the handoff, waiting, and overhead coordination delays implementation over many iterations.

Figure 7.3 component teams lead to sequential life cycle

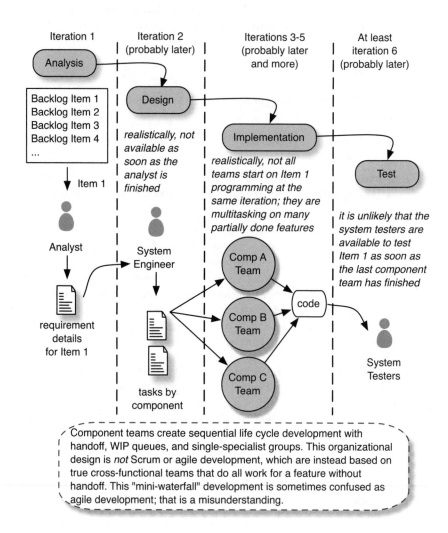

Component teams create sequential life cycle development with handoff, WIP queues, and single-specialist groups. This organizational design is *not* Scrum or agile development, which are instead based on true cross-functional teams that do all work for a feature without handoff. This "mini-waterfall" development is sometimes confused as agile development; that is a misunderstanding.

## Limits Learning

Consider this thought experiment, although it will never be achieved: Option 1—Everyone working on the product can do everything well. Option 2—Every person can do one (and only one) small task extremely well, but nothing else. Which option allows faster feature throughput? Which option has more bottlenecks? Which offers more adaptability? Although the perfection vision of option-1 isn't possible, viewed along a continuum of desirability, we want to encourage a learning organization that is moving in that direction—reducing bottlenecks, people learning one area well, then two, …

Observations:

❏ Developing multi-skilled people takes plenty of learning opportunities and close work with different kinds of experts.

❏ More specifically, developing *programmers* who can help in several components requires a variety of experiences and mentors.

❏ Data shows an extraordinary variance in individual programmer productivity—studies suggest an average of four times faster in the top versus bottom quartile [Prechelt00].

There's a strong link in software development between what you *know* and what you can *do well*—software is the quintessential knowledge-sensitive profession. In short: There are great business benefits if we have skilled developers who are constantly learning.

This learning has preconditions, of management responsibility:

❏ slack[5]

❏ a *structure* to support continual learning

– but there's a systemic flaw in component teams…

How do developers become skilled in their craft and broadly knowledgeable about their product? We asked Pekka Laukkanen—an experienced developer and creator of the Robot test framework [Laukkanen06, Robot08]—a question: "How do you become a great developer?" He thought about it carefully and answered: "Practice—and this means not just writing lots of code, but reflecting on it. *And reading others' code because that's where you learn to reflect on your own.*"

Yet, in traditional large-product groups with component teams, most developers know only a narrow fragment of the system, and most salient, they don't see or learn much that is new.

---

5. See *Slack* [DeMarco01] on the need for slack to get better.

And on the other hand, there are always a few wonderful people who know a lot about the system—the people you would go to for help on an inexplicable bug. Now, when you ask how that's possible, a common answer will be, *"He knows everything since he always reads everybody's code."* Or, *"He's worked on a lot of different code."* Interestingly, such people are more common in large open source products; there is a culture and value of *"Use the source, Luke"* [Raymond] that promotes reading and sharing knowledge via code.

Why does this matter? Because component teams inhibit developers from reading and learning new areas of the code base, and more broadly, from learning new things.

Contrast the organizational mindset that creates such a structure of limited learning with the advice of the seminal *The Fifth Discipline* [Senge94] in which MIT's Peter Senge summarizes the focus and culture of great long-lived companies: *learning* organizations. *Lean Process and Product Development* [Ward06] also stresses this theme; it summarizes the insight of Toyota's new product development success: *It's about creating lots of knowledge, and about continual learning.* And *Toyota Talent* [LM07] asks the question: "How does Toyota continue to be successful through good times and bad?" and answers "The answer is simple: great people," and

> *It is the knowledge and capability of people that distinguishes any organization from another. For the most part, organizations have access to the same technology, machinery, raw material, and even the same pool of potential employees as Toyota. The automaker's success lies partially in these areas, but the full benefit is from the people at Toyota who cultivate their success.*

Isao Kato, one of the students of Taichii Ohno (father of the Toyota Production System), said:

> *In Toyota we had a saying, "Mono zukuri wa hito zukuri", which mean "Making things is about making people." [Kato06]*

Yet what is the journey of the software developer in many large product groups? After graduating from university, a young developer joins a large company and is assigned to a new or existing component. She writes the original code or evolves it, becoming the specialist. There she stays for years—apparently so that the organization can "go faster" by exploiting her one specialty—becoming a single point of success or failure, a bottleneck, and learning only a few new things. The university did not teach her good design, so where did she learn good from bad? How can she see lots of different code? How can she see opportunities for reusable code? How can she help elsewhere when there's a need?

> Note that the problem is not specialization; it is *single*-specialization, bottlenecks, and team structures that inhibit learning in new areas. To create a learning organization, we want a structure where developers can eventually become skilled in two areas—or more. Component teams inhibit that.

Component team (and single-function team) organizations gradually incur a **learning debt**—learning that should have occurred but didn't because of narrowly focused specialists, short-term quick-fix fire fighting, lack of reflection, and not keeping up with modern developments. When the product is young, the pain of this debt isn't really felt. As it ages and the number of single-specialized teams— the number of bottlenecks—expands from 5 to 35, this debt feels heavier and heavier. Those of you involved in old large products know what we mean.

### Encourages Delivery of Easier Work, not More Value

Component specialists, like other *single*-specialists, create an organizational constraint or bottleneck. This leads to a fascinating suboptimization: *Work is often selected based on specialty rather than customer value.*

Component teams are faster at developing customer features that primarily involve their single-speciality component—if such single-component customer features can be found (not always true). For that reason, when people are sitting in a room deciding what to do next, features are often selected according to what available component teams can do best or quickest. This tends to maximize the amount of code generated, but does not maximize the value delivered.[6] Therefore, component teams are optimized for *quickly developing features (or parts of features) that are easiest to do, rather than of highest value.* We once saw a component team assigned to code their small part of a low-priority customer feature that was not due for more than 18 months in the future, simply because it was easier to plan that way.

Figure 7.4 lower-value work chosen

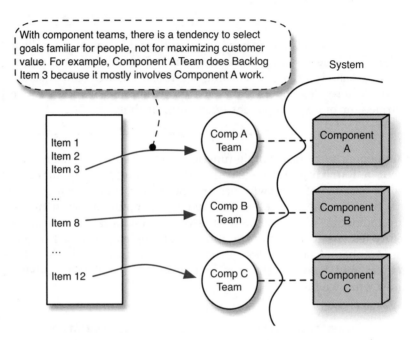

Interestingly, this sub-optimization is often invisible because 1) there isn't prioritization based on a customer-value calculation or the prioritization scheme consists of bizarre super-coarse-grained variants such as "mandatory" versus "absolutely mandatory"; 2) component teams tend to be busy fixing bugs related to their component; and, 3) there is plenty of internal local-improvement work. Everyone appears very busy—they must be doing valuable work!

---

6. Not only do more lines of code (LOC) *not* imply more value, more code can make things worse. Why? Because there is a relationship between LOC and defect rates and evolution effort. More code equals more problems and effort. Great development groups strive to *reduce* their LOC while creating new features, not increase it. Since component teams have a narrow view of the code base, they don't see reuse or duplication issues.

The sub-optimization becomes clear when we create a real Product Backlog, sorted by a priority that includes value (Figure 7.4).

## The Resource Pool and Resource Manager Quick Fix

One quick-fix way that traditional resource management tackles the priority problem is by creating projects according to which specialists are required and available [McGrath04]. Project managers select people from a specialist **resource pool** and release them back when finished. This gives rise to **project groups** or **feature projects**, usually with matrix management. In such organizations one hears people called 'resources' as though they were machine parts and human or team dynamics had little importance on productivity or motivation (which is not the case).

*project versus product p. 238*

Thus, with a resource pool, management twists the organization around single-specialist constraints. It seems to work well on paper or in a project management tool. But people are not machine parts—they can learn, be inspired or de-motivated, gain or lose focus, etc. In practice, resource pool and feature project management has disadvantages:

- **lower productivity due to non-jelled project groups**—there is clear evidence that short-lived groups of people brought together for a project—a "project group"—are correlated with lower productivity [KS93].

- **lower motivation and job satisfaction**—I often lead a "love/hate" exercise with many people in an enterprise to learn what they, well... *hate*. In large groups focused around resource pools and project groups, "we hate being part of a resource pool thrown into multiple short-term groups" is always at or near the top.

*work redesign p. 234*

- **less learning**—more single-specialization as people seldom work/learn outside their area.

- **lower productivity due to multitasking**—with resource pool management it is common to create partial 'resource' allocations where a person is 20% allocated to project-A, 20% to project-B, and so forth.[7] This implies increasing multitasking and—key point—lots of multitasking reduces productivity in product development, it does not improve it [DeMarco01].

❑ **lower productivity and throughput due to increased handoff and delay waste**—the people in the temporary group are often multitasking on many projects. If that's the case, it leads to another productivity/throughput impact: Since they are not working together at the same time on the same goal, there is delay and handoff between the members.

❑ **lower productivity and increased handoff and delay due to physical dispersion**—the project group is rarely co-located in the same room; members may be in different offices, buildings, or even cities (and time zones), and have little or no relationship with each other; physical and time zone dispersion of a task group impacts productivity [OO00].

❑ **lower productivity and higher costs due to more managers**—if each temporary project group has a project manager (usually in a matrix management structure), costs are higher and productivity lower because of the inverse relationship between management count and software productivity.

*Go See p. 52*   Observe the relationship between the lean "Go See" attitude and the belief that it is skillful to have resource pools that optimize around single-specialist constraints. People that do not spend regular time physically close to the real value-add workers may believe in resource pools and short-lived project groups because it appears on paper—as with machine parts—to be flexible and efficient. Yet those frequently involved in the real work directly see the subtle (but nontrivial) problems.

### Promotes Some Teams to Do "Artificial Work"

A corollary of the disadvantage of *encourages delivery of easier work, not more value* is illustrated by an example: Assume the market wants ten features that primarily involve components A–T and thus (in the simplest case) component teams A–T. What do component teams U–Z do during the next release? The market is not calling for high-value features involving their components, and there may even

---

7. Or worse. We've even seen 10% partial project allocations!

be *no* requests involving their components. In the best case, they are working on lower-value features—because that is all they can do. In the worst case, there is an explicit or more frequently a subtle implicit creation of artificial work for these teams so that component team U can keep busy doing component-U programming, even though there is no market driver for the work.

With component teams and large product groups there is often a resource manager who tries to keep the existing teams busy ("100% allocated") by choosing and assigning this low-value or artificial work, or by asking the underutilized teams for advice on what to do. Their focus is the *local optimization* of "everyone doing their best"—generating code according to what people know, rather than generating the most value. And the work is sometimes 'redesign': If we don't have anything new, we'll redo what we did before.[8]

### More Code Duplication and Hence Developers

We once visited a client with many component teams and discussed the link between this structure and code duplication. The client asked, rhetorically, "Do you know how many XML parsers we have?"

Consider duplication: Good code is free of it, and great developers strive to create *less* code as they build new features, through constant refactoring. It's difficult to see duplication or opportunities for reuse in a code base with single-component specialists, because one never looks broadly. Single-component specialists increase duplication. And so the code base grows ever larger than necessary, which in turn demands more single-component specialists...[9]

*see Legacy Code in companion book*

---

8. Improving existing code is a good thing; our point is different.
9. Code-cloning statistics based on (imperfect) automated analysis of large systems shows around 15% duplicated code [Baker95], but this is probably an underrepresentation because such tools don't robustly find "implicit duplication" of different-looking code that does the same thing. *Anecdote*: I've done refactoring (to remove duplication) on large systems built by component teams, removing explicit and implicit duplication; reduction averaged around 30%.

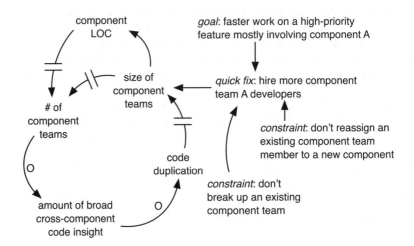

Figure 7.5 system dynamics of component teams and number of developers

## Ever-Growing Number of Developers

Component teams create several forces to increase the number of developers. One reason examined previously is the increased code bulk due to duplication. A second reason involves the mismatch between the existing component teams and the high-priority work, as explained next and summarized in the system dynamics diagram, Figure 7.5.

Component teams become boxes in the formal organization structure, each with its own manager. Several component teams form a subsystem group or department with a second-level manager. This leads to an interesting dynamic...

**Example**: **Current release**—A high-priority goal involves mostly work in component or subsystem A, and therefore component-A or subsystem-A groups work on it. They hire more people in the belief it will make them go faster. Component-C team has lower-priority goals and does not need or get more people. **Next release**—A high-priority goal involves primarily work for component C. Now, they are viewed as the bottleneck and so hire more people (see Figure 7.6).

We could have moved people from one component team to another, and gradually taught them (through pair programming) to help, instead of hiring more people. But this rarely happens. The other component team already has work chosen for the release, so they won't wish to lose people. And there is a fear it will take too long to learn anything to be helpful. Also, the mindset is that "it would be a waste of our specialist to move her to another component team." Finally, moving people is inhibited by political and management status problems—many managers don't want to have a smaller group (another force of local optimization). Conway formulated this well:

> *Parkinson's law [Parkinson57] plays an important role... As long as the manager's prestige and power are tied to the size of his budget, he will be motivated to expand his organization. [Conway68]*

Thus, the component-A team will grow, as will the component itself. It may even eventually split into two new components, and hence two new teams. The people will specialize on the new components. In this way large product organizations tend to grow even larger.

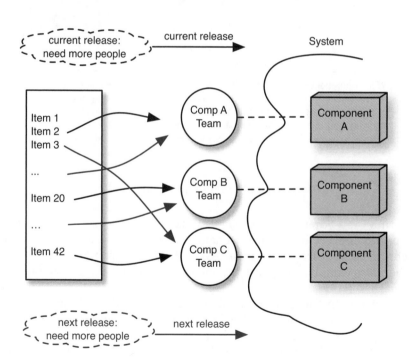

Figure 7.6 ever-growing size with component teams

Figure 7.7 chal-
lenges in planning—
coordination

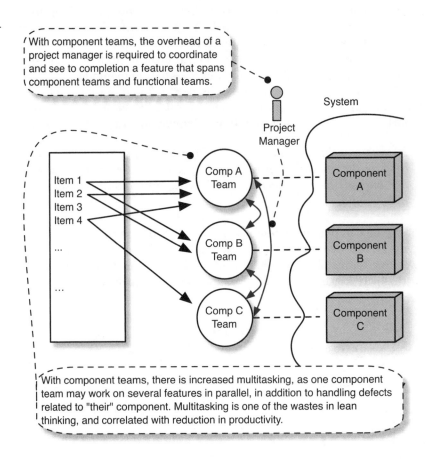

With component teams, the overhead of a project manager is required to coordinate and see to completion a feature that spans component teams and functional teams.

With component teams, there is increased multitasking, as one component team may work on several features in parallel, in addition to handling defects related to "their" component. Multitasking is one of the wastes in lean thinking, and correlated with reduction in productivity.

### Problems in Planning and Coordination

Scrum (and other agile methods) strive for an integrated product at the end of every iteration with demonstrable customer functionality. For most features this involves multiple component teams and therefore complicates planning and coordination between teams.

**Example**: In the next iteration the goal is to do Product Backlog items 1, 2, 3, and 4. Backlog item 1 (customer feature 1) requires changes in component A and B. Item 2 requires changes in component A, B, and C, and so forth. All teams depend on one another in the iteration planning and need to synchronize their work during the iteration (see Figure 7.7)—a task that is often handled by a separate project manager. Even if we successfully plan the complex interdependencies for this iteration, a delay in one team will have a ripple effect through all component teams, often across several iterations.

### Delays Delivery of Value

Value can be delivered only when the work of multiple component teams is integrated and tested. Figure 7.3 illustrates how component teams promote sequential life cycle. So what? With a component team organization, the work-in-progress (WIP) from a team usually waits several iterations before it can be combined into a valuable feature. This WIP, like all inventory, is one of the wastes in lean thinking; it hides defects, locks up an investment, reduces flexibility, and slows down the delivery of value. And in addition to the straightforward sequential life cycle reasons already discussed, component teams delay delivery as follows...

**Example**:

1. Item 1 in the Product Backlog involves component A. Component team A will work on their part of item 1 next iteration.

2. Item 4 involves components A and C. Since component team A is busy with item 1, they do not work on item 4.

3. Item 4 is the highest goal involving component C. Component team C therefore works on their part of item 4 next iteration.

❑ *First problem:* Not every team is working on highest value.

❑ *Second problem*: After the iteration, item 4 (which needs code in components A and C) can't yet be integrated, tested, and delivered, because of the missing component A code. Item 4 delivery has to wait for component team A.

Organizations try to solve this problem by the quick fix of creating a role, called **project manager** or **feature manager**, for coordinating the work across teams and/or by creating temporary **project groups** whose far-flung members multitask across multiple concurrent feature goals. Such tactics will never fundamentally resolve the problem or support rapid development, since the problem is structural—baked into the organization, built into the system.

### More Poor Code/Design

*see Design in companion*

Perhaps the greatest irony of component teams is this: *A mistaken belief behind their creation is that they yield components with good code/design.* Yet, over the years we have looked closely at the code across many large products, in many companies, and it is easy to see that the opposite is true—the code in a component maintained by a single-component team is often quite poor.[10] For example, we will sit to start pair programming with a component team member (who knows we'll be looking for great code), and with a slightly apologetically grin the programmer will say, "Yeah, we know it's messy, but *we* understand it." What is going on?

- ❏ **limited learning**—as discussed above, developers are not exposed to vast amounts of different code; this limits their learning of good design.

- ❏ **familiarity breeds obfuscation**—when I stare at the same complicated, obfuscated 10,000 lines of code month after month it starts to be familiar and 'clear'; I can no longer see how complicated it is, nor does it especially bother me, because of long exposure—so I am not motivated to deeply improve it.

- ❏ **obfuscation and duplication-heavy large code bases breed job security**—some *do* think like this, especially in groups where line management are not master programmers, not looking at the code, not encouraging great, refactored code.

- ❏ **no outside pressure to clarify, refactor, or provide many unit tests for the code**—no one other than the team of five component developers (who are long familiar with the complicated code) works on it; thus there is no pressure to continually refactor it, reduce coupling, and surround it with many unit tests so that it is clear and robustly testable for other people to work on.

---

10. New developers joining an existing component team (i.e., component) also report this observation.

The perpetuation of belief that component teams create great code is an indicator of a lack of "Go See" behavior by first-level management. If they were master developers (lean principle "my manager can do my job better than me") and regularly looking in depth across the code base, they would see that on average, *more—not less—fresh eyes on the code makes it better.*

## Summary of Disadvantages

- promotes sequential life cycle development and mindset
- limits learning by people working only on the same components for a long time—the waste of underutilized people
- encourages doing easier work rather than most valuable work
- promotes some component teams to do "artificial work"

- causes long delays due to major waiting and handoff wastes
- encourages code duplication
- unnecessarily promotes an ever-growing number of developers
- complicates planning and syn-chronization
- increases bottlenecks—single points of success are also single points of failure
- fosters more poor code/design

## Platform Groups—Large-Scale Component Groups

In large product organizations, there often exist one or more lower-level platform groups distinct from higher-level product groups. For example, in one client's radio networks division a platform group of hundreds of people provides a common platform to several market-visible products (each involving hundreds of people). Note that the platform group and a higher-level product group that uses it are essentially two very large component groups. There is no absolute constraint that a separate platform group must exist; for example, the software technologies and deployment environment are the same in both layers. A higher-level developer could in theory modify code in the lower-level 'platform' code—the boundary is arbitrary.

So, the long-term organizational change toward feature teams, large-scale Scrum, and less handoff waste implies that an artificially constructed platform group may merge into the customer-product groups, with feature teams that work across all code. This is a multi-year learning journey.

## TRY...FEATURE TEAMS

Most drawbacks of component teams can be resolved with feature teams (defined starting on p. 149). They enable us to put the requirements analysis, interaction design, planning, high-level design, programming, and system test responsibilities within the team[11], since they now have a whole end-to-end customer-feature focus. Planning, coordinating, and doing the work are greatly simplified. Handoff and delay wastes are dramatically reduced, leading to faster cycle time. Learning increases, and the organization can focus on truly high-priority market-valued features. And because multiple feature teams will work on shared components, sometimes at the same time, it is essential that the code is clean, constantly refactored, continually integrated, and surrounded by unit tests—as otherwise it won't be possible to work with.

> **Note a key insight**: Feature teams shift the *coordination challenge* between teams *away* from upfront requirements, design, and inter-team project management and *toward* coordination at the code level. To see this, compare Figure 7.7 and Figure 7.8. And with modern agile practices and tools, *coordinating at the code level is relatively easy*. Naturally, developers and managers unfamiliar with these practices don't know this, and so continue with upfront responses to the coordination challenge.

---

11. Ideally, customer documentation is also put within the team.

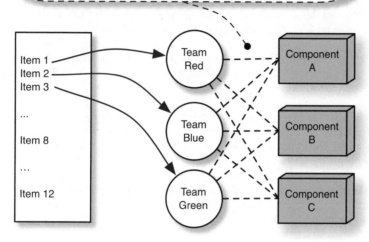

Figure 7.8 feature teams shift the coordination problem to shared code

As the shift to shared code coordination illustrates, a feature team organization introduces new issues. In traditional development these seemed difficult to solve. Fortunately, there are now solutions.

The following sections analyze these challenges and illustrate how modern agile development practices ameliorate them, thus enabling feature teams. Challenges or issues of feature teams include:

- broader skills and product knowledge
- concurrent access to code
- shared responsibility for design
- different mechanism to ensure product stability
- reuse and infrastructure work
- difficult-to-learn skills
- development and coordination of common functional (for example, test) skills that span members of many feature teams
- organizational structure
- defect handling

## Feature Teams versus Feature Projects

Feature teams are not feature projects. A **feature project** is organized around one feature. At the start, the needed specialists (usually developers from component teams or a resource pool) are identified and organized into a short-lived group—a virtual **project group**. The specialists are usually allocated a percentage of their time to work for the feature project. Feature teams and feature projects have important differences:

**Long-life teams**—A feature team, unlike a project group, may stay together for several years. The *team* has an opportunity to jell and learn to work together. A well-working jelled team leads to higher performance [KS93].

**Shared ownership**—In a feature team, the whole team is responsible for the whole feature. This leads to shared code ownership and cross-learning, which in the long run increases degrees of freedom and reduces bottlenecks. In feature projects, developers only update their particular single-specialty section of code.

**Stable, simple organizational structure**—Feature teams offer a simple structure; they are the stable organizational units. Traditional project teams are ever-shifting and result in matrix organizations, which degrades productivity.

**Self-managing; improved cost and efficiency**—Feature teams (and Scrum) do not require overhead project managers, because coordination is trivial.

### Broader Skills and Product Knowledge

This is the opposite of the *limits learning* problem of component teams. The feature team needs to make changes in any part of the system when they are working on a customer feature.

First, not all people need to know the whole system and all skills. The Product Owner and teams usually select a qualified feature team for a feature, unless they have the time and desire for a 'virgin' team to invest in some deep learning in less familiar territory. In the common case, the team members together need to already know enough—or be able to learn enough without herculean effort—to complete a customer-centric feature. Notice that feature teams *do* have specialized knowledge—that's good. And, since learning is possible, they are slowly extending their specializations over time as they take on features that require moderate new learning, strengthening the *system* of development over time (see Figure 7.9). This is enhanced by more pair-work and group-work in a team with various skills. We move beyond false dichotomies such as "specialization good, learning new areas bad" and "generalists good, specialists bad."

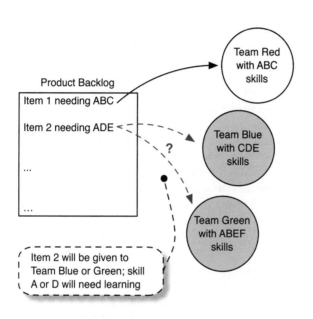

Figure 7.9 specialization is good, learning is good

Learning new areas of the code base is not a profound problem for "moderately large" products, but beyond some tipping point[12] it starts to be a challenge.

One solution is **requirement areas**. In traditional large product development, component teams are usually grouped within a major subsystem department. Similarly, when scaling the feature team organization, we can group feature teams within a **requirement area**—a broad area of related customer requirements such as "network performance monitoring and tuning" or "PDF features." To

*requirement
areas p. 217*

---

12. It depends on size, quality of code, and unit tests, …

clarify: A requirement area is not a subsystem or architectural module; it is a domain of related requirements from the customer perspective.

What's the advantage? Most often, a requirement-area feature team will *not* need to know the entire code base, since features in one area usually focus across a semi-predictable subset of the code base. Not always, but enough to reduce the scope of learning. Requirement-area feature teams provide the advantage of feature teams without the overwhelming learning challenge of a massive code base.[13]

But stepping back from the 'problem' of requiring broader knowledge: Is it a problem to avoid, or an opportunity to go faster?

A traditional assumption underlying this issue is the notion that assigning the existing best specialist for a task leads to better performance. Yet this is an example of *local optimization* thinking—no doubt locally and short-term it seems faster for code generation, but does it increase *long-term* systems improvement and throughput of highest market-valued features? In addition to the obvious bottle-necking it promotes (thus slowing throughput of a complete feature), does it make the organization as a whole speed up over time? As previously explored in the section on the disadvantages of component teams:

> *Product groups that repeatedly rely on single-skill specialists are limiting learning, reducing degrees of freedom, increasing bottlenecks, and creating single points of success—and failure. That does not improve long-term system throughput of highest market-valued features or the ability to change quickly.*

There is an assumption underlying concerns about broader product knowledge: The assumption is that it will take a *really* long time for a developer to learn a new area of the code base. And yet, in large product groups, it is not uncommon for an existing developer to move to a different component team and within four or five months be comfortable—even shorter if the code is clean. It isn't trivial, but neither is it a herculean feat. Programmers regularly learn to work

---

13. A requirement-area feature team may eventually move to a new area; we haven't seen that yet.

on new code and in new domains all the time; indeed, it's an emphasis of their university education.

Still, to dig deeper: Why is it hard to learn new areas of the code base? Usually, the symptom is incredibly messy code and bad design—a lack of good abstraction, encapsulation, constant refactoring, automated unit tests, and so forth. That should be a warning sign to increase refactoring, unit tests, and learning, not to avoid new people touching fragile code—to strengthen rather than to live with a weakness.

Learning new code and changing an existing code base is indeed a *learnable skill*. It takes practice to become good, and people in feature teams get that practice and learn this skill.

*potential skills*
*p. 206*

Returning to the apparent quick-fix, short-term performance advantage of choosing the best existing specialist for a task, this "common sense" has also been questioned in a study [Belshee05a].

Development ran with one-week iterations. Each iteration the team experimented with new practices. One experiment involved task selection. A traditional approach may be called *most qualified implementer*—the specialist who knows most about a task works on it. The team experimented with a task selection method called *least qualified implementer*—everyone selects the task they know least about. Also, task selection was combined with frequent pair switching, called **promiscuous pairing**, each 90 minutes. First, the initial velocity did not drop significantly. Second, after two iterations (two weeks) the velocity increased *above their previous level*. The benefit of increased learning eventually paid off.

Belshee explains the above result with a concept called *beginner's mind*. *"Beginner's Mind happens when the thinker is unsure of his boundaries. The thinker opens himself up and thoroughly tests his environment... The whole mind just opens up to learning."* [Belshee05b]

An experience report from Microsoft related to these practices:

> *The principles laid out in Belshee's paper are not for the faint of heart. They require dedication, commitment and courage. Dedication is required of each team member to strive for self*

*improvement. Commitment is needed for each team member to ensure the values and principles will be followed and the team will hold itself accountable. Courage, because the emotions that Promiscuous Pairing invites will be not unlike the most fun and scariest roller-coaster ever experienced. [Lacey06]*

The studies illustrates the potential for acceleration when an organization invests in broadening learning and skill, rather than limiting it through dependence on bottlenecks of single-specialists.

### Concurrent Access to Code

As illustrated in Figure 7.8, one important difference between component teams and feature teams is that the dependency and coordination between teams shifts from requirements and design to code. Several people may concurrently edit the same source code file, typically a set of C functions, or a class in C++ or Java.

With weak or complex version-control tools and practices, common in the 1980s and still promoted by companies such as IBM, this was a concern. Fortunately, it isn't an issue with modern free tools and agile practices.

*see Continuous Integration in companion*

Old-generation and complex (and costly) version control systems such as ClearCase defaulted to **strict locking** in which the person making a change locked the source file so that no one else could change it. Much worse, vendors promoted a culture of avoiding concurrent access, delaying integration, complex integration processes involving manual steps, integration managers, and tool administrators. This increased costs, complexity, bottlenecks, waiting, and reinforced single-team component ownership.

On the other hand, the practices and tools in agile and in open source development are faster and simpler. Free open source tools such as Subversion[14] default to **optimistic locking** (no locking),

---

14. Subversion is likely the most popular version control tool worldwide, and a de facto standard among agile organizations. *Tip*: It is no longer necessary to pay for tools for robust large-scale development; for example, we've seen Subversion used successfully on a 500-person multisite product that spanned Asia and Europe.

and more deeply, have always encouraged—through teaching and features—a culture of simplicity, shared code ownership, and concurrent access [Mason05]. With optimistic locking anyone can change a source file concurrently. When a developer integrates her code, Subversion automatically highlights and merges non-conflicting changes, and detects if conflicts exist. If so, the tool easily allows developers to see, merge, and resolve them.

An optimistic-locking, fast, simple tool and process are required when working in an agile development environment and are a key in eliminating problems related to concurrent access to code.

Optimistic locking could in theory lead to developers spending inordinate time merging difficult changes and resolving large conflicts. But this is resolved with **continuous integration** and **test-driven development**, key practices in scaling agile and lean development.

When developers practice **continuous integration** (CI) they integrate their code frequently—*at least* twice a day. Integrations are small and frequent (for example, five lines of code every two hours) rather than hundreds or thousands of lines of code merged after days or weeks. The chance of conflict is lower, as is the effort to resolve. Developers do *not* normally keep code on separate "developer branches" or "feature branches"; rather, they frequently integrate all code on the 'trunk' of the version-control system, and *minimize* branching. Furthermore, CI includes an automated build environment in which *all* code from the hundreds of developers is endlessly, relentless compiled, linked, and validated against thousands of automated tests; this happens many times each day.[15]

*see Continuous Integration in companion*

*parallel releases p. 209*

In **test-driven development** every function has many automated micro-level unit tests, and all programming starts with writing a new unit test before writing the code to be tested. Further, every feature has dozens or hundreds of automated high-level tests. This leads to thousands of automated tests that the developer can rerun locally after each merge step—in addition to their continual execution in the automated build system.

*see Test in companion*

In lean thinking terminology, CI replaces big batches and long cycle times of integration (the practice of traditional configuration man-

---

15. Note that this implies driving down the build time of a large system.

agement) with *small batches and short cycles* of integration—a repeating lean theme.

## Shared Responsibility for Design

In a traditional component team structure, each component has an owner who is responsible for its design and ongoing "conceptual integrity." On the other hand, feature teams result in shared ownership. This could—without the practices used in agile methods—lead to a degradation of integrity. All that said, it must be stressed that in reality, code/design degradation happens in many groups anyway, regardless of structure; recall the reasons component teams ironically often live with obfuscated code (p. 172).

Continuous integration (CI) implies *growing* a system in small steps—each meant to improve the system a little. In addition to integration of all code on the trunk multiple times daily and non-stop automated builds running thousands of automated tests, CI with ongoing design improvement is supported by other practices:

*see Design in companion*

❑ **evolutionary design culture**—since (as Conway points out) the initial design vision is rarely great, and in any event since software is ever-changing, encourage a culture in which people *view the design or architecture as a living thing* that needs never-ending incremental refinement

  – a sequential life cycle with a single upfront architectural or design phase gives the false message that the design is something we define and build *once*, rather then continually refine every day for the life of the system

❑ **test-driven development**—drive code development with automated micro-unit tests and higher-level tests; each test drives a small increment of functionality

  – this leads to hundreds of thousands of automated tests

❑ **refactoring**; a *key step*—after each micro-change of a new unit test and related solution code, perform a small refactoring step to improve the code/design quality (remove duplication, increase encapsulation, ...)

- refactoring implies always leaving the code a little better than we found it

- note that *design quality means code quality*; there is no real 'design' in software other than the source code [Reeves92]

These CI practices support continuous design improvement with feature teams, and the 9$^{th}$ agile principle: *Continuous attention to technical excellence and good design enhances agility.* Plus, there are strong connections between these agile practices and the lean principles *Stop and Fix, Continuous Improvement*, and the kaizen practice of endless and relentless small steps of improvement—in this case, *"kaizen in code."*

*be agile p. 139*

Successfully moving from solo to shared code ownership supported by agile practices doesn't happen overnight. The practice of **component guardians** can help. Super-fragile components (for which there is concern[16]) have a component guardian whose role is to teach others about the component ensures that the changes in it are skillful, and help remove the fragility. She is *not the owner* of the component; changes are made by feature team members. A novice person (or team) to the component asks the component guardian to teach him and help make changes, probably in design workshops and through pair programming. The guardian can also code-review all changes using a 'diff' tool that automatically sends her e-mail of changes. This role is somewhat similar to the **committer** role in open source development.[17] It is another example of the lean practices of regular mentoring from seniors and of increasing learning.

Another possible practice is establishing an **architecture code police** [OK99]; to quote, *"The architecture police is responsible for keeping a close check on the architecture."* Note that since the only real design is in the code, architecture code police are responsible for continually looking at the *code* (not at documents), identifying weaknesses, and coaching others while programming—they are master-

---

16. A typical reason for concern about delicate components is that the code is not clean, well refactored, and surrounded by many unit tests. The solution is to clean it up ("Stop and Fix"), after which a component guardian may not be necessary.

17. But the roles are not identical. Guardians (or 'stewards') do more teaching and pair programming, and allow commits at any time. Committers also teach, but less so, and control the commit of code.

programmer teachers. Architecture code police are a variant of component guardians; they are responsible for overall code quality. But no single person is responsible for a specific component. Warning: This practice could devolve into a separate "PowerPoint architects" group that is not focussed on the code, and not teaching through pair work.

A related practice is used at Planon, a Dutch company building workplace management solutions. The co-creator of Scrum, Jeff Sutherland, wrote: *"We have another Scrum company that has hit Gartner Group's magic [leaders]"* [Sutherland07]. They have multiple feature teams, each consisting of an architect, developers, testers, and documentation people. There is also one lead architect, but he is *not* responsible for defining the architecture and handing it over to the team. Instead, he is *"the initiator of a professional circle, that includes all architects, to keep the cross-team communication going."* Planon's term *professional circle* is a **community of practice**, in which people with similar interest form a community to share experiences, guide, and learn from each other [Wenger98, WMS02]. At Planon, they have a community of practice for different specialists such as architects, testers, and ScrumMasters [Smeets07].

*community of practice p. 252*

*see Design in companion*

Another practice to foster successful shared design is the **design workshop**. Each iteration, perhaps multiple times, the feature team gets together for between "two hours and two days" around giant whiteboard spaces. They do collaborative **agile modeling**, sketching on the walls in a creative design conversation. If there are component guardians or other technical leaders (that are not part of the feature team) who can help guide and review the agile modeling, they ideally also participate. See Figure 7.10.

For broad architectural issues **joint design workshops** (held repeatedly) can help. Interested representatives from different feature teams (not restricted to 'official' architects) spend time together at the whiteboards for large-scale and common infrastructure design.[18] Participants return to their feature team, teaching joint insights in their local workshops and while pair programming.

---

18. Solutions for multisite joint design workshops are explored in the *Design* chapter.

Handoff and partially done work (such as design specifications) are wastes in lean thinking. To reduce this and to encourage a culture of teaching, it is desirable that design leaders not be members of a separate group that create specifications, but rather be full-time members on a feature team who also participate in joint design workshops as a *part-time architectural community of practice*.

Figure 7.10 design workshop with agile modeling

### New Mechanisms for Code Stability

Code stability in a component team organization is attempted with component owners. They implement their portion of a customer feature in their component, hopefully keeping it stable. Note that stability is an ideal rather than an assured consequence of this approach. It is common to find large product groups where the build frequently breaks—often as a consequence of the many coordination problems inherent to and between component teams.[19]

With feature teams, new—and just plain better—stability techniques are used. Massive test automation with continuous integration (CI) is a key practice. When developers implement new functionality, they write automated tests that are added to the CI system and run constantly. When a test breaks:

*see Test and Continuous Integration in companion*

1. The CI system automatically (for example, via e-mail or SMS) informs the set of people who might have broken the build.

---

19. We have seen many examples of a three-month or worse 'stabilization' phase in traditional large products that used component teams.

2. Upon notification, one or more of these people stop, investigate, and bring the build back to stability.

- this CI attitude illustrates the lean principle of *Stop and Fix*

### Infrastructure and Reuse Work

In a component team organization, goals such as a reusable framework or improving test automation are usually met by formation of a temporary project group or with an existing component team.

In a feature team organization with Scrum, these major goals are added to the Product Backlog—an exception to the guideline to focus on adding customer-feature items, since these goals span all features.

This backlog infrastructure work is prioritized by the Product Owner in collaboration with the teams. Then the infrastructure work is *given to an existing feature team*, as any other backlog item. This team works on infrastructure for a few iterations (delivering incremental results each iteration) and thus may be called an **infrastructure team**, a temporary role until they return to normal feature team responsibility.

### Difficult-to-Learn Skills

*potential skill
p. 206*

A feature team may not have mastery of all skills needed to finish a feature. This is a solvable problem if there is the **potential skill** [KS01]. On the other hand, some skills are really tough to learn, such as graphic art or specialized color mathematics. Solutions:

- ❏ **fixed specialist for the iteration**—This creates a constraint in the iteration planning; all work related to that skill needs to be done by the feature team with the specialist (who may be a permanent or temporary visiting member).

  - A good Stop and Fix approach to working with the specialist is that he is a teacher and reviewer, not a doer

- ❏ **roaming specialist**—During the iteration planning several teams request help from a specialist; she schedules which teams she will work with (and coach) and roams between them.

❑ **visit the specialist at her primary team**—the specialist physically stays with one feature team that needs her most (for the iteration) and invites other people to visit her for mini-design workshops, review, and consultation.

Solo specialists are bottlenecks; avoid these solutions unless team learning is not an option. Encourage specialists to coach, not do.

### Coordinating Functional Skills: Communities of Practice

An old issue in cross-functional teams is the development and coordination of functional skills and issues across the teams, such as testing skills or architectural issues. The classic solution, previously introduced, is to support **communities of practice** (COP) [Wenger98, WMS02]. For example, there can be a COP leader for the test discipline that coordinates education and resolution of common issues across the testers who are full-time members of different feature teams and part-time members of a common testing COP.

*communities of practice p. 252*

### Organizational Structure

In a component- and functional-team (for example, test team) organization, members typically report to component and functional managers (for example, the "testing manager"). What is the management structure in an agile-oriented enterprise of cross-functional, cross-component feature teams?

In an agile enterprise, several feature teams can report to a common feature team's line manager. The developers and testers on the team report to the same person. Note that this person is not a project manager, because in Scrum and other agile methods, teams are self-managing with respect to project work (11$^{th}$ agile principle).

*organizational structure p. 241*

### Handling Defects

In a traditional component team structure, the team is usually given responsibility for handling defects related to their component. Note that this inhibits long-term systems improvement and throughput by increasing interrupt-driven multitasking (reducing productivity) for the team, and by avoiding learning and reinforcing the weakness and bottleneck of depending upon single points of success or failure.

On a large product with (for example) 50 feature teams, an alternative that our clients have found useful is to have a rotating maintenance (defect) group. Each iteration, a certain number of feature teams move into the role of maintenance group. At the end of the two or three iterations, they revert to feature teams doing new features, and other feature teams move into maintenance. Lingering defects that aren't resolved by the timebox boundary are carried back to the feature team role and wrapped up before new feature work is done.

As an additional learning mechanism, consider adding the practice of handling defects with pair programming, pairing someone who knows more and someone who knows less, to increase skills transfer.

## TRANSITION

In his report on feature teams in Ericsson [KAL00], Karlsson observed, *"Implementing daily build and feature teams in an organization with a strong [traditional] development process, distributed development and a tradition of module [single component] responsibility is not an easy task."* It takes hard work and management commitment.

There are several tactics for transitioning to feature teams:

- ❑ reorganize into broad cross-component feature teams

- ❑ gradually expand team responsibility

### Reorganize into Broad Cross-Component Feature Teams

One change tactic is to reorganize so that, collectively, the new teams have knowledge of most of the system. How? By grouping different specialists from most component areas (Figure 7.11).

A variation is that a new team is formed more narrowly with specialists from the *subset* of most components typically used in one (customer) **requirements area**, such as "PDF printing." This approach exploits the fact that there is a semi-predictable subset of components related to one requirements area. It is simpler to achieve and reduces the learning burden on team members.

*requirement areas p. 217*

When one product at Xerox made the transition to feature teams, it started out by forming larger (eleven- or twelve-member) teams than the recommended Scrum average of seven. The advantage was that a sufficiently broad cross-section of specialists was brought together into feature teams capable of handling most features. The disadvantage was that twelve members is an unwieldy size for creating a single jelled team with common purpose.

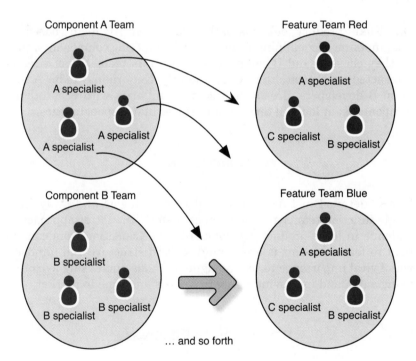

Figure 7.11 moving to feature teams

## Gradually Expand Teams' Responsibility

For some, reorganizing to full-feature teams is considered too difficult, although in fact the impediments are often mindset and political will. As an alternative, take smaller steps to gradually expand teams' responsibility from component to "multi-component" teams to true feature teams.

Simplified example: Suppose an organization has four component teams A, B, C, and D. Create two AB teams and two CD teams from the original four groups, slowly broadening the responsibilities of the teams, and increasing cross-component learning. A customer feature will still need to be split across more flexible "multi-component" teams, but things are a little better. Eight months later, the two AB and two CD teams can be reformed into four ABCD teams... and so on.

One Nokia product took this path, and formed AB teams based on the guideline of combining from closely interacting components; that is, they chose A and B components (and thus teams) that directly interacted with each other. Consequently, the original team A and team B developers already had some familiarity with each other's components, at least in terms of interfaces and responsibilities.

## CONCLUSION

Why a detailed justification toward feature teams and away from single-function teams and component teams? The latter approach is endemic in large-product development. The transition from component to feature teams is a profound shift in structure and mindset, yet of vital importance to scaling agile methods, increasing learning, being agile, and improving competitiveness and time to market.

## RECOMMENDED READINGS

❑ *Dynamics of Software Development* by Jim McCarthy. Originally published in 1995 but republished in 2008. Jim's book is a true classic on software development. Already in 1995 it emphasized feature teams. The rest of the book is stuffed with insightful tips related to software development.

❏ "XP and Large Distributed Software Projects" by Karlsson and Andersson. This early large-scale agile development article is published in *Extreme Programming Perspectives*. It is a insightful and much under-appreciated article describing the strong relationship between feature teams and continuous integration.

❏ "How Do Committees Invent?" by Mel Conway. This 40-year article is as insightful today as it was 40 years ago. It is available via the authors website at www.melconway.com.

❏ *Agile Software Development in the Large* by Jutta Eckstein. This is the first book published on the topic of scaling agile development. It describes the experience of a medium-sized (around 100 people) project and stresses the importance of feature teams in large-scale development.

❏ "Promiscuous Pairing and Beginner's Mind" by Arlo Belshee. This article is not directly related to feature teams or large-scale development but it does contain some fascinating experiments that question some of the assumptions behind specialization.

## Chapter

## Book

# Chapter

**8**

# TEAMS

*One man alone can be pretty dumb sometimes, but for real bona fide*
*stupidity, there ain't nothin' can beat teamwork.*
*—Edward Abbey*

Teams to lean are like bricks to buildings. They are so basic, people even forget to mention them. Toyota expert, Jeffrey Liker:

> *Toyota sincerely believes that teams are more effective and efficient than the sum of individuals, and that when they are given the skills and systems of problem solving, the sky is the limit [LH08].*

But teams are the core building block for large product development—and team structure has a huge impact on productivity and cycle time. This chapter covers different team-related subjects and their influence on organizing work.

| **Team has** |
|---|
| ❏ a shared work product |
| ❏ interdependent work |
| ❏ a shared responsibility |
| ❏ a set of working agreements |
| ❏ responsibility for managing the outside-the-team relationships [SJS03] |
| ❏ distributed leadership [Katzenbach98] |

## TRY…SELF-ORGANIZING TEAMS

Self-organizing teams are the basis of Scrum and a widespread modern management practice. They go by different names such as self-managing, self-directing, and empowered, but the idea is the same. And what is that? Well, *the team has the authority* to design, plan, and execute their task and to monitor and manage their work process and progress [Hackman02]. In other words, the team—rather than a (project) manager—has the responsibility of deciding how to work.

In a healthy self-organizing team, the leadership role is also shared among team members—a hard thing for traditional management to change. Preston Smith, author of the first book on flexible product development [Smith07], notes that a *"measure of a self-organizing team is how frequently the leadership changes [in the team]."*

What does it mean to share leadership among team members? At the MIT leadership center, Peter Senge and three other MIT professors did a four-year study called *"leadership in the age of uncertainty."* One of their key assumptions was that leadership *"should permeate all levels of the firm"* [Ancona05]. They identified four leadership capabilities: (1) making sense of the world around us, (2) developing relationships within and across the organization, (3) creating a vision of the future, and (4) creating new ways of working together [Malone05]. In a self-organizing team, all members constantly exercise these capabilities and, depending on the situation, one team member takes a more or a less strong leadership role.

*Avoid…Manager not taking responsibility for creating the conditions needed for teams to self-organize*

We worked with some product groups who, when moving to self-organizing teams, gathered the people and said, "From today you are self-organizing; go and do your job." Afterwards, they sat back and waited. The team was confused and their productivity plummeted. Self-organizing teams do not just happen, they need the right environment. The organization is responsible for supporting the team development by creating the conditions needed for teams to succeed. Switching to self-organizing teams means the job of the traditional manager changes from directing the team to creating these conditions.

In Scrum, the ScrumMaster is responsible for creating the environment a team needs to succeed. To avoid confusion, Scrum introduced a new role instead of changing the responsibilities of existing roles. The change from a traditional (project) manager to a ScrumMaster is a change in mindset and attitude. Often, traditional managers experience a loss of power, or what we call "illusion of power." Some helpful references related to this change are included in this chapter's recommended readings section.

The foundation of Scrum is the work of Nonaka and Takeuchi [NT86], who studied innovation and knowledge creation in Japan. Their conclusion: Innovative new product development is done by self-organizing teams. According to them [NTI84], self-organizing teams require to be:

❑ autonomous

❑ cross-functional

❑ challenged

Autonomy is already covered and a later section covers cross-functional teams. The third requirement is…

## TRY…SET CHALLENGING BUT REALISTIC GOALS

The one thing all team literature seems to agree on is this: A team needs a *challenging performance goal*. Why? A clear goal results in a shared-work product with all team members sharing responsibility. This binds the team together and challenges people to cooperate, learn, and work as a team. The result: The combined contribution exceeds the sum of the individual contributions—a truly high-performing team.

In the work of Nonake and Takeuchi, the teams were responsible for the whole product. Other studies showed that when the team is responsible for the end-to-end result, their internal motivation is higher [HO80]. Feature teams and requirement areas create this end-to-end focus, thereby, increasing the teams' internal motivation and creating the conditions for challenging and meaningful goals.

*feature teams p. 149; requirement areas p. 217*

Figure 8.1 Scrum
has cross-functional
teams

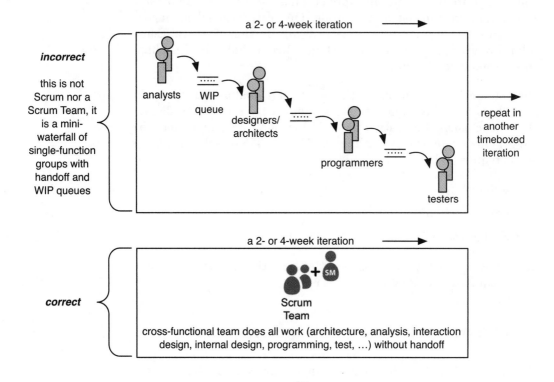

## TRY...CROSS-FUNCTIONAL TEAMS

Self-organizing teams are *cross-functional* (or *multifunctional*). A cross-functional team is a *"group of people with a clear purpose representing a variety of functions or disciplines in the organization whose combined efforts are necessary for achieving the team's purpose"* [Parker02].

*Avoid...Single-function specialist teams*

Why are cross-functional teams important? Imagine having a single-function specialist design team, a single-function specialist implementation team, and a single-function specialist test team. These teams 'optimize' their work according to their specific function—a local optimization. They hand off work to "the next team"—another lean waste. And they create queues between the teams, which increases the total cycle time, and reduces the feedback loop, thus decreasing the learning opportunities (see Figure 8.1). Cross-functional teams avoid these wastes by letting the team *see the whole*.

By definition, a Scrum team is cross-functional. Its members include at least product marketing (Product Owner), software development, and testing. A cross-functional team implies breaking the organizational barriers between development and testing by putting them in the same team. For most organizations we worked with, this was already a major change. However, when traditional product development literature mentions cross-functional teams, they are not talking about specializations inside the product development function; instead:

> *Cross-functional means that team membership includes all the key functions involved in the project, usually Engineering, Marketing, and Manufacturing, at a minimum [Smith07].*

True cross-functional integration in large product development is rare. Instead, we have frequently encountered *cross-functional project management groups* with management representatives of the different functional areas. *They do not work.* Some examples:

❏ *Most organizations turn such important cross-functional decisions over to a management group, but this arrangement is usually slow to react in a turbulent environment. Such groups do not convene often enough or quickly enough to deal with constant change. In addition, they do not have information at hand regarding decisions the team faces today. The team would have to brief them, which wastes precious reaction time. When a team is encountering constant change, it needs the capability to make cross-functional trade-off decisions internally, which means that it needs an internal cross-functional composition [Smith07].*

❏ *Ford had formed cross-functional planning groups of senior managers and senior staffers to think about future technology needs. One reason for forming the groups was to provide guidance for research work, which they did. But the executives wrongly assumed that the groups would also naturally serve as a link between research and the operating engine-development groups, thereby making sure the latter would tap the former's knowledge. But those links never materialized at the working level [BCHW94].*

❏ *Cross-functional project teams ... do not guarantee effective development. Even good "teamwork" may not be enough. In one American company ... we found a very coherent "project team" with a high level of team spirit. But the team consisted only of liaison people from each department; none of the working engineers responsible for creating actual drawings and prototypes was included. The liaison team was effectively an enclave that tended to be isolated from the working engineers, who referred to the liaison members as "the team people." It took extensive clinical study to recognize that this high integration at the liaison level masked a lack of integration across the development organization [CF91].*

❏ A large telecom company we worked with formed *program management teams* consisting of project managers from the different functions. These project managers commanded single-function specialist teams, resulting in a traditional sequential life cycle with huge queues between teams. There was never any true cross-functional integration and the "cross-functional program management team" served as another structure for traditional command-and-control management.

*Avoid...IBM* ❏ Another very large company we worked with was 'advised' to use this kind of management structure by IBM who sold them their *integrated product development solution*. This boiled down to using a stage-gate sequential life cycle process with a cross-functional management team. This team was controlled by a product development team leader who commanded the different single-specialist project group managers. Ironically, the IBM integrated product development material [Mugge04] refers to the same sources as this book. The earlier two stories about the lack of true integration came from these.

Clark and Wheelwright, authors of *"Revolutionizing Product Development"* [CW92]—the classic work on product development—simply conclude that *"True cross-functional integration occurs at the working level."* An ideal cross-functional team includes all functions needed for shipping the product. This is not possible in large product development. For example, only a few teams include hardware- or manufacturing-related people, and thus these teams do the work most related to these functions. Other functional groups that spend even less effort in product development, such as HR, are best left out of the team and in a supporting role.

The first step for most organizations is to integrate analysis, interaction design, software architecture, programming, and testing. They need to realize that in the long run, to become faster and more agile, other functions also need to be integrated in the teams. They need to remember that "*Successful implementation of multifunctional teams requires a fundamental redesign of the entire organization*" [Meyer93].

## TRY...LONG-LIVED TEAMS

Creating high-performance teams takes time. It's sad that currently the most common way of structuring work is by projects. Once the team finally manages to reach a level of high-performance, they are broken up and the individuals are assigned to new project teams. We worked with one of the first Scrum teams in China that was broken up when they finished their project work. In their retrospective, the most important item that came up was "We finally know how to work together and now we get split up." Ironically, the reason for breaking up well-working teams is 'efficiency.' Efficiency is often incorrectly measured by an "increase in resource utilization" (remember the baton and the runner). But, does this really improve the overall efficiency or is this another local optimization?

If you are truly interested in performance, then it is unskillfull to break up high-performing teams. Instead of regrouping teams to fit the work, you can regroup the work to fit the teams. For example, when using feature teams you give features to existing teams instead of regrouping the teams for each feature. The teams are considered the "unit of organizing work."

How long should a team stay together? Ralph Katz—a professor of entrepreneurship and innovation—studied the relation between team performance and team longevity. His research shows that R&D teams increase their performance until they reach a peak after working together for four years [Katz82] (Figure 8.2).[1] After this, their performance dropped, probably because of the lack of fresh ideas. Therefore, keep teams together as long as possible. But sometimes rotate members across teams to create new insights. Of course, self-organizing teams can decide to rotate their members themselves.

Figure 8.2 team performance over time

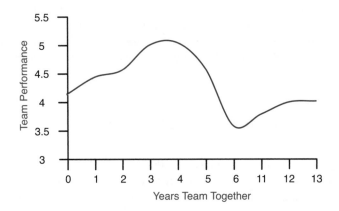

## Try...Team Owns the Process

One reason for the increase in performance over time is improvement in the team's process. A Scrum team owns their process and is expected to improve it. In Toyota, every team member is expected to not just execute his task, but to also be responsible for improving his team's work. The team member handbook at Toyota states:

*All team members are expected to take part in developing and designing new ways of doing their work that continue to improve the job and productivity as well as the quality of our product. In the process, team members also learn to work effectively as a team and to help their fellow team members, when necessary, to perform their job duties [LH08].*

---

1. Team performance was measured by interviewing people involved and then rating their response on a seven-point scale.

Figure 8.3 large-scale Scrum teams

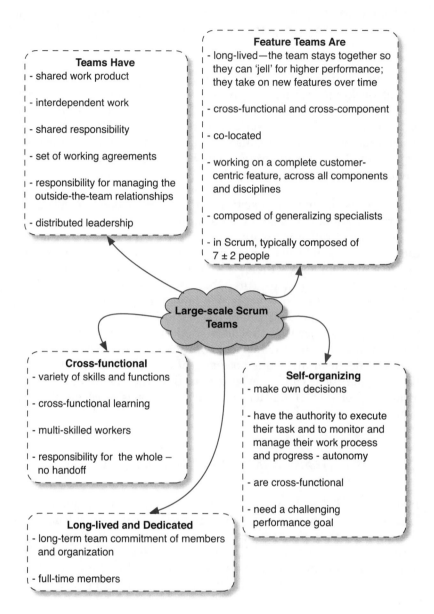

**Feature Teams Are**
- long-lived—the team stays together so they can 'jell' for higher performance; they take on new features over time
- cross-functional and cross-component
- co-located
- working on a complete customer-centric feature, across all components and disciplines
- composed of generalizing specialists
- in Scrum, typically composed of 7 ± 2 people

**Teams Have**
- shared work product
- interdependent work
- shared responsibility
- set of working agreements
- responsibility for managing the outside-the-team relationships
- distributed leadership

**Large-scale Scrum Teams**

**Cross-functional**
- variety of skills and functions
- cross-functional learning
- multi-skilled workers
- responsibility for the whole – no handoff

**Self-organizing**
- make own decisions
- have the authority to execute their task and to monitor and manage their work process and progress - autonomy
- are cross-functional
- need a challenging performance goal

**Long-lived and Dedicated**
- long-term team commitment of members and organization
- full-time members

Of course, team members only improve their process if they feel they own it. When people are regrouped frequently, it is hard to get this kind of ownership. The result is that people "just do their job," follow the process, and a huge potential in performance and job satisfaction is lost.

*Definition of Done p. 313*

How can multiple teams work together if every team has their own way of working? Multiple teams need to agree on cross-team **working agreements**—standards. The Scrum "Definition of Done" is an example of a multi-team working agreement. Over time, the working agreement evolves because teams reflect, learn, and improve. Important: No separate group owns the cross-team working agreement; the teams own them together.

When transitioning an existing product development group to Scrum, the set of basic agreements is not yet established. Neither is there a way of reflecting working agreements nor a way of changing them. To kick-start the transition, management can take one team's agreements and make them the multi-team working agreements without having consensus. After this, they need to *let go* and let the teams evolve these agreements. We have seen this in a large radio network telecom product where the "Definition of Done" set for all the teams was based on that of a single team. This "Definition of Done" was above most teams' capabilities and resulted in a temporary slowdown in all teams because they had to learn and expand their capabilities. One drawback was that the teams did not feel ownership of the "Definition of Done," so it was hard for them to evolve it.

## TRY...TEAM MANAGES EXTERNAL DEPENDENCIES

In traditional development it is common for someone outside the team—a project manager—to manage the external dependencies for the team so that the team can focus on their work. Surprisingly, according to the results of long-time team researcher and MIT professor Deborah Ancona, teams with an internal and *external* focus outperform teams with solely an internal focus. She calls these teams X-teams.

*High-performance teams manage across their boundaries, reaching out to find the information they need, understand the context in which they work, manage the politics and power struggles that surround the team initiative, get support for their ideas, and coordinate with the myriad other groups that are key to a team's success [AB07].*

She is not alone in this. An article published by Manchester Business School reviewed research on cross-functional teams and their success factors. The researchers found that *"teams need to be educated to consider boundary management as an important part of their task"* [HGG00]. Harvard professor and long-time team researcher Richard Hackman suggests establishing two outward-looking working agreements, of which the first one is:

*Members should take an active, rather than a reactive, stance towards the environment in which the team operates, continuously scanning the environment and inventing or adjusting their performance strategies accordingly [Hackman02].*

What are the implication for large product development? They are profound! *First*, each team needs a clear goal so that they know their boundaries. Establishing customer-focused feature teams helps. It results in code-focused, cross-team communication. *Second*, the organization needs to make it crystal clear that the teams themselves are responsible for coordinating their work with other teams. A team's success must be measured by the whole product's success to prevent local optimization. Removing official coordination roles such as project managers makes it clear to the team that coordination is their responsibility. *Third*, establish a whole product-wide continuous integration system. This creates the visibility teams need so that they can coordinate their work. The health of the product must always be visible to everybody.

*see Continuous Integration in companion book*

Coordination roles, such as the project manager role, tend to result in inward-focused teams who blame their failures on the coordinating person or on the other teams. They are victims. Removing these roles makes it crystal clear that teams are responsible for coordinating their work—managing their boundary.

The problem with coordination roles was painfully visible when we worked with a telecom messaging product. This product used Scrum and had ScrumMasters creating the conditions for self-organizing teams, but they refused to remove the project manager role. The result? The project manager became responsible for the coordination among teams and even for the communication to the Product Owner. He became stressed and overloaded with work. When we told him that his role is not needed, he laughed, and pointed out the amount of work he was doing. He did not realize that his role attracted the work, and that the work—the major bottleneck in the product group— would disappear if his role was removed.

Another product group did remove project managers and let the teams coordinate their work. One of the line managers of this group reflected on this change and said, "Nobody ever missed them, and I have fifty percent more 'free' time."

## TRY...DEDICATED TEAM MEMBERS

Avoid non-dedicated team members or "partial allocation." A team member who is in multiple teams does not have the same commitment and shared responsibility as the other members. "Part-time people equate to part-time commitment. Part-time commitment leads to team failure" [Jensen96]. To the maximum amount possible, all members are 100 percent allocated—fully dedicated to their team. The amount of management waste that disappears is amazing. In the past, we worked with some traditional sequential life cycle product groups and saw that the amount of time managers were spending on "allocating resources" was non-trivial.

## TRY...MULTI-SKILLED WORKERS

In Scrum, a team develops the product in priority order—based on customer value. This results in a mismatch between the selected Product Backlog Items and the skills of the team, especially with long-lived dedicated teams. For example, the next iteration the team works on Backlog Item one and two. These items require work in ABC and ADE. However, the team consists of specialists in ABCEFG. There is no D specialist and there is no work for the F and G specialist (see Figure 8.4). What to do?

Figure 8.4 mismatch between Backlog Items and skills on the team

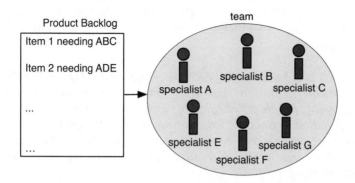

Product Backlog

| Item 1 needing ABC |
| Item 2 needing ADE |
| ... |
| ... |

team

specialist A
specialist B
specialist C
specialist E
specialist F
specialist G

This mismatch is common. It means team members need to step out of their knowledge area and learn new skills. Learning multiple skills—developing multi-skilled workers—creates flexibility and understanding of each others job. Multi-skilled workers are common and important in Toyota:

> *Cross-training...has many purposes and benefits. To have members know as many skills as possible and to rotate among the team helps teamwork... and helps the team make improvements in order to raise their capabilities and improve productivity for the company. It also helps the flexibility... If a person already knows four or five jobs... [he] will be able to move to a new team and set of jobs and quickly and efficiently learn to perform them. On the other hand, if... [he] only learns one job and gets wedded to that job, or spends years developing the seniority to get assigned to an easy job, ... [he] will not want to move, thereby reducing flexibility [LH08].*

When we talk to senior management about learning and multi-skilling, they tell us they worry about efficiency. When people are learning, they are slower. Therefore, the view is that it is more efficient to have the specialist work on the specialist things. This might make sense from a traditional Tayloristic[2] manufacturing mindset (though Toyota uses multi-skilled workers in manufacturing to increase efficiency), but from a product-development-as-knowledge-

---

2. Many old-fashioned management practices have been influenced by Frederick Taylor's scientific management [Taylor11].

creation perspective [NT95], this kind of thinking is *silly. Learning is the major activity in product development.* In the long run, reducing learning reduces efficiency—not increases it. Sherman, in *Fortune Magazine*:

> *Workers will be rewarded for knowledge and adaptability. Specialization is out, a new-style generalism is in. The most employable people will be flexible folk who can move easily from one function to another, integrating diverse disciplines and perspectives... people will need the ability not only to learn fundamentally new skills but also to unlearn outdated ways [Sherman93].*

*Potential skill*—How can this work in large-scale product development? The key is to think about *potential skill* instead of actual skill. A person has a potential skill when he can learn the skill in a reasonable amount of time. For example, people with a computer science degree can learn a new programming language within a reasonable amount of time. Even more important, when they already know five programming languages, then learning the sixth is even faster. Therefore, people should be selected to teams for potential skill rather than the teams being changed to utilize current skills. That way, people grow in their jobs and teams are kept together for a long time. When do you know your team is working well and learning? One perspective:

> *You will know your teams are working the day an engineer begins sounding like a marketer, or vice versa. Effective teams operate like a small startup in that people take whatever role is required, with little regard to function or rank. Leadership roles will also rotate when the team is working at peak effectiveness. The designated leader will step back and let leadership emerge from the parties either most knowledgeable or responsible for the issue under discussion. There is not an absence of leadership, but rather an increase and balance of leadership from all team members [Meyer93].*

NSN has a central support coaching group, called *Flexible Company*, for agile development. The group was created as a cross-functional team with specialists from development, testing, quality management, CMMI, and some other areas. Each Monday morning the group held a meeting dedicated to learning. Lots of conflict—learning—happened during this meeting. The result? After a couple of months the areas started blurring and people outside this team could no longer recognize the original specialization of the persons.

## TRY...TEAM MAKES DECISIONS

Self-organizing teams make their own decisions. However, many people grew up in a command-and-control environment where management made decisions for them. What happens when such people move to self-organizing teams? Endless discussion without decisions. This is painful. A ScrumMaster can help the team learn how to make decisions. There are many decision-making methods, such as voting, consensus, and "expert decides." A team *agreement* on how to make decisions is more important than the specific decision-making method. That said, most healthy teams apply some kind of consensus decisions making method [KLTFB07]

We worked with a product group building network optimization products; they had fallen in the not-know-how-to-make-decisions trap. After a discussion of their current problems, it was obvious that they knew how to solve their problems except that they could not agree with each other on the solutions. We introduced the *Decider protocol* [MM02], which is a quick and easy way of making consensus decisions. This helped the team move forward because finally they could agree on which solution to implement for their problems.

Paul Nagy is a ScrumMaster in NSN Hungary. In one design meeting, his team could not make a decision. The team was split exactly fifty-fifty on the two design alternatives they had. After long discussions, they desperately asked their ScrumMaster, Paul, to decide for them. He asked the team to explain the two alternatives. Then he grabbed his wallet, took out a coin and flipped it. "Heads... alternative one," he said. The team looked at him angrily and said, "You did not even think about it!" He answered, "You asked me to make the decision." The team never asked him to make a decision again—they always made it themselves.

## TRY…OPEN TEAM CONFLICT

People working together creates conflict. That is not a bad thing. But conflict needs to be resolved. Unresolved conflict has a negative impact on team performance and creates a dysfunctional team atmosphere [Lencioni02]. Resolved conflict, on the other hand, creates learning and trust, both of which have a positive impact on performance. Conflict is an opportunity for the team to improve their performance, and hence a good thing.

Team conflict keeps a ScrumMaster busy. Without *apparent* conflict, the team is in trouble. You, as ScrumMaster, need to discover why. Are members avoiding discussion? Is something hidden? Are members truly committed to the team? When there is conflict in the team, a ScrumMaster observes the team to make sure they resolve the issues. Good teams resolve their own conflict; teams who were just formed need help. Well-working teams naturally have conflict but can express and resolve it.

We have worked with teams all over the world, and cultural differences are fascinating to us. North-East Asia (China, Japan, and Korea) has a very strong conflict-avoidance culture. People would rather shut up than create "social instability." When working with or in these cultures, it is important to realize this and to sometimes open the needed conflict.

## EFFECTS ON ORGANIZATION

Self-organizing cross-functional teams have a major impact on the organization. To repeat an earlier quote,

> *"Successful implementation of multifunctional teams requires a fundamental redesign of the entire organization" [Meyer93].*

*organizational impact p. 241*

Some points are covered here, but most of the organizational impact is discussed in the *Organization* chapter.

### Avoid...Phase-based "resource allocation"

In traditional sequential life cycle development, each phase has phase specialists. For example, requirement specialists in the requirements phase, design specialists in the design phase, and developers in the implementation phase. The requirement specialist would only be on the release in the beginning—she was only allocated in the requirement phase.

Scrum is not the waterfall. There are no phases. With its self-managing, cross-functional, long-lived feature teams, it balances the "resource need" over the release. The same people stay on the release from the beginning until the end.

### Avoid...Parallel releases (a symptom of imbalanced groups and work)

In traditional development, when a requirement analyst finished analyzing the requirements, what would she do? Would she wait for the testing to be finished so that the next release can be started? No...

Most organizations want to achieve a high "resource utilization." Therefore, when the requirement analyst has nothing to do, she can start analyzing the requirements for the *next* release. That way, the 'resources' are used 'efficiently' and the time-to-market is improved. However, as seen in *Queuing Theory*, cycle time *increases* when "resource utilization" is high in a system with variation.

*queuing theory*
*p. 93*

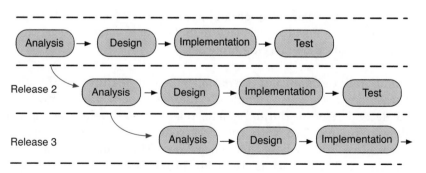

Figure 8.5 parallel release for so-called efficient resource usage, a local optimization "watching the runner rather than the baton"

Wishful thinking. Learning happens and requirements change. When the product is in a later phase, the requirement analyst is needed again. She spends her time on the previous release, thereby delaying the next release. Parallel releases increase waste—a lot. It causes multi-tasking, handoff, and extra processes. Ironically, the (misunderstood) "father of the waterfall" warned about this in his classic paper that was incorrectly used to justify waterfall development [Royce70, Larman03].

Parallel releases caused problems for many products we worked with. Product groups frequently decide "to do the next release with Scrum." Scrum requires a cross-functional team from *day one*. However, the testers are still busy testing the previous release, and thus they are not included in the 'cross-functional' team. The result? Even with good intentions, the product group reverts to sequential development.

*see Requirements and Continuous Integration in companion*

Without parallel releases, does the time-to-market degrade? The opposite is true. The removal of the waste in product development decreases the cycle time and therefore improves the time-to-market. But some products have large features for which development takes longer than one release. This is common in the telecom industry. The trick is to split up the large feature and deliver parts of it over multiple releases. These feature parts are integrated, included, and released, though they might be disabled from use until complete.

### Avoid...Staircase branching (a symptom of imbalanced groups and work)

Functional teams and sequential life cycle development leads to parallel releases. Parallel releases lead to waste—and one of these wastes is caused by merging branches.

Traditional development scenario: When a feature in the first release has been coded completely, the developers start working on the second release. But, of course, release two development is not allowed to interfere with the first release. Thus, they create a release-two branch based on release one. The same happens with the release three, which is created by branching from release two.

We have seen this branching model with many large products and call it the "branch early" strategy. Berczuk and Appleton, in their classic *Configuration Management Patterns* [BA03] call it staircase branching (Figure 8.6).

Figure 8.6 staircase branching

This branching model maximizes waste. It causes developers extra work to synchronize all changes over all branches. We have seen products where developers spend most of their time on these synchronizations. What is the alternative? *Branch as late as possible.* Keep developing on the mainline and only branch off just before the release (Figure 8.7). This requires the development to use continuous integration.

Figure 8.7 mainline development branching model

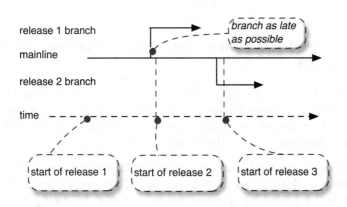

### Avoid...Projects in product development (a symptom of imbalanced groups and work)

Valtech often does relatively short-term *projects*. A client orders a ten-month project and when it is done, it is done. Xerox, Ericsson, Microsoft and many other companies develop *products*. A product has many releases and the code base stays around for a long time.

Traditional development with single-function teams, phase-based "resource allocation" and staircase branching *leads to using* **projects** for product development. Every definition of the word *project* (for example, [PMBOK04]) includes its temporal nature, resulting in a focus on short-term goals. Using projects for product development is fraught with local optimizations—short-term over long-term thinking.

Self-organizing, cross-functional, "resource-balanced," feature teams work iteratively on the mainline by selecting work from a Product Backlog: This leads to a better balance between long and short-term goals that are needed for product development. The concept of *project* does not belong in this type of product development.

One large multisite product group has completely abandoned the concept of project in development. All feature teams get their work from the Product Backlog, and at certain points the Product Owner decides to release.

## CONCLUSION

These different—but proven—team concepts cause major change in organizations.

- ❑ Self-organizing teams require a change from command-and-control management to manager-teacher. Instead of focusing on what people do, management should focus on how to create the environment for the teams to succeed.

- ❑ Cross-functional teams require breaking functional boundaries and working together across the whole organization to optimize delivering customer value. Instead of boxing people in functional groups, management should focus on cross-functional learning.

- Long-lived dedicated teams require giving work to existing teams and letting them decide how to do it. Instead of considering individuals to be the unit of performance, the focus needs to be on complete teams.

## RECOMMENDED READINGS

When switching to cross-functional teams, changing management style is difficult. Luckily, a lot of excellent material has been written on this subject.

- *Leading Teams*, by Richard Hackman. Harvard professor Richard Hackman is a long-time team researcher. His book is currently our favorite team-related book. It has a strong focus on helping management in their change to team-based work.

- *Leading Self-Directed Work Teams*, by Kimball Fisher. This book has a strong focus on the change in role when one becomes a team leader of a self-directed team.

- *The Project Manager's Bridge to Agility*, by Michele Sliger and Stacia Broderick. Michele and Stacia are two Scrum Trainers and also PMI-certified PMPs. Traditional project managers will find here an explanation of the difference in thinking from a PMI PMBOK perspective. When reading it, please read their "agile project manager" as ScrumMaster.

Some texts on team in general.

- *The Wisdom of Teams*, by Jon Katzenbach and Douglas Smith. This is probably the most popular team reference and certainly worth reading.

- *The Five Dysfunctions of a Team*, by Patrick Lencioni. Written like a novel, it covers well the need for conflict in teams.

Cross-functional teams are described mainly in product development literature. Some good texts:

- *Fast Cycle Time*, by Chris Meyer. Recently republished (2007), this is a true classic on product development and talks about cross-functional (multifunctional) teams in detail.

- *Revolutionizing Product Development*, by Steven Wheelwright and Kim Clark. Another classic in product development literature; has one chapter on cross-functional integration.

Some texts related to software development teams:

- *Software for Your Head*, by Jim and Michele McCarthy. Jim and Michele spent years in 'boot camps' to find the most efficient ways for teams to work. They documented this as a set of protocols in this book.

- *Peopleware*, by Tom DeMarco and Tim Lister. This classic on the importance of people in software development also has a couple of chapters focusing on teams.

# Chapter

---

# Book

# REQUIREMENT AREAS

*To be stupid, selfish, and have good health are three requirements for
happiness, though if stupidity is lacking, all is lost.*
*—Gustave Flaubert*

A product with more than five or ten feature teams is difficult for

❑ teams…to work on the whole product

❑ the Product Owner…to work with so many teams

Therefore, feature teams are scaled up by grouping related teams in
a **requirement area**. Like a feature team, a requirement area is
customer centric; it is not an architectural sub-system. It is a set of
features that are strongly related from the customer perspective.
For example, *network management* and *performance*. The set of features is put in an **Area Backlog** and managed independently from
other areas' features. Requirement areas do *not* map directly to specific architectural components.

### Try…One Product Owner and one Product Backlog

Delivering low-value features is a waste. Lean thinking and Scrum
focus on delivering high customer value, and that requires having
visibility to overall development. Therefore, every product—no matter its size—needs *one* Product Owner (PO) and *one* Product Backlog
(PB). But this can lead to

❑ the PO dealing with too many teams

❑ the PB becoming too large

❑ teams working on the whole system

**PO dealing with too many teams**—With all the tasks the PO needs to do, it seems impossible for him to work with more than a couple of teams. How to solve this? One way is for teams to take over the clarification of Product Backlog Item (PBI) work by including subject matter experts on the team. An alternative is for someone to assist the PO with clarification work. He joins the **Product Owner Team** but does not make decisions related to prioritization. Using these techniques, one PO can work with up to five or ten teams. More than that will cause information overload for the PO and makes iteration planning difficult.

**PB becoming too large**—Lean thinking promotes small batches and short cycles. We suggest that each team have at least four PBIs for each iteration that they can complete independently within that iteration. With 50 teams this leads to a PB with 200 PBIs just for one iteration. Prioritizing 200 PBIs per iteration is too much work for one PO.

**Teams working on the whole system**—Feature teams are good, and so is learning new parts of the system. But too much learning without delivering value is not. This can happen when teams work on completely unfamiliar features. They have no opportunity to specialize and this affects teams' velocity. How to strike a balance?

## TRY...REQUIREMENTS AREAS

*Try...Affinity clustering or diagram for finding requirement areas*

**Requirement areas** are customer-centric categories of PBIs. Example requirement areas: for a digital press printer, *color workflow* and *transaction printing*; for an internet portal area, *ads* and *news*; for a telecom system, *protocols, performance,* and *network management* (see Figure 9.1). Discovering the requirement areas is surprisingly easy. For example, in Berlin we once simply wrote PBIs on cards, spread them on the floor, and asked the PO and others to group them—affinity clustering into the requirement areas.

Figure 9.1 requirement areas in PB

| Product Backlog | |
|---|---|
| **Backlog Item** | **Requirement Area** |
| IPv6 | protocols |
| performance 10x | performance |
| HSDPA | management |
| performance stats | protocols |
| configuration of cells | management |
| new NMS solution | continuous integration |
| speed-up of build | upgrades |
| improved upgrading support | management |
| stability to 99.999% | reliability |

Note: An Area Backlog is a *view* into the PB based on the requirement area (Figure 9.2). Each PBI belongs to one Area Backlog, and vice versa.

Area Backlog Items are finer-grained than PBIs. The PB contains fewer items and they are more coarse-grained, making it manageable. Remember though, when a large item is split the priority of the resulting fine-grained items is not the same. When this difference is big, then it must be reflected in the PB so that it is visible to the PO.

Figure 9.2 Area Backlogs

| Product Backlog |
|---|
| IPv6 |
| performance 10x |
| HSDPA |
| performance stats |
| configuration of cells |
| new NMS solution |
| speed-up of build |
| improved upgrading support |
| stability to 99.999% |

| Performance Area Backlog | |
|---|---|
| performance 10x | switch hardware |
| performance 10x | optimize DSP |
| ... | ... |

| Protocols  Area Backlog | |
|---|---|
| IPv6 | simple connect |
| IPv6 | data sending |
| HSDPA | failed call |
| ... | ... |

The Area Backlog Items are split, clarified, and prioritized independently of the other Area Backlog Items. This is done by a separate person—an **Area Product Owner** (APO). She specializes in a customer-centric area and acts as PO in relation to the teams for that area (see Figure 9.3).

Figure 9.3 APO works on Area Backlog

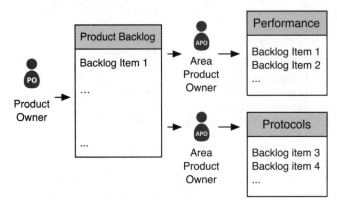

see Product Management in companion book

*Product Owner Team*—The APOs and the PO together form a team—the **Product Owner Team**. This team makes product-wide prioritization decisions, but the PO always has the final decision. Also, scope and schedule decisions stay with the PO—he decides when to release what.

Teams are distributed over the requirement areas based on the PB priority (see Figure 9.4). Areas are of different size in terms of effort and so they contain a different number of teams. Too-small areas are not a good idea because they result in many backlogs and many APOs. The overview is lost and teams develop low-value features. Rather, prefer a couple of small areas combined in one broader area—increasing the flexibility within this area. On the other hand, too-large areas are difficult for one APO. To strike a balance, consider a minimum of four and a maximum of ten teams per area.

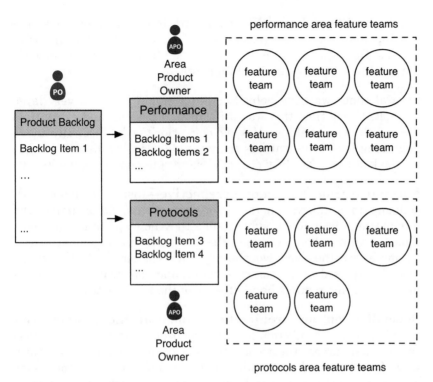

Figure 9.4 feature teams working on areas

performance area feature teams

**Product Backlog**

Backlog Item 1

...

...

**Area Product Owner**

**Performance**

Backlog Items 1
Backlog Items 2
...

**Protocols**

Backlog Item 3
Backlog Item 4
...

**Area Product Owner**

feature team

feature team

feature team

feature team

feature team

feature team

feature team

feature team

feature team

feature team

feature team

protocols area feature teams

Each team works in one area and focuses on related features. In relation to the area teams, the APO acts as the PO in iteration planning and reviews. It is almost like the area is a separate product. Every PBI fits by definition in exactly one area and therefore the areas can work independently—from a requirement perspective. However, from a *code* perspective teams need to coordinate and synchronize their work with other areas. The areas are scaled-up groups of feature teams, so all the inter-team code coordination issues discussed in the *Feature Teams* chapter must be considered.

Requirement areas make it possible to

❑ have one PO and one PB

❑ specialize from a customer perspective

❑ specialize on a part of the system

**Have one PO and one PB**—Even with hundreds of people in the development, you can keep one PO who makes product-wide prioritizations. He works with the Product Owner Team and therefore does not need to know the details of all areas.

Several times we have helped create a single PB for a very large product. Every time this was difficult and painful, and every time the result was striking. Having *one* prioritized PB finally made delivering low-value features truly visible. One PO discovered that for the last two years fifty people were working on low-value items.

**Specialize from customer perspective**—Instead of teams specializing in a subsystem (a set of components; for example, the "adaptations framework subsystem") they now specialize in a customer domain. For example, the "network management area." Teams share the same vocabulary with customers. They can be directly involved in the communication and clarification of requirements, and this reduces handoff—one of the lean wastes.

**Specialize on an architectural part of the system**—This sounds like a contradiction to what has been written above, because requirement areas are a customer view and not an architectural view. In other words, a requirement area does not map one-to-one with a specific architectural subsystem. But fortunately, in most products requirement areas do not map N-to-N either. Features in the "color workflow" area are seldom randomly scattered across the entire code base. *Most* work in one requirement area is likely to be in a few predictable architectural subsystems. The teams specialize in these subsystems 'accidentally' because most work in most area-features is repeatedly in the same family of subsystems. This technical specialization speeds up the development without the restriction of component ownership as found in traditional large-scale development (see sidebar). An analogy is "a point of gravity." Several subsystems are at the center of the area. The further away from the center, the less likely they need to be changed.

### Try…Moving whole teams between areas

Scenario: The area where a team works used to have many high-priority items. But priorities change over time and now the items in the area are a lower priority. Consequently, teams move between areas. New areas are created and old areas cease to exist; areas shift slowly over time.

The PO monitors the difference in PBI priorities between areas. When the difference is too large, he moves a well-working, high-performing feature team from one area to another. The whole team together, as a stable long-lived team, learns the new area. This slows a team down for some time, but they deliver higher-value features. In the early days they will be asking for lots of help from the other teams in that area.

Feature teams doing infrastructure work either have their own area or, when the infrastructure area is small, are included in another area. For example, teams may work in a combined area called "Protocols and Continuous Integration Infrastructure."

## TRANSITIONING TO REQUIREMENT AREAS

Changing to requirement areas is a big step. Two options are all-at-once and gradual-via-**Development Areas.**

### Try...An all-at-once transition to requirement areas

When transitioning all at once, you need to:

1. create requirement areas in the backlog

2. create Area Backlogs and assign APOs

3. move the feature teams in the areas

Take the skills of the existing feature teams into account when moving them in the requirement areas.

Most large changes are best done gradually. That said, we worked with a few product groups who took a gradual approach and the extra trouble was not worth it. Therefore...

### Avoid...Development areas

Some product groups took an intermediate step in the change to requirement areas by combining traditional scaling (see sidebar) with feature teams. They created the areas based on the subsystem department's architectural components—called **Development Areas**—with what they called "development area feature teams" (these were not real feature teams).

It turned out that the Development Areas structure did not make the change easier. They had and continue to have component-team problems such as

❑ PBIs need to be split based on architectural components before they are added to the Area Backlog

❑ work on the Area Backlog Items needs to be coordinated and synchronized

❏ PBI analysis, in which the item is split and put in the Area Backlog, needs to be done before the development iteration.

❏ PBI testing needs to be done separately from the development areas, in separate testing teams

These "development area feature teams" are actually "multi-component" teams that span more components but still do not do true end-to-end customer features. It is a step in the right direction but does not go all the way.

Each of the above component-team problems was 'solved' by adding a role or team to the organization: architect, feature coordinator, project manager, or system-testing team. These extra roles—plus delivering value slower with more hand off and more sequential development—are costs of a more gradual change.

One product group moved gradually from development areas to requirement areas by blurring the boundaries between the development areas. When a PBI covered multiple development areas, the product group would find out which development area was most affected and then move the whole item to that Area Backlog. When the priorities were unbalanced, they would expand the responsibility of an area so they could work on high-priority items.

Avoid development areas unless it is impossible to move directly to requirement areas. The drawbacks quickly outweigh the advantage of a gradual change.

## TOOLS

What tool supports managing large backlogs? Use a simple spreadsheet. Not because a spreadsheet is so good; just because it is better than the alternatives.

We have seen a PB of a multisite product in three countries with four hundred people managed with spreadsheets. In this product, there were inconsistencies in the backlogs, so the head of development asked the PO, "Would buying a new tool help with the backlog?" The PO responded insightfully, "I don't think the tool is the problem." When managing backlogs, the tool is seldom the problem.

Avoid these tools:

- ❏ traditional requirement management tools
- ❏ tools optimized for reporting

*Avoid...*
*Traditional*
*requirement*
*management*
*tools*

**Traditional requirement management tools**—These tools are often database-based. This makes it hard to have one forced-ranked list as in a PB. A common solution is to have a priority column. But this does not work well and leads to an increase in effort needed to maintain the backlog.

*Avoid...Tools*
*optimized for*
*reporting*

**Tools optimized for reporting**—Many tool vendors understand that it is senior management who decides whether or not to buy a tool. Therefore, many tools—including most "agile tools"—are optimized for reporting rather than for real value work. Developers or POs find the tool awkward and report that it slows them down, but senior management see the reports they want—an obvious sub-optimization. Notice that such tools may inhibit the lean *Go See* practice.

## CONCLUSION

Requirement areas provide a consistent way to scale up Scrum and feature teams for very large product development. They are also a major organizational change. There are ways of moving to requirement areas gradually, but avoid them since their drawbacks outweigh their advantages.

# Chapter

# Book

# ORGANIZATION

*Most organizations have what appear to be suicidal tendencies.*
*—Philip Crosby*

*The subject of the organization is large, likewise this chapter.*
*Yet it is a fraction of what needs to be explored. The recom-*
*mended readings are relatively extensive to encourage study.*

We have regularly been asked, "Since Scrum is a development method, why would it lead to organizational change?" The answer is that Scrum contains concepts and practices that challenge traditional organizational assumptions. Self-management and cross-functionality of teams are high-impact examples—though neither idea originates from Scrum. They have been applied in different contexts for decades and their impact on organizations is widely publicized.

*self-managing*
*cross-functional*
*teams p. 194*

This chapter suggests deep and challenging changes in organizational design. These changes relate to assumptions behind organizations and how they should act. Adjusting organizational structure is relatively easy, but changing mindset takes time, discussion, introspection, and learning. Large organizations are…large. They employ thousands of people, all with ideas about organizations—changing organizational assumptions means changing *people's* assumptions, one at a time. This is a slow process, years in the making. Bear this in mind when reading this chapter. We know some topics seem far from reality in most organizations, but a vision directs the gradual change. Be patient and good humored.

We who are introducing large-scale Scrum are not alone. The changes in organizational assumptions are happening in many companies and industries. Companies adopt new structures and different management styles to compete in the new knowledge and innovation-driven world. Management guru Gary Hamel in *The Future of Management* put it like this:

> *These new realities call for new organizational and managerial capabilities. To thrive in an increasingly disruptive world, companies must become as strategically adaptable as they are operationally efficient. To safeguard their margins, they must become gushers of rule-breaking innovation. And if they're going to out-invent and outthink a growing mob of upstarts, they must learn how to inspire their employees to give the very best of themselves every day. [Hamel07]*

### Top Ten Organizational Impediments

To ensure that we highlighted important topics, we asked a group of agile development experts working in and with large companies about the most challenging organizational impediments. Mike Cohn, author of two popular agile development books, and Clinton Keith, a Scrum trainer specializing in game development, both replied with a reference to their article "How to Fail with Agile" [CK08]. Their 20-point list of impediments focuses more on the team level than the organizational level, but it's worth reading. We aggregated the other responses in the *top ten organizational impediments*.

**10.** Jeff Sutherland, co-creator of Scrum, considers the **failure to remove organizational impediments** the main obstacle in large organizations. A common reason for not removing impediments is "That's the way we've always done business." We also frequently hear, "We won't change because we invested so much in this."[1]

**9.** Peter Alfvin, an experienced development manager involved with introducing lean principles at Xerox, and Petri Haapio, head of the agile coaching department at Reaktor Innovations, both mention **centralized departments looking for cost 'savings' and 'synergy' that leads to a local optimization** as an impediment. Their examples included a centralized tool department forcing one tool, leading to slower development caused by the wrong tool for a job; furniture police forcing cubicles to standardize and minimize cost,

---

1. The investment includes both money and reputations.

leading to inefficient workplaces; IT department limiting video conferencing to lower network traffic, leading to less communication.

**8.** Sami Lilja, global coordinator of agile development activities at Nokia Siemens Networks, noticed that some organizations **consider learning a waste of time and money**. He believes this opinion is a major impediment because those organizations educate and coach people only "when there is time for it." This view results in a vicious fire fighting cycle—mistakes made because of constricted developer skills, hasty emergency repairs, management unwillingness to allot time to analyze earlier mistakes, more mistakes made...

**7.** Larry Cai, a specialist at Ericsson Shanghai, mentions *functional organizations* as one of the largest impediments. They create barriers for communication and abet finger-pointing among units.

**6.** Esther Derby, consultant, coach, expert facilitator, and author of two books related to organizational learning, considers **systems that foster local optimization over global optimization** a major barrier. She gave several examples, including *Management by Objectives* (MBO) and budgeting systems.

**5.** Mike Bria, a former agile coach at Siemens Medical Systems, mentioned "do-it-yourself home improvement" as an impediment. He highlighted the problem attitude of "we know how" after people read one or two books. In other words, the problem of **failure to learn from outside expertise.** The same is mentioned by Lasse Koskela, the author of *Test-Driven*—unwillingness to look outside the organization.

**4.** A. *(name removed on request)*, a Scrum trainer at one of the largest e-commerce sites, mentioned **individual performance evaluation and rewarding** as a major obstacle. They frustrate developers and managers, hinder team performance, and foster command-and-control management.

**3.** Lü Yi, a Scrum trainer and department manager of a large development group in Nokia Siemens Networks in Hangzhou, considers **"commitment games" and unrealistic promises** to be the main organizational obstacle. They lead to shortcuts, continuous fire fighting, and legacy code. We cover this topic in more detail in the *Legacy Code* chapter of the companion book.

**2.** Diana Larsen, expert facilitator and, together with Esther Derby, the author of *Agile Retrospectives*, simply stated, "**Assuming it's all about developers**." We have seen this frequently—people who do not think they need to change because agile and lean involves only developers. They ask, "Why would it affect me?"

**1**. Almost everybody cited *"silver bullet thinking and superficial adoption"* as a major impediment. Dave Thomas, founder of OTI, large-scale lean product development consultant, and managing director of ObjectMentor, mentioned the misunderstanding of equating agility and productivity, and the lack of educated executives. This leads to the belief that meaningful problems can be solved by saying "we do agile" and going through the motions, with no deep understanding or change by the leadership team—cargo cult process adoption. Ironically, this leads to no real change and no real result, and the eventual predictable abandonment of lean principles or agile development because "that doesn't work."

A related impediment is the wishful thinking that significant improvement in large product groups can and will happen 'fast,' within only a few years, rather than what we see as the more likely five or ten years—if there is sustained executive support.

The remainder of the chapter explores some of these organizational obstacles and what you can do about them. It is structured around the "Star Model"[2] created by organizational design expert Jay Galbraith [Galbraith93]. The strategy of an organization drives the five other elements of the model: task, people, rewards, processes, and structure. The better these elements are aligned, the larger the organizational capability (see Figure 10.1).

---

2. Since 1994, Galbraith made minor updates to the Star Model. We chose the older version since it structured the chapter well.

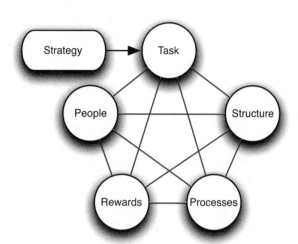

Figure 10.1 Star Model for organizational design

This model explicates why adopting Scrum requires change in the whole organization. Scrum directly alters the processes and structure elements. The organizational capability then decreases unless the other elements in the model are adjusted accordingly.

## PURPOSE AND STRATEGY

Organizations are created with a **goal**— a purpose. For example, Toyota's goal is to *"strive for cleaner and safer car making, and work to make the earth a better place to live"* [Toyota08]. Profit and market share are needed for reaching this broader goal. The founder of the Visa organization, Dee Hock, stressed the importance of a goal and wrote that a *"purpose is a clear, simple statement of intent that identifies and binds the community together as worthy of pursuit."* Their vision: *Digital money* [Hock99].

But not any goal will do for the enterprise that wants to endure and attract great people. According to quality thought-leader W. Edwards Deming, the goal of an organization should not merely be something short-sighted or monetary, such as maximizing next year's profit; it needs to be long term and deeply purposeful. The first of Deming's famous 14 points states that companies should *"create consistency of purpose toward improvement of product and service, with the aim to become competitive and to stay in business, and to provide jobs"* [Deming82]. Less successful companies define their goal only in terms of market share, profit, or shareholder value. Reasonable pedestrian aspirations, but such goals rarely *inspire* people.

A **strategy** describes how to reach that goal. It includes the markets the company wants to be in and the type of products it wants to offer. Also how the company expects to get there. It might include competing on the basis of time or agility, continuous improvement, or perfection. The interest in Scrum flows directly from a strategy, and this drives the organizational elements in the Star Model.

## TASK

*feature teams p. 149*

This section examines designing the work. In Scrum, teams finish complete customer-centric Product Backlog items each iteration. This has a big impact on the organization of work, as discussed in earlier chapters. Here, *features* and the *feature team* structure are explored from a different perspective—that of *work redesign*.

### Try...Work redesign

Is the potential of people at work fully realized? During the sixties and seventies, this was a frequently asked question. Organizations had grown to mammoth proportions, and because of specialization, jobs became monotonous. It was common to hear statements such as *"it is clearly a waste of human resources to place bright people in bad jobs because we fail to recognize their potential"* [O'Toole77], or *"as division of labor increases in complexity in large-scale organizations, individual roles may seem to lack organic connection with the whole structure of roles, and the result is that the employee may lack under-standing of the coordinated activity and a sense of purpose in his work"* [Blaumer64].

This led to the "Work Redesign" movement. Its goal? Make jobs more challenging by enlarging (enriching) them—by broadening responsibilities. How? By redesigning the work so that it maximizes the skills of the people and the *intrinsic* motivations [HO80].

In a seminal book from the 1980s, *Work Redesign*, Harvard professor Richard Hackman envisioned two alternative futures.

| Alternative 1 | Alternative 2 |
|---|---|
| • job responsibilities broaden | • jobs become more specialized |
| • decision making is delegated to the worker | • use of command-and-control management increases as information technology increases information |
| • focus on intrinsic motivation increases | • focus on extrinsic rewards such as incentives |
| • self-managing teams are commonplace | • focus on individual efficiency |
| • fewer levels of management—leaner organizations | • more supervision |

Hackman sadly predicted alternative 2 as the likely future. We think he was right. Consider today's resource management functions, over-specialization, the focus on trying to 'maximize' resource utilization, and the increasing emphasize on bribes or rewards to influence workers.

But work has changed. More automation *did* lead to increased responsibilities. And perhaps the biggest change is the mass emergence of *knowledge workers*.

Did these changes make the work more challenging? No. In the 21$^{st}$ century, it is still common to find statements such as *"Despite all our gains in technology, product innovations and world markets, most people are not thriving in the organizations they work for. They are neither fulfilled nor excited. They are frustrated... Can you imagine the personal and organizational cost of failure to fully engage the passion, talent and intelligence of the workforce"* [Covey04], or *"Billions of people show up for work every day, but way too many are sleepwalking. The result: organizations that systematically under-perform their potential"* [Hamel07]. Nothing has changed.

We are at the same crossroads as 30 years ago. We have the choice between the same two alternative futures. However, in today's fast-changing, global economy, alternative 1 is the only one that allows our organizations to survive.

The only sustainable way to compete in the "flat world" [Friedman06] is to realize and utilize the *full potential* of *all employees*. If you don't, your competitor in Singapore will. How? The principles of *work redesign* still apply. Restructure today's knowledge work so that it is *meaningful* and encourages growth and *learning*, instead of putting 'resources' in a specialized single-function box.

The five work design (or redesign) principles are

- ❏ combine tasks
- ❏ form natural work units
- ❏ establish client relationships
- ❏ vertically load the job (empowerment)
- ❏ open feedback channels

These principles, first elucidated in the 1980s, are still relevant to knowledge workers today and in the future. Use them to structure work. Organizing in *feature* teams instead of component teams is one example of how you can apply work redesign principles.

### Try...Distinguish between products and projects

Most product development is organized as *projects*—every new product release is a new project. Organizations manage development by managing projects with tools such as a project management office or project portfolio management. Each project is led by a project manager, has its own management structure, and has clear goals about what content must be finished when. Projects are managed independently of one another. Organizing product development in this

*parallel releases*
*p. 209*

project-oriented manner had certain advantages when a traditional sequential life cycle was used.

Should the notion of *projects* really be the *hammer* that changes the whole world to *nails*? In fact, no. It is beneficial to distinguish between product and project development.

| *Product* Development | *Project* Development |
|---|---|
| people work on the product over multiple releases | at the end of the release, people work on a different project |
| development continues until not profitable, preempted by new technology (or disrupted [Christensen03, Levitt60]) or all valuable features are implemented | end of project is clear (usually, after one release) |
| content decisions are "now or next release?" | content decisions are "in or out?" |
| different releases are not independent | projects are independent |
| short-term-view decisions (local optimizations) lead to long-term problems such as legacy code | making short-term-view decisions are not (apparently) harmful |
| same code base is used over multiple releases | every project has a different code base. (Though parts might be shared, that leads to "product-like" problems) |

*see Legacy Code in companion book*

Making the explicit distinction between project and product is not new. In the classic book on matrix organizations, the authors point out, "*Because the temporary nature of program or project management—completing a task within cost, schedule, and performance targets—the objectives of the project manager is to go out of business. Product management is oriented in an almost opposite direction. It aims to take an opportunity—an idea, a service, a technology, a prod-*

*uct, or a brand—and make it as profitable, extensive and long-lived as possible*" [DL77].

The distinction between product and project development is not always clear. For example, after you have delivered the project, your client asks for new features in a new release. This way, the project gradually changes to a product. Having shared components among projects is another common example in which the differentiation between product and project is unclear. The shared components are the organization's product. Still, making the distinction is worthwhile because…

### Avoid…Projects in product development

*Try…Continuous product development*

This tip expands the prior one and relates to one made in the *Teams* chapter. Expressed positively, this tip is *Try…Continuous product development.*

The work in different specialization areas levels out as a result of Scrum. For example, whereas previously you needed testing at the end of a release cycle or project, now testing is needed evenly throughout the life of the product, day after day, iteration after iteration. This removes one important reason for using *projects* in *product* development—"resource management." Before, you had to find new work for a requirement specialist after the requirements phase finished, but now he can stay on the product—in a feature team—doing leveled work each iteration until the product is retired. There is no need to move people between projects; there are long-lived teams for the product.

*continuous product development in Scrum p. 322*

An alternative way of organizing product development work—the Scrum model—is to think of it as continuous flow rather than as a series of long projects. This is **continuous product development**. The teams add value to the product iteration by iteration, and when enough value is added to warrant a release, the Product Owner simply releases the product. From the teams' perspective, the development just continues…forever. In the perfection vision of Scrum, in which it is possible to release at the end of any iteration, no extraordinary shift is involved in releasing on Friday and starting a new release on Monday. It's just the next iteration. Even if lingering finalization work is done in a Release Sprint, this is handled by the

*see Planning in companion*

Product Owner and the stable teams within the normal Scrum rhythm; no special overhead is required.

There is no project anymore—nor a project manager or other person responsible for just one release. There is only the stable Product Owner responsible for each release as the years pass. The management structure for the product group does not change between releases, it stays the same...'forever.' See Figure 10.2.

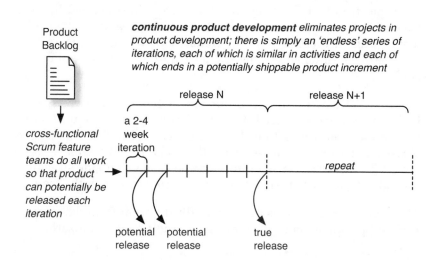

Figure 10.2 product development in a continuous flow without 'projects'

Product Backlog

*continuous product development eliminates projects in product development; there is simply an 'endless' series of iterations, each of which is similar in activities and each of which ends in a potentially shippable product increment*

release N  release N+1

*cross-functional Scrum feature teams do all work so that product can potentially be released each iteration*

a 2-4 week iteration

repeat

potential release  potential release  true release

This continuous product development is made possible by an even distribution of planning over the release—continuous product backlog refinement or *rolling wave planning*—instead of large upfront release planning meetings. The main tool for this is the Product Backlog that stays up-to-date at all times and gradually is refined. Using the Product Backlog, the Product Owner is always able to answer the critical questions, "What is the next release date?" and "What is the release content?"

*see Planning in companion*

### Try...Give projects to existing teams

The *Teams* chapter explores the concept of long-lived teams—keep teams together *forever*. In product development, it is not hard to imagine how that works. But what about *project*-oriented work?[3]

*long-lived teams p. 199*

Isn't the short-lived team disbanded and distributed when the project finished? There is an alternative.

Most organizations use *individuals* as the unit for allocating work. An alternative that fits well to Scrum is to use *teams* as the "unit of performance." Thus, when a new project is started, it is staffed with an existing team instead of separate individuals.

The skills of the existing team will never match the skills needed in the new project. This skill mismatch might slow down the start of the project, but in the long run, the performance gained by long-lived teams balances out this slowdown. Using teams as the performance unit also creates an environment in which people—all the time—are continuously facing challenges to learn and acquire new skills.

There are situations in which difficult or tedious-to-learn, specialized new knowledge is needed quickly. For example, perhaps there is a fixed-date contractual deadline in eight weeks. The stable team already knows some things about the domain and technology, but not all. In this case, consider inviting one or more outside specialists (probably from other teams) to physically co-locate with the team.

*Avoid...Resource pools with resource management*

This stable-team model is fundamentally different from the resource pool and resource management of some traditional organizations.

*organizational processes p. 255*

What if various projects are so small that each would only consume a few days of an available team? This is discussed in the *Processes* section.

---

3.  We mean true one-time project work; not product work being inappropriately treated as sets of projects.

## STRUCTURE

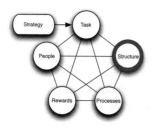

The structure section describes how Scrum influences the organizational structure. At the heart of Scrum are self-managing cross-functional teams. The impact of adopting teams on organizational structure and roles is extensively reported. For example, one report on team-based organizational design states, *"Teams violate the logic of the design of a bureaucratic, hierarchical, segmented organization"* [MCM95].

### Try...Keep the organization as flat as possible

The principle behind self-managing teams is to give teams more management responsibility. The team becomes responsible for doing and managing the work and work process.

It ought to be obvious, though painful, that you therefore need fewer managers. Not only that, the role of management changes significantly from managing the work to creating the conditions for teams to thrive—from command-and-control to manager-teacher.

Removing people from management roles is hard work. Organizational systems (such as HR policies) change and the remaining managers need education and coaching. The product groups we have worked with have underestimated the amount of coaching that is needed.

How many employees report to one manager? Late Japanese quality expert Kaoru Ishikawa thought one hundred was about right. *"Man is by nature good... Through education and training, subordinates become reliable, and the span of control becomes larger and larger. My ideal is to have one supervisor for every one hundred workers"* [Ishikawa85].

When is your organization ready for fewer managers?

You cannot simply tell the team to take more responsibility and expect them to do so. They will have to learn how. A chief architect of a team starting their third Sprint once told us, "We had forgotten what the word responsibility means. Before Scrum, we just did the tasks assigned to us but we never really took responsibility for them."

*Try...Make the organization slightly flatter than it can handle.*

Most people "grew up" in traditional command-and-control organizations. Therefore, it is hard for them to take more responsibility while their traditional manager is around. Similarly, it is hard for managers to change their role toward their earlier subordinates [Fisher99]. You can break this deadlock by making the organization slightly flatter than it can handle. As an example, *"One organization we studied discovered that it could not take a gradual approach to changing management roles. Assessment data revealed that as long as teams had managers, they simply did not become self-managing. This company then eliminated two-thirds of the management structure and found that self-management emerged quickly"* [MCM95].

We worked with one product group that used natural attrition to shrink the overhead. The change to Scrum made some managers uncomfortable and they left. Their positions were not refilled but removed by expanding the responsibilities of the current managers.

*Try...Invite managers to join teams to do development work*

What to do with a manager surplus? Before managers became managers, they often did real product work and most have not yet lost that capability. Therefore, you can ask if they would like to join a development team. Inviting people to leave management roles gives a strong and needed message that not all career paths should lead to becoming a manager, and reinforces the lean thinking vision of most valuing the hands-on value work. We worked with one person who, after five years in a management role, moved back to technical product work. He has become a well-respected technical expert who contributes and innovates faster than many others.

*queuing theory and small batches p. 100*

We worked at one large embedded-systems organization that clearly had more managers than needed. The reason? *Performance appraisals.* Human Resources (HR) required two performance appraisals per year at fixed times—a large batch indeed. The effect of this was that managers did nothing but review performance and resulting paperwork for two full months a year. An inefficient system. Start improving it by helping HR people learn about queuing theory and small batches. A larger can of worms in this situation is the very notion of performance appraisals; we open the lid on that can in the *Rewards* section.

### Avoid...Functional units

The traditional way of structuring organizations is around functional specializations such as test, development, architecture, and product marketing—functional units. One driving motive for this is to provide functional learning and related professional development. However, there is usually little time for learning since people are always working on products; the intent is not fulfilled.

*organizational impediment #7: "functional organizations" p. 230*

Functional units have drawbacks. They lead to local optimization of functions. Also, the perspective of functional specialists is frequently limited, with miscommunication and misunderstanding as a result. The drawbacks of functional organizations outweigh their benefits.

A funny (well, to us) example of a local optimization occurred in a large product group organized around functional units. Each of the functional units set improvement targets for themselves. The manager of the *testing* unit suggested that they could improve the testing by...testing later. He said (to paraphrase), "By delaying testing until the end, the software will be in a better shape and the testing will take less time." We guess we do not have to deconstruct on how many levels this is an *insanely bad idea*.

Deming recommended, *"Break down barriers between departments. People in research, design, sales, and production must work as a team, to foresee problems of production and in use that may be encountered with the product or service"* [Deming82]. Thus, an alternative to functional organizations is to...

### Try...Scrum teams as organizational unit

In several organizations, we have been able to influence the organizational design. Based on these experiences, we can give a concrete example of an organizational structure. However, none of the product groups we work with have implemented exactly this structure, although our clients reading this section will find it familiar. The example is a combination of the different structures we have encountered. Most product groups focus on development; therefore, the focus of this section is on development structure rather than on sales, marketing, and finance—topics for some future material.

Figure 10.3 product group structure with Scrum Teams and requirement areas

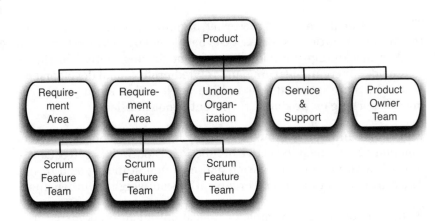

The example organizational structure (Figure 10.3) has four units:

❑ Requirement Area unit

❑ 'Undone' unit

❑ Service and support unit

❑ Product Owner Team

These units are discussed in detail below.

**Try…Organize around requirement areas**

*requirement areas p. 217*

Structure the product group primarily by requirement areas and related Scrum feature teams—a **Requirement Area unit**. Each unit has a requirement area manager whom the feature teams "report to." His (or her) prime role is to support new feature teams that join the area. He will probably also have work stemming from organizational policies such as budgeting, performance appraisals, and so forth.

The main advantage of this structure is that it keeps the organization simple and flat. People are not distracted by organizational complexity, policies, and politics. It increases the *focus* on the real product work. And since a Requirement Area represents a large domain of features relevant to customers (such as transaction printing), the product group is *organized toward the customer perspective*, not by an internal perspective (such as architectural components or functions).

A 'disadvantage' of this structure is that there are changes in Requirement Areas over time—not every month, but non-trivially. What kind?

*Try...Keep the formal organization flexible*

- ❏ teams move from a less to a more valuable area

- ❏ an area ceases to exist—there are no more high-value items

- ❏ a new area is created (3D printing, ...)

These changes in the Requirement Areas need to be reflected in the formal organization. This by itself is not a problem. However, some HR practices or IT systems make frequent changes in the organization difficult, or the Requirement Area manager does not want a reduction in the number of people that report to her—a reduction in status. These impediments need to be dealt with.

### Try...Eliminating the 'Undone' unit by eliminating 'Undone' work

The goal of a group using Scrum is to create a Potentially Shippable Product Increment each iteration—there is no more work to be done. The Product Owner can then decide whether or not to ship it. This is trivial for a one-team web application. But for organizations with large embedded systems with piles of legacy code, being able to produce a product increment each new iteration that is *honestly potentially shippable* takes years—if not decades—*of continuous improvement*. Even though reaching this goal is frequently deemed impossible, it should still be the goal of organizations with lots of legacy code, and the current "Definition of Done" is the measure of progress to this perfection challenge. By improving the skill of their people, automating their tests, improving their build times, cleaning their legacy, and other improvement activities, those organizations

*see "Definition of Done" in Planning in companion*

can gradually expand the "Definition of Done" until it is *honestly* potentially shippable.[4]

'Undone' work is the activities that need to be performed before an iteration starts, or between the end of the iteration and the actual deployment to production use ('release'). This work is unfortunately often not performed by the Scrum teams and instead undertaken by a separate organizational unit—the **'Undone' unit**. Typical activities undertaken by this unit are higher-level testing, architecture documentation, customer documentation, and so forth.

In lean thinking terms, this unit specializes in the waste of *partially done work*. They create it or consume and finish it—the WIP unit.

Over time, the group improves their ways of working. As they do, their "Definition of Done" expands, and work and people move from the 'Undone' unit into the Requirement Area units. The improvement goal of delivering a Potentially Shippable Product Increment results in gradually eliminating the 'Undone' unit—the goal of the 'Undone' unit should be to remove themselves.

**Try...Service and support unit**

Scrum teams are responsible for all work needed to create a Potentially Shippable Product Increment. Sometimes it is useful to move supporting work to a separate unit. Beware this decision, since it can lead to over-specialization and bottlenecks. Such a unit can offer support for

❑ maintaining a shared resource

❑ tools and infrastructure

❑ facilitation and coaching

---

4. "Is it all honestly done?"... "Oh yeah, definitely!"... "Great, let's ship it tomorrow."... "Well, actually there is just one tiny thing left..."

## Maintaining a Shared Resource

A shared resource does not mean people but *things*. Large embedded systems have special testing equipment that must be shared among the teams: for example, an expensive telecom network element or production digital printer press.

Each Scrum team reserves the testing equipment when it is needed. And even when there is a lab support group, the Scrum team is still responsible for keeping the test environment clean.

A test lab support group can boost the productive use of these scarce shared resources by, for example, applying queuing theory to reduce the average wait time for the equipment.

*queuing theory p. 93*

## Tools and Infrastructure

Tools and infrastructure support for tools are difficult to get right. We all have the experience of being forced to use bad tools or being unable to install our favorite profiler because it requires administrator rights. On the other hand, doing all tool and infrastructure activities within the Scrum teams might be wasteful.

*impediment #9 "central organizations leading to local optimizations"*

An example of a tools support role is a 'toolsmith' who keeps himself up-to-date with the latest tools information. He can help you find a tool, or perhaps 'build' and install some open source server application.

A tool support group, if it exists, should *support, not decide,* the tools used. Conforming to a central-tool-group-approved list will locally optimize for conformance to a tool budget or other narrow objective, while sub-optimizing value throughput or cycle time. Such lists often reflect the limited insight of tool 'specialists' speculating in an ivory tower. Instead, provide support for the tools that the developers *choose* to use—the tools that they find effective. If you have internally developed tools, make sure that the source code is accessible to the people who use the tool so that they can improve it themselves when needed—*internal open source*.

*Try...Internal open source for internal tools*

Another common example of infrastructure support is a Software Configuration Management (SCM) specialist. He maintains the

SCM system, creates new repositories, and facilitates the creation of standards. SCM specialists are trouble when they *control* the use of the SCM system. Their role is to *facilitate* the creation of SCM agreements, not to decide on them—the feature teams decide what is most efficient.

## Facilitation and Coaching

*impediment #8 "considering learning a waste"*

Facilitation support is a valuable resource to Scrum teams. Experienced and skilled facilitators can improve meetings and team communication practices. Such a facilitator should pair with the team's ScrumMaster so that the ScrumMaster learns advanced facilitation techniques and becomes more efficient in her work.

Facilitation support for Communities of Practice (CoP) is also indispensable for their success. This support includes setting up forums or discussion groups, facilitating meetings or gatherings, and helping the CoP coordinator find ways to grow the community.

Practices such as test-driven development require a lot of coaching—it is a major change in development style and can only be done with pair programming coaches. These coaches can be located in the support organization, joining different teams each Sprint.

## Caution!

*impediment #9 "centralized organizations leading to local optimization"*

Support organizations should support, not control. All too often, they optimize *their work* and make decisions that should be made by people who work on products. By taking this responsibility away from Scrum teams, the *support* mutates into a *burden*. Make sure to focus on support!

## Try...Product Owner Team as organizational unit

*Product Owner Team p. 220; see Product Management in companion*

The Product Owner Team is composed of 1) the Product Owner, 2 the Area Product Owners, and 3) perhaps others who clarify the requirements for teams (and, for some reason, are not in a team). The Product Owner team members make cost, schedule, content decisions for the whole product. Plus, they maintain the Product Backlog and other artifacts needed for communicating the product's vision.

## Avoid...Project Management Office

Some organizations have a Project Management Office (PMO) or a Program Management Office (PMO). Their activities *"range from providing project management support functions to actually being responsible for the direct management of projects"* [PMBOK04]. By looking at this description, it ought to be obvious that the PMO is no longer needed (at least, not for development work) when Scrum is adopted. Most project management responsibilities are moved into the teams. Scrum support comes from the team of hands-on agile coaches (who are not managers) in the service and support organization. Responsibilities of releases, metrics, and other schedule- or content-related issues move to the Product Owner Team.

*impediment #9 "centralized organizations leads to local optimization"*

Most agile literature recognizes that a traditional PMO is not needed in an agile and lean development organization. Unfortunately, not all of it concludes that the PMO role should be removed, but instead recommends that it be changed to...something else. Changed how? Some suggest that the "agile PMO" would provide training and support for agile projects [SB08, TN07]. It gets worse: One author even suggested that the "agile PMO" *"most likely needs to be expanded [more people] from its traditional model"* [Kreb08].

*Avoid...So-called Agile PMO*

Changing responsibilities of an existing organizational unit is arguably more 'safe' than removing it. But is it a good idea?

Imagine you work as a 'programmer.' The predictions about artificial intelligence and automatic programming have finally come true—programming is no longer needed. Does it make sense to keep the 'programmer' job title but change the responsibilities? That would be illogical. When a role does not include programming, why call it programmer?

Naturally, the same applies to the PMO. When Scrum has been adopted and the PMO does not—or at least, should not—do project-management-related things, then calling this unit a PMO is illogical. It is interesting to examine why this change is difficult for organizations.

Likewise for "project manager." When a role does not include project management, do not call it project manager. We have seen good Scrum adoptions where the organization kept calling a true Scrum-

Master a "project manager" even when the team and Product Owner took over all project management responsibilities. Perhaps people do not like the name 'ScrumMaster'; call it a *team leader*—a common term in self-managing team literature [Fisher99, Hackman02].

Keeping a title but changing the responsibilities is a sure way to create miscommunication, misunderstanding, and the recognition by people that there is some dysfunction. Remove the PMO.

### Avoid...Fake ScrumMasters

*impediment #1 "silver bullet thinking"*

The preceding tip mentioned introducing real ScrumMasters yet inconsistently sticking with an irrelevant project manager title. The opposite is unfortunately more common: Changing the title of someone to 'ScrumMaster' while he acts like—and is encouraged by the organization to act like—a project manager. Fake ScrumMasters.

This is an instance of *cargo cult process adoption*—adopting pieces of an idea, such as names, without understanding the underlying principles. Consider: "We adopted Scrum. Our Sprint length is the length of our project. The Product Owner decides the items in the Sprint and the project manager acts as ScrumMaster. He makes the Sprint Backlog and assigns the tasks to people in the team." Hearing variations of this saddens us.

Fake ScrumMasters—most commonly, project managers or team managers—fill the world with misunderstandings by resisting change and refusing to learn. They create an illusion that the organization is actually trying to improve and in that way turn good ideas into management fads and more organizational dysfunction.

### Avoid...Matrix organizations in product development

A matrix organization is an organizational structure where some people report to two managers—or even more. In product development, a matrix with one or more project managers and a functional manager is very common.

Matrix organizations tend to increase the amount of management in an organization. This, according to the research of Capers Jones, decreases the overall productivity in software development. To repeat an earlier quote, *"The matrix structure tends to raise the management head count for larger projects. Because software productivity declines as the management count goes up, this form of organization can be hazardous for software"* [Jones01].

A reason for matrix organization was an "information-processing overload" for managers [DL77]. Matrix organizations have more managers so that they can share the information-processing load. Self-managing teams solve this problem by moving management responsibilities to the teams.

### Try...Self-organized team creation

How to create teams?[5] The people in the organization know their own skills and their own interests best, so they can organize themselves into teams.[6] This is a startling practice for traditional command-and-control management groups who automatically assume that they know better than the workers how to form suitable teams. Sometimes they *do* know better. Sometimes not.

We worked with one product group in Asia wherein the manager of a department did the following. He defined three rules: Teams must 1) be cross-functional, 2) be cross-component, and 3) consist of seven to nine people. All one hundred people met in one large room. The manager put flip-chart paper on the wall for each potential team. He explained the three rules and offered an exact two-hour timebox for the people to decide how to form teams. If unresolved after that time, he said that he would decide. For almost two hours it was chaotic but in the final stretch people formed into ten teams.

After a year, the department manager still considered it a good way to form teams. However, upon reflection, he realized it did have drawbacks. For example, all the "agile enthusiasts" formed enthusiastic agile teams and the "agile skeptics" formed skeptical teams. Not surprisingly, the enthusiastic teams were much faster and more

---

5. We do not cover how Product Owners work together to decide which teams work for which products.
6. These are sometimes called "self-designing teams."

successful in adopting agile practices. He speculated that adopting practices might have been faster by mixing the people better.

In another product group, the manager did not give *any* guidelines and simply asked the people to "form teams." In the first attempt, the programmers created a 40-person programming 'team' and testers created a 30-person testing team! The manager explained that this was not acceptable and that the teams need to be cross-functional. In the second attempt, the people successfully formed cross-functional teams.

These stories and mishaps highlight a principle of lean thinking: the importance of a culture of manager-teachers who are deeply experienced and knowledgeable in lean principles, and can act as skillful coaches. The self-organizing teams concept does *not* imply that no advice or coaching comes from experienced and talented managers.

### Try...Form self-organizing teams based on skill

The previous tip was consistent with classic self-organization. It has the drawback of potentially forming sub-optimal teams of people who all think alike. Or the strongest people may decide to form their own "A team" and hence deprive others of the coaching these talented people could offer—reduced organizational learning.

As an alternative, management can form the teams according to skills and experience. This *might* balance the teams better. One weakness is that it assumes that the decision maker's opinion of skill and balance is insightful. Another drawback is that people can feel uncomfortable being forced into a self-organizing team; this makes taking team responsibility difficult.

### Try...Cultivate Communities of Practice

*Communities of Practice are groups of people who share a concern, a set of problems, or a passion about a topic, and who deepen their knowledge and expertise in this area by interacting on an ongoing basis [WMS02].*

**Communities of Practice** (CoP) are rooted in self-organization. They do not appear on an organization chart. Participation is voluntary—people engage because they have a passion to learn or contribute.

Organizations cannot form or put together CoPs like they can form departments or projects. But organizations can promote them and provide support—facilitators, IT infrastructure, budget.

CoPs and Scrum work well together; both embrace volunteering and self-organization. A CoP needs an informal leader, called a **CoP coordinator**, who emerges from the group because of a passion for the subject. A part of cultivating CoPs is to support the CoP coordinators. Sometimes coordinating activities becomes a full-time role, and the coordinator may then move to the *Support unit*. However, be wary of full-time CoP coordinators; ironically, they can lose touch with their practice by no longer…practicing.

We worked with a multinational organization that had a ScrumMaster CoP that was cultivated by the centralized support organization. It consisted of hundreds of ScrumMasters discussing Scrum-related issues on their mailing list. Every year, they organized an internal Scrum Gathering, which was held as an **OpenSpace** conference.[7]

### Try…Use CoPs for functional learning

Many organizations come to awareness of CoPs through the transition to cross-functional teams and the elimination of the matrix. We were coaching at Lockheed-Martin some years ago during their early days of agile adoption. Project or product groups had previously (usually) been organized into functional teams (analysts, testers, and so on). Lockheed-Martin people realized that when they transitioned to an agile approach, abolished matrix management, and adopted long-lived cross-functional teams, there could be a problem in learning or knowledge sharing related to one function. For example, they asked, *"How will all the specialist testers learn—as a group—about a new testing practice, when they are distributed to different cross-functional teams?"* Because of this question, they discov-

---

7. **OpenSpace** is a style of organizing large discussions rooted in the concept of self-organization [Owen97].

ered CoPs and put in place a support system to cultivate their growth.

Alternatives to CoPs include formal organizations such as councils and study groups [HKL93]. However, we recommend CoPs as an excellent informal approach to functional learning. *"People who work in cross-functional teams often form communities of practice to keep in touch with their peers in various parts of the company and thus maintain their expertise"* [WMS02].

The learning culture of Toyota is to "spread knowledge laterally." This practice is called *yokoten*. The person who learned something novel or improved a practice is responsible for sharing this. Toyota people are supported in active sharing and pro-active seeking for ideas and practices across groups and sites. The concept of CoP is similar to yokoten.

Is a CoP not a matrix organization in new clothes? No, there are clear conceptual differences between them.

> *Communities of practice provide a fundamental different approach toward the same goal. The matrix structure only focuses on the distribution of authority and the coordination of resources by multiplying reporting relationships. It does not create different structures for different purposes. Whereas a matrix has reporting relationships on both arms, communities of practice provide a different kind of structure for focusing on knowledge. They are based on collegial relationships, not reporting relationships. Even community leaders [CoP coordinators] are not your bosses; they are your peers. This combination of formal and informal structures is fundamentally different from a matrix. [WMS02]*

## PROCESSES

We discuss processes elsewhere when they strongly relate to another element in the Galbraith star model. For example, the *performance appraisal* process is covered in the *Rewards* section. Here, we consider noteworthy processes that do not fit neatly in another section, including *portfolio management, stage-gate®,* and *budgeting.*

Many processes have a clear relationship to *Structure*. For example, both performance appraisal and budgeting processes are arranged by organizational structure.

Scrum is a product-development framework by which the teams evolve their own processes. This section does not cover Scrum or processes inside development—these are covered in other chapters and the companion book. However, this section *does* cover portfolio management and stage-gate. These are valid for both product development and projects, but to simplify phrasing, we write *product* unless we mean only a *project.*

**Portfolio management**—The product portfolio is the set of all the products in the organization. Management of this portfolio implies selecting, prioritizing, and killing products [PMI06]. Many organizations are not disciplined at prioritizing products—they want to do it all. The predictable outcome is that they get little or nothing done— too many products, too little focus [AMNS96]. Portfolio management is the process to solve this problem. Its goals are [CEK01]

❑ *maximize the total value*—working on most valuable?

❑ *balance*—balancing types, markets, risks, and life span?

❑ *strategic alignment*—support the strategy?

Traditionally, organizations attempt to achieve these goals by holding long and intensive portfolio management meetings, typically twice a year. The portfolio of products is reviewed and re-prioritized; some live, some die.

**Stage-gate**—How do you ensure that product development is on track and that one product is still important? A stage-gate process [Cooper01] tries to answer these questions by dividing the development into five stages with checkpoints (called gates) between them. At the gates, a management team checks development progress and the product's relevancy. Based on these, they make a go/kill decision—fund the next stage for the product or not?

Stage-gate recognizes that uncertainty is high when product development starts and that it (usually) decreases over time. Therefore, the investments in early stages are relatively small, while the latter stages have larger investments. Thus, management makes smaller investment decisions when the risk is high and larger investment decisions when the risk is low.

A pivotal aspect of stage-gate is a focus on marketing and product management. It recognizes that products fail 'simply' because they were not what the customer wanted. Consequently, stage-gate emphasizes in-depth, high-quality market study in the early stages.

Portfolio management and stage-gate differ in that the former involves a set of products whereas the latter's focus is one product. One commonality is that they both make go/kill decisions.

With these definitions in place, on to some organizational tips that support scaling lean and agile product development...

### Try...Merged product backlog for a set of products

Traditional high-level work prioritization is based on *products* and not features. This creates a coarse-grained view—and decisions. The relative priority of individual features is not considered.

Coarse-grained product prioritization leads to a local optimization in which the low-priority items of a high-priority product are implemented instead of the *essential* items of a lower-priority product.

We have worked with some smaller (100-person) companies for which this was a problem. Their solution? Merge the Product Backlogs of different products into one Product Backlog for the whole company. The CEO acted as the Product Owner. This works especially well when the different products non-trivially share a common code base or platform—common for smaller companies.

When the organization has one Product Backlog and one Product Owner for the whole company, then the prioritization aspect of portfolio management and prioritizing the Scrum Product Backlog are the same activity. However, it is now done on the feature level—avoiding the previous local optimization.

What if your organization is larger than one hundred people, involving many products and tens of thousands of new features? Although we have no experience in this, a company (or division) Product Backlog can be scaled up with Requirement Areas.[8] That is, if merged feature-level prioritization is overwhelmingly long and detailed (and it would be for some of our clients), we speculate that at least *Requirement-Area-level* prioritization across a set of products is manageable and useful; for example, deciding that the *power management* Requirement Area in one or more products is more important than adding *color workflow* support to product X.

*Requirement Areas p. 217*

### Try...Team works on multiple products

This tip is a corollary to the previous one.

We worked with an anti-virus company that had one large product and many small products. Each of the latter required only one or two people, so the company formed one- or two-person 'teams' and tried to use Scrum. Did not work well.

An alternative is—as the prior tip suggested—to merge the smaller Product Backlogs into one. Then form long-lived stable Scrum teams of around seven people, and let them work on the combined Product Backlog. During one iteration, a team might do four features for large-product X and one for small-product Y.

As mentioned, this works best when the different products share a common code base.

---

8. A merged Product Backlog view can easily be created with a spreadsheet tool that links to other Product Backlog spreadsheets.

## Avoid...Stage-gate processes (if Scrum is adopted)

Most large organizations have adopted some variant of stage-gate process for their product development. Stage-gate processes are definitely an improvement over no processes at all, and their emphasis on good, early market analysis is commendable.

One key intention behind stage-gate is to make go/kill decisions related to a product. But *the gates are not the only means to make these decisions* in the stage-gate model. Although not everybody is aware of this, the creator of stage-gate, Robert Cooper, proposes *two* options for making these decisions [CEK01]:

❑ Option 1: *Gates dominate*—go/kill decisions are made at the gates and confirmed at the portfolio management meetings.

❑ Option 2: *Portfolio review / management meeting dominates*—go/kill decisions are made in portfolio management meetings and only rarely at the gate review meetings.

Cooper recommends the first option when there is low change, and the second option when the environment changes frequently—common and appropriate for software-intensive systems development, as Cooper explicitly points out. To quote:

> *The result of the portfolio-review-dominates approach is a more dynamic, constantly changing, portfolio of projects. The method may suit faster-paced companies, such as software, IT, and electronics firms, but it requires a much stronger commitment by senior management to the decision process. [CEK01]*

Companies adopting large-scale Scrum probably belong to the second case and thus would choose the second option.[9]

Not surprisingly, Cooper does not recommend that the entire stage-gate framework be dropped if option 2 is adopted. His view is that even though the gates may no longer be used or useful for go/kill decisions in domains such as "software, IT, and electronics firms," he assumes—because his background does not include Scrum—that the

---

9. These days, "constantly changing environment" is almost certainly the norm rather than the exception.

gates are still important for assuring that *development is on track*. That is, even if the go/kill question is removed, three important questions remain to be answered during each gate meeting.

- ❑ Are the deliverables in place and of sound quality?

- ❑ Is the project on time and within budget?

- ❑ Does the project remain a good investment? [CEK01]

These are excellent questions. So excellent that in Scrum a good Product Owner asks himself exactly these questions *at the end of each iteration*. And because each iteration involves real development and a Sprint Review showing concrete deliverables, the Product Owner has extraordinary, high-quality, realistic information to answer these questions.

Scrum has replaced the traditional, long-cycle stage-gates with a 'gate' at each two-week iteration. The traditional stage-gate meetings do not add any more value when Scrum is used. This is another example in lean and agile methods of moving to shorter cycles and smaller batches.

To summarize: When an organization (1) holds frequent and short portfolio management meetings, and (2) all products use short time-boxed iterations, then using a stage-gate process is arguably simply unnecessary overhead. Hence, if the alternatives are in place, you can...avoid stage-gate.

*Caution*: As mentioned, one intention of stage-gate is to include skillful marketing work early in product development. This is unequivocally a good idea. When avoiding or replacing stage-gate with Scrum and frequent portfolio reviews, make sure marketing is still involved from the beginning.

Stage-gate also has some weaknesses:

- ❑ it promotes large-batches and thus delay [Smith05].

- ❑ it favors large-investment decisions over frequent small ones.

- ❑ it tends to turn into waterfall development (see below).

- ❑ it examines individual products rather than the portfolio.

❑ it advocates go/kill decisions rather than increasing or decreasing the investment.

### Avoid...Especially...*traditional* stage-gate

Unknown to most, Cooper's stage-gate of today is not the stage-gate of yesterday. *"The notion of a rigid, lock-stepped process is dead! Rather, today's fast-paced NextGen Stage-Gate system is adaptable and flexible"* [Cooper07].

The world is changing, everybody is learning, and so are the creators of stage-gate. The latest model is perhaps the fourth generation— the count is unclear as the latest is "next generation stage gate."[10]

Evolving the stage-gate model is salutary, yet naturally creates confusion... *In every discussion or communication, one needs to clarify which generation the other person refers to.* This is quite important. The recommendations from 1993 are different from the ones in 2001, and the 2008 ones are different again.

Unfortunately, many companies 'installed' their stage-gate process years ago and did not bother keeping up with Cooper's evolution. Make sure your company is aware of these developments and learns about "the fourth generation" or "the NextGen" stage-gate.

### Avoid...Stage-gate becoming a waterfall

If a stage-gate process remains in place, make sure it does not become a sequential life cycle.

In the description of 'NextGen' stage-gate [Cooper08], Robert Cooper lists misconceptions about stage-gate. In the *"not a functional, phased review process,"* he explains that every stage should be cross-functional. Most of the stage-gate processes we have seen in large organizations resemble a sequential life-cycle process (requirements finished and handed off to a design team, ...), so this is indeed a common misconception.

---

10. Perhaps the *next* generation will be called *post-modern stage-gate*.

The stage-gate process itself shares some of the blame for this misconception. Even in the 2008 generation, three of the stages are *Business Case*, *Development*, and *Test*. For most people, this resembles a waterfall and thus, it does not come as a surprise that most stage-gate processes evolve into a sequential life cycle process.

The stage-gate model is generic—for any kind of product. In the context of *physical* product development, such as a washing machine, there is naturally a final *Test* stage that follows *Development* (although good mechanical engineers know to also test early during development). But an insight of ever-growing appreciation is that software is a unique novel domain. Many of our old physical-product-development notions of how to work are unnecessary or ill-conceived. The ability to eliminate test-at-the-end through continuous integration and acceptance test-driven-development are examples. The creators of stage-gate are not unaware of these techniques.

### Try...Beyond budgeting

*The transformation [of finance's traditional role and practices] requires reexamining and, probably, abandoning some of the vestiges of finance's previous management control tools. In particular, several companies in Europe and North America have **questioned their use of the annual operating budget**, a management tool introduced at General Motors nearly a century ago by CEO Alfred Sloan and CFO Donaldson Brown. Although the operating budget was a great innovation at the time, **today's dynamic and highly volatile environment has made an annual fixed operating plan an anachronism**. The counter-reaction to the high preparation cost, in time and money, of the annual budget and its inflexibility in light of rapidly changing external circumstances and internal opportunities has launched the Beyond Budgeting movement. [Bogsnes09] (emphasis added)* *this relates to impediment #6 "local optimization over global optimization"*

The above quotation is from Robert Kaplan, a well-known thought leader in the world of finance and management accounting, Harvard Business School professor, creator of the *balanced scorecard*, and member of the Accounting Hall of Fame. Some in the accounting and finance field are not yet aware of the coming sea change in financial and accounting practice that Kaplan cites: the **Beyond Budgeting** movement that profoundly changes the budgeting process.

There is non-trivial influence from financial policies on the way product development can be done, and on the degree of adaptability. For example, traditional accounting emphasizes maximizing resource utilization rather than maximizing value throughput. An annual operating budget can constrain investment in a new product or feature opportunity that was not foreseen (or foreseeable) when the budget was created.

The annual ritual of speculating what applications will be built over the next year (and their content and cost) is based largely on wishful thinking and assumptions that seldom play out in reality. The dedication of large sums of money to these far-future conjectures inhibits financial adaptability and skillful use of capital. For example, perhaps some budgeted future applications should have lower priority than new ideas discovered during the year. The highly speculative estimates force wasteful padding of application budgets, to avoid complaints. Complaints for deviation from the original budget (and rewards for *appearing* to comply with it) engenders management opacity and gaming of the numbers—and less transparency means less ability to inspect and adapt in Scrum. Small application investments cannot be shifted with agility month by month as new learning arises. Investment risk is large, not small. Contrast this with the classic investment risk management practice of *dollar cost averaging,* where one spreads out smaller investments over many (often monthly) periods, adjusting choices as fresh information emerges.

The annual budgeting cycle is far out of sync with the bi-weekly or monthly cycle of results and decision making in Scrum. Plus, a slow annual cycle does not exploit the new opportunity for real fine-grained control through transparency and adaptability that Scrum offers. Traditional accounting lags behind this evolution in product development responsiveness.

More broadly, notice that the annual budgeting process involves big batches and long cycle times, decidedly un-lean practices that inhibit enterprise adaptation and organizational learning. With the insight of queueing theory, it is also easy to see that a massive-batch budgeting process is inefficient.

Short frequent cycles of investment decision making (versus an annual budget) seem 'wasteful' to traditional financial managers because of the high transaction cost (overhead) of each approval cycle. But as examined in the "Indirect Benefits of Reducing Batch Size and Cycle Time" section on page 112, the move to short frequent cycles engenders out-of-the-box thinking of radically different and more efficient mechanisms—in this case, *Beyond Budgeting*...

The Beyond Budgeting movement started in 1970 at Handelsbanken bank in Sweden. CEO Jan Wallander decided to eliminate the traditional management 'controls' that he could see did not work well, including budgets, hierarchy, and individual rewards. Since 1972, the bank has consistently been more profitable than the average of competitors, and is among the most cost efficient in the world.

Another well-publicized example of Beyond Budgeting was the elimination in 1995 of the annual operating budget at Borealis, the largest European petrochemicals company. This initiative was led by Bjarte Bogsnes, the head of finance and accounting (who has also served as a director of HR). Bogsnes started with the *local* goal of dramatically improving financial management systems. He has since gone on to lead toward a *system* goal and to communicate the need for a *system* change in management values and practices to realize the enterprise goals of Beyond Budgeting.

In the 1990s a group of financial management researchers and practitioners realized that the traditional annual budget was an outdated and inadequate practice. They formed the Beyond Budgeting Round Table (BBRT[11]), a Community of Practice of companies (including StatoilHydro, the 59th largest company in the world in 2008) that were moving...beyond budgeting. This CoP also led to the books *Beyond Budgeting* [HF03] and *Implementing Beyond Budgeting* [Bogsnes09].

---

11. See also www.bbrt.org.

These financial leaders came to the same realization behind the agile development movement: Many traditional ideas of management (including financial management) are ineffective or counterproductive and merely create an illusion of control—at least in today's world of accelerating business change and competition based on knowledge workers. This is the point emphasized by management guru Peter Drucker:

> Uncertainty—in the economy, society, politics—has become so great as to render futile, if not counterproductive, the kind of planning most companies still practice: forecasting based on probabilities. [Drucker92]

The response in the Beyond Budgeting movement is to replace the "illusion of control" fostered by detailed planning and annual budgets with a new set of mechanisms that emphasize transparency and adaptive processes. Jeremy Hope, a founding member of the BBRT, summed up the vision of Beyond Budgeting in a phrase stunningly reflective of the message of Scrum: "Transparency is the new control system."

Beyond Budgeting recognizes certain myths and false dichotomies in traditional financial management, including

- ❏ no centralized control = chaos and anarchy
- ❏ good performance = hitting the budget numbers
- ❏ no budget = cost explosion
- ❏ no individual bonus = no performance
- ❏ more details = more quality

In companies adopting Beyond Budgeting, one early step involves the management team learning the evidence to deconstruct these myths. They also examine other ideas behind traditional financial management and move to new models. These include the following:

**Trust and transparency**—Move to a high-trust and high-transparency model with employees. This includes trust related to spending and investment. It does not mean the end of safeguards to inhibit betting the bank on currency speculations.

**Cost management**—Abandon the belief that a cost budget is the only or the most effective way to manage costs. Stop creating an annual operating budget.

**Target setting and evaluation**—Move from absolute to relative targets. Use holistic evaluation in which real leaders do in-depth, nuanced, qualitative evaluation of performance rather than simplistic "did you hit the numbers?"

**Bonus**—Stop individual bonuses. Research shows they do not work, they locally sub-optimize performance, and they increase "gaming the system." If bonuses are 'necessary,' use group-based sharing.

**Rhythm or Cadence**—Traditional financial practices create an uneven rhythm (or no rhythm) in planning, evaluation, and adaptation. The cycle is too long. Move to short cycles (for example, monthly or quarterly) and establish an even cadence.

**Quality**—Traditional budgets try to do too much, consolidating three goals: (1) good targets, (2) good forecasts, and (3) good resource allocation. Trying to serve all masters leads to no master being well served—traditional budgets are a poor solution to improving quality in these goals. Beyond Budgeting *separates* all three.

**Efficiency**—One study estimates that 25,000 person-days are spent in annual budgeting for each one billion USD in revenue. It is an extraordinarily wasteful process with limited benefit.

Moving from these myths and issues to solutions, Beyond Budgeting offers a new model based on 12 principles.

**Leadership Principles:**

1. *Customers*. Focus everyone on improving customer outcomes, not on hierarchical relationships.

2. *Organization*. Organize as a network of lean, accountable teams, not around centralized functions.

3. *Responsibility*. Enable everyone to act and think like a leader, not merely follow the plan.

4. *Autonomy*. Give teams the freedom and capability to act; do not micromanage them.

5. *Values*. Govern through a few clear values, goals, and boundaries, not detailed rules and budgets.

6. *Transparency*. Promote open information for self-management; do not restrict it hierarchically.

## Process Principles:

7. *Goals*. Set relative goals for continuous improvement; do not negotiate fixed performance contracts.

8. *Rewards*. Reward shared success based on relative performance, not on meeting fixed targets.

9. *Planning*. Make planning a continuous and inclusive process, not a top-down annual event.

10. *Controls*. Base controls on relative indicators and trends, not on variances against plan.

11. *Resources*. Make resources available as needed, not through annual budget allocations.

12. *Coordination*. Coordinate interactions dynamically, not through annual planning cycles.

There is an extraordinary similarity between these principles and the lean or agile families of principles. Beyond Budgeting is the financial management model that complements agile development.

This introduction only scratches the surface. In-depth study of the resources is necessary to understand the detailed practices and start the implementation journey.

## REWARDS

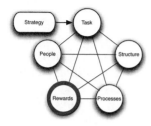

The next two sections examine a *topic* bursting with opinions, taboos, and assumptions—Human Resources (HR) policies and practices. *Teams* drive agile development but traditional HR practices focus on *individuals*. This causes systemic conflict. HR practices need to change to consider and foster real teams. Practices such as rewarding and performance review are based on assumptions that are not supported by the evidence available. This section investigates some of these assumptions.

### Try...Engage HR

HR practices are a major obstacle in numerous large organizations we have worked with. Only a few have succeeded in changing them. But you will never succeed changing HR practices without engaging the HR specialists in your organization.

HR specialists consider it their job to improve the situation of the employees in an organization. They do this according to what they were taught and assumptions they have. You cannot expect them to suddenly change because of "this lean thing." HR, like any other supporting function, needs to be educated in why lean affects their policies. HR should be your partner, not your enemy.

In some organizations, we have invited HR people to participate in Scrum courses and in product groups' agile-adoption workshops so that they could start to appreciate the ideas and changes. This helped them change policies to fit better to self-managing teams. One HR specialist even used Scrum principles to manage HR work.

### Try...Ask HR for credible research evidence

Convincing the specialists in the global corporate HR ivory tower might turn out to be futile even when you provide them with experience reports, research, literature, and other evidence. They might have some basic assumptions that are hard to change. There-fore...ask for the evidence upon which they base their practices and assumptions.

And what kind of evidence? Stanford professors Pfeffer and Sutton are two proponents of evidence-based management, which recom-mends the use of evidence from academically credible empirical research as the foundation for policies and practices. They especially set their sights on HR practices, as the currently popular practices are *inconsistent* with evidence [PS06a, PS06b, PS06c].[12]

We asked for evidence related to the HR practices at one company that emphasized individual target setting. Their reply was, "There are articles to prove anything." But they failed to provide *any* arti-cles to support their policies, and successfully avoided further dis-cussion.

However, they *did* ask the agile-support group to remove from the intranet the group's advice on dealing with individual target setting, because it was in conflict with HR policies. One of this company's corporate values is...*Openness*.

The rest of this section contains tips for changing HR practices. But because changing them seems *impossible*, this section also provides tips for dealing with HR practices that cannot yet be changed.

### Avoid...Incentives linked to performance

*impediment #4 "individual performance evaluation"*

Rewarding people for their performance is a common practice, but what are the assumptions behind it? It assumes that people are

❑ in control of their performance

❑ motivated by rewards, which leads to improved performance

*systems thinking p. 9*

Both assumptions are questionable. Most work, especially product development, is interdependent. Quality guru Deming frequently pointed out that everybody was part of a larger system and therefore does not have full influence on their performance. What is the effect

---

12. For more, see www.evidence-basedmanagement.com.

of promising rewards for work that people cannot fully influence? De-motivation. Alfie Kohn, author of the provocative book *Punished by Rewards*, therefore recommends to *"decouple the task from the compensation"* [Kohn93].

Assuming it was possible to create performance measurements over which people had full control, then their motivation and performance would surely increase by putting an incentive on this target. Not so.

Psychologist Frederick Herzberg, author of one of the most popular *Harvard Business Review* articles, "One More Time: How Do You Motivate Employees," explains that incentives create *movement*, not motivation. Giving a reward for a job well done motivates a person for the reward but not for the job. This is an important distinction— the motivation is short term and the focus is on the reward, not the job [Herzberg87].

Is there anything wrong with creating *movement* instead of motivation? Not by itself, but rewards have the side effect of decreasing the *intrinsic motivation* and the very performance that managers hoped to improve. Deming said:

> *What they [the present style of rewards] do is to squeeze out from an individual, over his lifetime, his innate intrinsic motivation, self-esteem, dignity. They build into him fear, self-defense, extrinsic motivation. We have been destroying our people, from toddlers on through the university, and on the job. We must preserve the power of intrinsic motivation, dignity, cooperation, curiosity, joy in learning, that people are born with. [Deming94]*

Deming is not the only one warning us against rewards. A great deal of research establishes the harm of pay-per-performance. Stanford professor Jeffrey Pfeffer concludes, *"The evidence for widespread dissatisfaction with such pay plans is pervasive. Both employees and company survey data suggest that the likelihood of success is low and the odds of problems and dissatisfaction are high"* [Pfeffer07].

Michael Beer, professor at Harvard Business School, studied 13 pay-per-performance experiments at HP. Every single one of them failed.

*"Managers came to believe that employees were too focused on pay and insufficiently focused on the task"* [BC04].

Toyota Japan does not link rewards to individual performance. The only bonus they pay is based on the performance of the whole company. *"Pay is the same for all within a given classification, and bonuses (as a percentage) are the same for all members"* [LH08].

What can you do if your company insists on pay-per-performance?

### Try...De-emphasize incentives

Managers love to play with the incentives tool. *"Tinkering with pay appears to be easier than fixing organizational culture and leadership capabilities"* [Pfeffer07]. But emphasizing incentives creates a fascinating organizational dynamic (Figure 10.4).

Figure 10.4 focus on incentives increases dissatisfaction

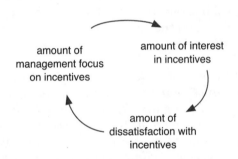

Pfeffer states in his *Harvard Business Review* article, "Six Dangerous Myth about Pay," *"Emphasizing pay as the primary reward encourages people to come and stay for the wrong reasons"* [Pfeffer98]. By emphasizing incentives, managers increase their importance. Potential motivation is short-lived and in the longer term the result is discontent with the reward system. This triggers managers to once again change and emphasize incentives, without realizing the downward spiral of incentive dissatisfaction. When you cannot remove the incentive system, at least de-emphasize it [Poppendieck04]. Emphasize other aspects that *increase* intrinsic motivation, such as challenging and meaningful work, learning, achievement, and personal growth.

*challenging work p. 195; work redesign p. 234*

## Avoid...Putting incentives on productivity measures

'Productivity' is a popular incentive target..."Rewarding high productivity undoubtedly improves performance" is a common assumption. Even if this were so, it implies that measuring knowledge worker productivity is even possible.

Several ways of measuring productivity in software development have been proposed. One of the first and unfortunately still widely used 'productivity' metrics is lines of code (LOCs) per time period.

What will happen if one puts an incentive on LOCs? More lines of code will be generated—but is that desirable? We worked with a client for which a programmer, in response to a small change request in existing functionality, *copied* a 20-thousand-LOC module, changed 50 lines, and said "done!" He did this repeatedly and was declared the productivity hero.

We worked with one product group in Hungary who added a feature and refactored the code to eliminate duplication. The result: more functionality and fewer total LOCs. So, did they have *negative* productivity? Over beer, we have speculated whether "lines of code removed" would be a good productivity metric. But when we look at the entries of the Obfuscated C competition,[13] we changed our minds.

Capers Jones has spent most of his career deconstructing and discrediting LOC measurements as productivity measures [Jones08]. The alternatives are elegant but hard to measure. And whether they measure all aspects of productivity is doubtful [Fowler03].

The conclusion: "Productivity metrics" are measuring only part of the output. In that case, would putting incentives on these metrics improve part of the output? Perhaps, but not without an important drawback. Rob Austin, in *Measuring and Managing Performance in Organizations,* created a model for examining incentives. He distinguishes between *full* and *partial* measurements and shows that partial measurements lead to optimizing effort toward the metric instead of toward the goal; this is called measurement dysfunction.

---

13. The Obfuscated C competition has made writing ugly code an art form. See www0.us.ioccc.org/main.html

For example, the goal in software development is not more LOCs but more functionality—more LOCs are not necessarily more functionality. LOCs are only an indirect measure of functionality. The more indirect, the larger the distortion in output.

*secret toolbox; see Legacy Code in companion book* In software development, measurement dysfunction makes *incentives for productivity* more harmful than beneficial. They result in developers using the "secret developer toolbox" and therefore an increase of hazardous legacy code, leading to competitive problems.

### Try...Team incentives instead of individual incentives

You are not convinced that incentives are harmful? Or is your situation that you can't do anything about removing them?

At least, set *team* incentives rather than individual incentives for self-managing cross-functional Scrum teams. *"Talking about teamwork and cooperation and then **not** having a group-based component to the pay system matters because paying solely on individual basis signals what the organization believes is actually important—**individual** behavior and performance"* [Pfeffer98] (emphasis added).

Switching from individual to team-based incentives systems sounds easy, but in our experience even this change is difficult for large organizations. In one of them, the corporate HR stated, "If individual targets are set well, then they do not disturb teamwork." By stating this, they ignored the vast body of team literature, for example [Hackman02, MCM95, WBW91], that states individual incentives are a problem for self-managing teams.

Team-based incentives might also create resistance from employees. An example in a company moving to team based-incentives:

> In the organizations we studied, the more people were paid for individual performance, the more they felt fairly paid and satisfied with work, even though the performance of their teams was adversely affected! [MCM95]

This resistance changed over time as people came to see the team-based reward system as fair:

*As people work in team-based settings, they begin to adopt the logic of the new organization and perceive reward practices that are consistent with that new logic as fair. This change in viewpoint takes time. [MCM95]*

Toyota Japan does not use pay-per-performance, but when they expanded into North America, they knew the reward system had to be adjusted to Western beliefs. They created a metric for plant performance and linked it to rewards. Still, they were for team (or plant) performance rather than for individual results. *"All hourly employees receive the same percentage bonus. This fits the Western culture of rewards that are within control of the employees though it is not tied to individual performance"* [LH08].

### Try...Team-based targets without rewards

Just to make sure the earlier tips are not misunderstood, setting *targets* for teams is essential. Linking incentives to targets is not essential and is arguably harmful.

*challenging performance target p. 195*

### Avoid...Performance appraisals

 One sacred-incentive-cow sacrificed. Another relates to the (semi-)annual performance review/appraisal. Twice a year, every manager must review the performance of his subordinates, set their *individual* objectives, and discuss their individual learning. How do performance appraisals fit in a team environment?

*impediment #4 "individual performance evaluation"*

The thought-provoking book *Abolishing Performance Appraisals* examines the assumptions behind appraisals and the research about their effectiveness. They come to the startling conclusion that there is absolutely no evidence that they are worthwhile. Instead, they are usually more harmful than beneficial and it is therefore a good idea to stop them [CJ02].

What are the problems with performance appraisals? Numerous. It is not only the individual-focused aspect of appraisals that negatively influences teamwork. The whole concept of performance appraisals is rooted in command-and-control management assumptions, such as "managers are responsible for the results, targets, and personal learning of their subordinates." Or "managers can independently or effectively judge the performance of their subordinates." Or "managers need a formal process for giving feedback to their subordinates; otherwise, managers won't give feedback." Appraisals result in employees wondering why they did not receive this feedback before, or worse, disagreeing with their manager about their performance. Appraisals backfire and de-motivate.

There is nothing new or unique about this. Deming's 12th point of his famous 14 points to get *Out of the Crisis*, appeals for the removal of performance appraisals [Deming82]. Also, the third item on his list of *seven deadly diseases* of Western companies is *"evaluation of performance, merit rating, or annual review."* Quality guru Philip Crosby and Deming rarely agreed on anything except when it came to performance appraisals. Crosby's conclusion on appraisals: *"The result of all this is to make reviews counterproductive"* [Crosby84].

But you might wonder, "Without performance review, how do we know the amount of pay increase?" Toyota, as pointed out earlier, pays everybody the same within a given classification. So, then there is no need for an annual performance review to determine pay increase. The increase is decided for a certain classification and determined by the cost of living and market value of certain skills [Derby07b].

*Go See p. 52*

How can you know when to promote someone to a higher classification without an annual review? If your managers need an annual review to determine this, there is a lack of Go See behavior.

Are organizations without annual bonuses necessarily less attractive to employees? No. Most companies have a fixed compensation budget that consists of salary, incentives, and other benefits. This budget does not need to decrease; instead, the incentive part decreases and the other parts *increase*. Companies that abolished their incentive pay and performance appraisals frequently pay employees above market-average salaries [CJ02].

### Avoid...ScrumMasters do performance appraisals

A ScrumMaster evaluating the performance of the team or its individual members leads to a dysfunctional environment. *"Creating a higher status position (evaluator) is an impediment to the team self-organizing"* [Derby07a]. It destroys the openness and transparency that are so needed in self-managing teams.

### Try...Discuss with your team how to do appraisals

What do you do if it is impossible to get rid of appraisals? One alternative is to ask the team how to deal with them. Explain to them the problems with appraisals and why they need to do them anyway—HR policy.

### Try...Fill in the forms

De-emphasize appraisals. Explain to your team why they are dysfunctional and harmful. Fill in the needed forms and send them to HR. Focus on doing and improving the real work instead.

## PEOPLE

The first agile value highlights the importance of individuals—their skill, morale, and other qualities. The 10<sup>th</sup> Toyota Way principle emphasizes finding and developing exceptional people, and Toyota is extraordinarily careful in their hiring practices [LH08]. Lean product development emphasizes a culture of long-term, hands-on engineers with "towering technical excellence."

This last section offers people-related tips consistent with lean and agile principles. Suggestions cover job titles, career paths, hiring, and training.

## Avoid...Limiting peoples' perspective

This is a generalization of many of the following tips.

*impediment #2*
*"thinking it's all*
*about developers"*
Some organizational systems stimulate or force people to specialize in only one skill or function. The deep knowledge of a skillful specialist is unquestionably an important organizational asset. These systems also offer people a clear direction in their career. However, by doing so they limit the cross-functional learning pivotal for fast cycle time development and for agility. You do not want people to be exceptionally skillful in just *one* specialty. Products rarely need one specialty; they need an integration of talent from different areas.

Having excessively narrow specialists leads to communication and integration problems because those specialists do not understand or appreciate one another's domain. Thus, organizational systems need to support the creation of deep specialized knowledge *and* stimulate broad learning. It does not have to be a false dichotomy.

## Avoid...Job titles

Job titles promote hierarchy and specialization.

**Hierarchy**—Job titles reflect status and hierarchy that often leads to less openness within a group. You do not want John to agree with Charles simply because Charles has a higher position. You want John to agree because he thinks that is the best way forward. Removing hierarchy is critical when establishing self-organizing teams.

**Specialization**—Job titles also reflect specialization, which leads to a narrow perspective of work. For example, developer John will not help with (or learn about) testing tasks because "I am a developer, not a tester."

In Scrum, there are no predefined roles in the team because members of a self-organizing team think in terms of skill, not roles or job titles. For example, Sanjay does most of the testing because he is a true expert. However, when there are many testing tasks, John helps out—and learns more.

### Try...Create only one job title

An alternative to removing job titles is to define only one. Sometimes this is easier because it does not require a change of HR policy.

W. L. Gore is an unusual company that practices 'unmanagement' and 'unstructure' [MS95]. The size of every plant is limited to 200 people. When the unit grows above 200, it is split in two. The company has no organizational chart or formal hierarchy. Every employee has exactly the same job title: 'associate.'

### Try...Let people make their own titles; encourage funny titles

Another technique for removing status and hierarchy from job titles is to let all employees make up their own. Semco, an unconventional Brazilian company does this and they had three 'gods' working in the company. Having everyone select their own job title can lead to less resistance when a job title matters to people in their social environment.

### Try...(if all else fails) Generic title with levels

Suppose none of the preceding options is feasible in the short term because HR insists on job titles with gradations or levels. An alternative in some companies is to use a relatively generic title with a level, such as "R&D member—level 3."

### Try...Simple internal titles map to special external titles

In some societies, job title status and moving *up* is understandably critical to people. It is not very impressive to tell your mother-in-law, or next prospective employer, that your official job title is...team member. A solution that strikes a balance is to define both an internal and external title. The internal title may be *R&D member* but when a person leaves the company, something more special may be provided to help the person in the job market, such as *senior architect* or *senior manager*.

### Avoid...Job descriptions

Specific job descriptions and job titles lead to the same dysfunctions. Job descriptions might lead to people following them—the lean waste of under-realized talent or potential. This can also increase a blaming culture in which people look at the job descriptions to find the guilty party..."Well, he's the tester. It says on page two that he should have done that."

### Try...Simple general job descriptions

The time and energy that people use to define specific job descriptions may in fact significantly contribute to the *heat death of the universe*. For months, pages of detailed points are passed around and reviewed for the "Fault Manager" job description. We wonder if the person who finally does this job ever reads the list.

If removing job descriptions is not currently an option then at least make them simple, broad, and high level. For example, the description of "team member": *A team member has the shared responsibility for the outcome of an iteration*. High-level general job descriptions promote thinking, innovating, learning, and doing whatever is necessary to deliver the product, rather than strictly following limited responsibilities

### Avoid...Career paths

Large organizations promise their employees a future inside the company by providing road maps—career paths.

We have seen and coached many organizations with career paths, and in all cases they fomented de-motivation and disappointment and stifled the multi-talented potential of people. Employees became frustrated because they wanted to follow the path faster and this resulted in more single-specialization.

Large-scale Scrum can lead to major changes in career paths. One product group we worked with used to have three paths:

- Project manager career path—This ceased to exist after the move to Scrum.

- Management career path—This became less attractive in a flatter organization where management responsibilities moved to Scrum teams.

- Technical/engineering career path—Originally, this meant to move away from hands-on programming and become a "Power Point architect." Scrum renewed the focus on the real-value work of development.

Predefined career paths made these changes more difficult because they upset people who had bet their career on one particular path.

### Try...Job rotation

Job rotation—changing your job to a different functional domain—is an excellent way to create cross-functional learning. These 'rotations' can be for a few months or a few years.

I (Bas here) used to work in Nokia and always considered job rotation to be one of the strengths of the company. It was common to meet people who started their Nokia career in a completely different functional area. Why was this so common? One reason is the history. Nokia was founded as a paper company and transformed itself into a rubber company, then to a steel cable company, then to a consumer electronics company, and lately to a telecommunication company [Steinbock01]. I met people who joined Nokia when it was a steel cable company. My first manager moved from engineering to sales and back to engineering, and this gave him a broad perspective.

Nokia is not unique in this. Honda lets engineers work in a different department for one week every year [Galbraith93]. W. L. Gore encourages its 'associates' to find their own work [MS95]. And, Toyota uses job rotation as one way of broadening people's perspective.

*Acquiring experience in several job functions or aspects of business operation equips managers to make better system-wide decisions. It takes time to develop this competence and requires hands-on experience and multiple job rotations. [OST08]*

### Try...Start people with job rotation

When to start exposing people to a different functional areas? As soon as possible.

During their first year at Toyota, new people go through "general training," in which they build cars in the factory for a couple of months. They then work for a dealership to sell cars, even door to door (in Japan). This general training creates a broad feel for what their business is about. *"The message is clear: Each employee works for Toyota, not for a specific function"* [LM06b].

### Try...Hire the best

Great people are arguably the most important success factor in new product development. So companies that are serious about products invest time to make sure they hire the right people. For example, Microsoft and Google are famous for their strict hiring policies—and for talented developers.

Great developers attract more great developers. They love working in a challenging environment with peers who are doing the challenging. Therefore, one way of hiring the best is to...hire the best.

In 2000, Joel Spolsky, an ex-Microsoft Excel developer, was looking for a great place to work [Spolsky08]. But he could not find a company where a focus on great developers was paramount. So he decided to start his own company—Fogs Creek. What was his business plan?

Figure 10.5 Joel's business plan

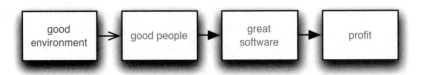

Eight years later, Joel is still proud of the way his company treats developers. They also build successful products and have been profitable ever since the company was founded. Their foundation: Hire great developers [Spolsky07].

### Avoid...Hiring when you cannot find the best

Though this tip seems obvious, it is not a common practice. In some large companies, the planned "head count" for a department determines how many people they should hire. And if the department does not hire them now, then they will not be allowed to hire them later. This policy triggers these departments to locally optimize and hire "the best available" instead of "the best." In product development it is better to hire a few great people than many average people. If you cannot find great people, then it's better not to hire at all.

### Try...Team does the hiring

How will you know whether a new hire will fit in a team? Involve the team in the hiring; better yet, let the team do the interviewing and let them make the final decision.

Michael Lopp, author of *Managing Humans*, feels that involving "some team members" is not good enough. He writes "*Everyone on the team needs to interview every candidate*" [Lopp07].

Semco, the extraordinary Brazilian company, practices **collective interviewing**. They internally broadcast upcoming interviews and invite anyone to join. Having thirty plus people interviewing one candidate is not an exception. The more important positions attract more interviewers and—they say—this leads to a better selection. In one instance, no interviewer showed up for an interview and therefore that position was cancelled. It must not be needed if no one was interested in acting as an interviewer [Semler03].

### Try...Long and in-depth hands-on evaluation

"So, are you a good programmer?"... "Well, pretty good. I've been programming for seven years. On my resume you can see the products I've worked on."... "Great! Next question. ..."

Not good enough. Talking about programming is easy. At ObjectSpace where I (Craig here) used to work, a candidate would have to spend six or more hours in a room with expert developers. During this period the candidate would have to sketch out (on the whiteboard) detailed design solutions for problems, and do relatively long and in-depth programming. The reviewers would carefully look at the code. If you want to hire great talent, inspect the real work of a candidate through some kind of long and in-depth, hands-on evaluation.

Although this tip used developer candidates as an example, it applies more broadly to other categories—digital electronics engineers, graphic designers, and more.

### Try...Pair programming with developer candidates

Arguably the most in-depth approach to really seeing what a developer candidate can create and how they work with others is to evaluate them through long pair programming sessions. The candidate may write great code but be difficult to work with. Pair programming with a developer starts to expose his or her true technical and social work skills. Pair a candidate for a half-day or one day with one or more potential future team members.

Nothing beats evaluating a candidate on real work. Therefore...

### Try...Trial iteration

How do you know if someone will really fit in with the team and has the right mix of skills? If the candidate passes the first round of pair programming evaluations, consider a second round of evaluation in which the candidate joins the team for one iteration. Of course, he would be compensated for working that iteration.

### Try...Lots of formal education and coaching

*impediment #5 "failure to learn from outside"*

Agile development and lean thinking involves new thinking tools, technical skills, behaviors, mindset, Scrum, test-driven development, continuous integration, self-managing teams...it's a non-trivial list.

The most common education mistake is: too little for too few.

Within the Xerox lean development initiative, on the other hand, each team goes through at least four weeks of in-depth education and coaching in lean principles, Scrum, and agile development skills, both in the classroom and at their team location.

In another product group we coached in adopting large-scale Scrum, 50 percent of the people went through a ScrumMaster course even they were not all going to serve as a ScrumMaster. It provided common broad understanding.

It is important that virtually everyone in the product group is well educated in the new non-technical topics—Scrum and lean thinking, for example. All people need a common understanding and vocabulary of the big picture. Plus, development staff need in-depth education and coaching in agile development skills.

Unequivocally, the large product groups that have been most successful in adopting agile and lean development focused on education and coaching.

### Try...Lots of coaching

Some ideas can be well taught in a classroom or workshop. Some cannot. A good example is test-driven development (TDD). We have given many TDD courses, but when we ask the participants after some months whether they use it, a frequent reply is, "The course was great! We really want to use this, but we are currently working with this legacy code and it doesn't apply there."

*impediment #5 "failure to learn from outside expertise"*

Well, it does apply there as well. This is an example of the kind of skill that requires coaching for weeks or months at the person's place of work, during their regular tasks.

The same is true for other practices. Educating a novice ScrumMaster while an expert coach facilitates the Sprint Retrospective is much more effective than a course in retrospective techniques. Have an experienced ScrumMaster come in and coach the team for the first few iterations and let other ScrumMasters observe.

Our advice to the organizations that we work with is to have some structured classroom education, but to primarily focus on using expert coaches who spend time with Scrum teams and the Product Owner Team during their Scrum events and during their day-to-day work.

## CONCLUSION

Lean and agile development principles and practices, self-managing cross-functional teams, and other related concepts *should* lead to non-trivial change in all elements of an organization. Otherwise, the implications of these have probably not been grasped. This change is caused by fundamentally different assumptions about workers, teams, work, and the way in which work should be structured.

Do not expect this to go fast; it will take years or perhaps decades—in fact, forever, considering the pillar of *continuous improvement*. A good sense of humor, an informal supportive community of practice, and patience is especially helpful in organizational improvement. Celebrate small steps forward. Especially in the work of organizational redesign, we encourage our clients to keep in mind systems thinking and the dynamic of local optimization.

## RECOMMENDED READINGS

This chapter covered many topics. Most were given cursory treatment; therefore this section has a relatively large set of recommended readings.

The task, structure, and process sections covered structuring tasks and forming the formal organization. Much has been written about organizational design, but not so much in an agile and lean development context. Some recommendations:

❑ *Work Redesign*, by Richard Hackman. A book written in 1980s and mainly focused on administration and factory work. But the ideas in this book are as insightful today as they were thirty years ago. In the last part, Hackman made predictions about the future of work that are surprisingly accurate.

- *One More Time: How Do You Motivate Employees?* by Frederick Herzberg. The first part of this classic article is about motivation and the hygiene/motivator theory. The last part looks at work redesign from a slightly different angle than that of Hackman.

- *Communities of Practice: The Organizational Frontier*, by Etienne Wenger and William Snyder. This is a *Harvard Business Review* article and is a short and easy-to-read introduction to the concept of CoP.

- *Cultivating Communities of Practice* by Etienne Wenger, Richard Dermott, and William Snyder. What, why, and how? These questions are answered with lots of practical examples.

The *Rewards* section covered topics related to incentives and appraisals, without diving into the details. Plenty of good material is available on this subject:

- *Six Dangerous Myths About Pay*, by Jeffrey Pfeffer. This short article not only covers the pay-per-performance myth, but also several other pay-related myths.

- *Punished by Rewards*, by Alfie Kohn. Are incentive systems the only reward-related problem or is more going on? Kohn takes a deep dive in the subject of rewarding at work and in the classroom. This analysis challenges some fundamental assumptions behind rewarding.

- *Abolishing Performance Appraisals*, by Tom Coens and Mary Jenkins. Are performance appraisals rooted in good insight, credible organizational research, and evidence? This analysis concludes that no evidence exists that they work and that the assumptions behind performance appraisals are shaky at best.

- *Measuring and Managing Performance in Organizations*, by Rob Austin. What happens if you give incentives but are not able to measure all the workers' output? This is one of the questions Rob Austin tries to answer in his book. His model shows that *measurement dysfunctions* are the outcome, ironically resulting in *poorer* performance.

One great way of learning about organizations is to study modern companies. Their ideas are not hypothetical. Organizations such as Google, W. L. Gore, Semco, and Visa are interesting cases to study:

- ❏ *Maverick*, by Richardo Semler. Semco, a Brazilian company from São Paolo has gradually *freed* its employees. Once a fairly traditional company, Semco went through a major change and became one the most studied companies in the world because of their innovative HR practices. *Maverick* describes this change.

- ❏ *Birth of the Chaordic Age*, by Dee Hock. "Self-management cannot happen in traditional industries such as banking." Not so. Dee Hock is the founder of Visa and describes how it was build on the principles of self-organization.

- ❏ *Business Without Bosses*, by Charles Manz and Henry Sims. What would happen without managers? Would there be total chaos? Not at W. L. Gore. They practice 'unmanagement' and do not have an organization chart at all. Chapter 6 of *Business Without Bosses* describes how W. L. Gore operates.

- ❏ *The Google Story*, by David Vise. One of the most successful companies of the last decade: Google. This book describes the history of Google and some of the interesting practices within Google. It is a little superficial, but still worth reading.

- ❏ *The Future of Management*, by Gary Hamel. "What will be the future role of management?" is the key question in Hamel's book. Chapters 4–6 study three companies with innovative organizational practices: Whole Foods Market, W. L. Gore, and Google.

# Chapter

# Book

# LARGE-SCALE SCRUM

*Cabbage: A familiar kitchen-garden vegetable
about as large and wise as a man's head.*
—Ambrose Bierce

Large-scale Scrum is Scrum.

It is not "new and improved Scrum." Rather, it is regular Scrum, an empirical process framework that can inspect and adapt to any method weight and work in a group of any size. **Large-scale Scrum** is a label—for brevity in writing—to imply regular Scrum plus the set of tips that we have seen work in large multiteam, multisite, and offshore agile development.[1] These tips are experiments to try in the context of the classic Scrum framework. That is why the tips start with "Try…", to suggest no more than an experiment.

Be dubious of messages such as "Scrum 2.0," "Scrum++," "Scrum#,", "UnifiedScrum," "OpenScrum," or "new and improved Scrum that should replace regular Scrum." They may miss the point of empirical process and the implications of Scrum. To reiterate a quote by Ken Schwaber, the co-creator of Scrum:

> *There will be no Scrum Release 2.0…Why not? Because the point of Scrum is not to solve [specific problems of development]… Scrum unearths the problems caused by the complexity and lets the organization solve them, one by one, over and over again. [Schwaber07]*

Regular Scrum is a simple framework that exposes organizational problems. We are not suggesting that new ideas cannot arise and improve the framework. But attempts to 'improve' it are most often

---

1. The companion book *Practices for Scaling Lean & Agile Development* consolidates many of these tips.

(1) avoidance of dealing with the weaknesses exposed when regular Scrum is really applied, (2) conformance to status quo policies or entrenched groups, (3) a belief in a new silver bullet practice or tool, (4) fuzzy understanding of Scrum and empirical process control, or (5) an attempt by the traditional consulting companies to take your money—"Accenture Scrum/Agile," "IBM Scrum/Agile," and so on.

Large-scale Scrum, as regular Scrum, is a framework for development in which the concrete details need to be filled in by the teams and evolved iteration by iteration, team by team. It reflects the lean thinking pillar of continuous improvement. It is a collection of suggestions for inspecting and adapting the product and process when there are *many* teams—at least two teams but also for groups of 500 or 1000 people.

It is said that Scrum is *easy to understand but hard to use* because it brings weaknesses to light. In the case of a small group adopting Scrum (for example, 7 people) within a large organization, the problems revealed and dealt with may be quite local. But in a larger product group (say, 500 people) adopting large-scale Scrum, systemic weaknesses are exposed in the organizational design—in structure, processes, rewards, people, and tasks. In this case, large-scale Scrum is a force for organizational change. This dynamic reflects the lean metaphor of lowering the water level—Scrum is a framework for making the rocks visible. Lowering the water is easy, the hard part is removing the rocks—especially when they involve organizational policy and structure.

This is why *thinking tools* and *organizational tools* are presented before this chapter. Sooner or later the existing enterprise structure will clearly be seen as limiting the success of maximizing ROI with large-scale Scrum. These tools are relevant to dealing with these enterprise limitations and the issues of organizational redesign that will be roused when large-scale Scrum is introduced.

## OVERVIEW

This chapter provides an overview of some suggestions for large-scale Scrum and points to related concepts and tips in the *Organizational Tools* section. Many "action tool" or practice tips (multisite,

offshore, design, requirements, coordination, planning, contracts, …)
are covered in the companion book.

The following descriptions only emphasize what is noteworthy in the
context of scaling. Regular Scrum elements are not explained unless
we felt that reiteration was useful. Basic Scrum knowledge is
assumed; see the *Scrum Primer* chapter for a synopsis.[2]

*Scrum Primer
p. 305*

For large-scale Scrum we suggest two alternative frameworks. One
is for up to about ten teams in a product group. The other goes
beyond that—scaling to at least many hundreds, if not thousands, of
people in a product group.

## TRY…LARGE-SCALE SCRUM FW-1 FOR UP TO TEN TEAMS

### Introduction

The first framework is appropriate for one Product Owner (PO) and
up to 'ten' teams. 'Ten' is not a magic number for choosing between
framework-1 and framework-2. The tipping point is context dependent; sometimes less. At some point the PO (1) can no longer grasp
an overview of the entire product and, (2) can no longer effectively
interact with the teams. When the PO is no longer able to focus on
high-level product management, something should change.

Before moving to framework-2, first consider if the PO can be helped
by delegating more work to the teams or by providing other domain
experts who can work with the PO. For example, requirements splitting and fine-grained analysis can be done by the teams or other
subject matter experts who support the PO. Encourage the teams to
directly interact with real customers to reduce handoff and reduce
the burden on the PO. Most project management should be done by
the teams. The PO does not need to be involved in low-level details;
they should be able to focus on true product management.

---

2. Terminology point: This chapter (and book) uses *iteration* rather
   than *Sprint* because of the former's familiarity and use in other iterative methods. We occasionally use the latter term when it is imper-
   ative in context.

Figure 11.1 large-scale Scrum, FW-1

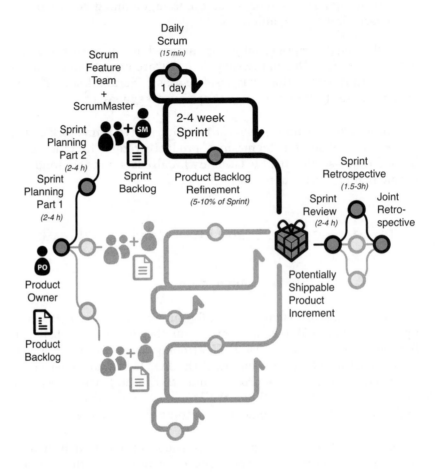

**Roles**

- ❏ Product Owner
- ❏ Scrum Feature Teams
- ❏ ScrumMasters

**Product Owner**—The Product Owner role and responsibilities are the same as in regular one-team classic Scrum. What are those? There has been some confusion, so it may be worthwhile to review…

*[The Product Owner] owns the vision for the total product portfolio, the business plan, the road map, and the dates. They are accountable for the revenue stream...The POs are business focused on product so there is not a one-to-one mapping to teams. [Sutherland08]*

*The Product Owner's focus is return on investment (ROI)...The Product Owner uses the Product Backlog to give the highest priority to the requirements that are of highest value to the business, to insert nonfunctional requirements that lead to opportunistic releases and implementations of functionality, and to constantly adjust the product in response to changing business conditions, including new competitive offerings. [Schwaber04].*

And from the *Certified ScrumMaster* course [Schwaber05], the Product Owner...

❏ *defines the features of the product, decides on release date and content*

❏ *is responsible for the profitability of the product (ROI)*

❏ *prioritizes features according to market value*

❏ *can change features and priority [every iteration]*

❏ *accepts or rejects work results*

In Scrum the PO is called "the single wringable neck" in terms of responsibility for product success or failure. The classic Scrum PO role has several classic *product manager* responsibilities, though they are distinguished from *only* being a traditional product manager by also using a prioritized and evolving Product Backlog and Scrum to maximize ROI, and by meeting with teams each iteration to present goals and to review the results. In a product group with existing product managers, the chief (or only) product manager serves as PO. Note that skillful *product management* expertise is critical to being an effective PO.

*see Product Management in the companion book*

In the case of internal application development (such as internal financial application rather than a product for the market), the PO role is played by one business customer, who often represents a group of users or stakeholders.

When there are multiple teams there are *many* Product Backlog items, and that means more work for the Product Owner. Therefore, he or she may be helped by the teams (a good first option), subject matter experts, business analysts, customer representatives, or other people in product management. These supporters may work within the Scrum Feature Teams or with product management (close to the Product Owner) to help with the myriad requirement details and other minutiae, ensuring that the Product Owner can focus on the big picture—the overall product.

As the name suggests, there is *one and only one* Product Owner for a product, whether there are five or fifty-five teams in the group. This is necessary to optimally prioritize the overall Product Backlog from a product perspective.

The companion book's *Product Management* chapter explores this role in more detail.

**Scrum Feature Teams**—These are normal Scrum teams that take whole customer-centric features from the Product Backlog and independently complete them. They are self-managing and cross-functional teams. Because they are *feature teams*, there should be little need for the teams to interact or coordinate, except at the level of integration of code, which is resolved through continuous integration. Scrum Feature Teams are explored in the *Feature Teams* and *Teams* chapters.

**ScrumMasters**—These are regular ScrumMasters that (1) act as Scrum-method coaches for their teams and the Product Owner, (2) help their team become a *real* team by facilitating conflict and removing obstacles, (3) help the Product Owner, (4) remind the team of their goal, and (5) bring change to the organization so that overall product development is optimized and maximum ROI is realized.

In the context of scaling and multiteam development, there are many opportunities for a team to require a representative at meetings. It is useful for a ScrumMaster to *not* act as the team representative. One Scrum goal is an engaged self-managing team; thus, a good ScrumMaster will avoid taking any management-like role or activity, including team representative. Other team members need to learn to take on all management-related roles and activities.[3]

## Artifacts

- ❑ Product Backlog
- ❑ Sprint Backlogs
- ❑ Potentially Shippable Product Increment

**Product Backlog**—This is a regular backlog. For scaling, *user story* format is especially well suited to express Product Backlog Items because of the ease of splitting user stories. The companion book's *Requirements* chapter explores this in more detail, especially focusing on how to split large user stories (for example, *one* user story that will take 150 people two years) into smaller ones—a common problem in large-scale development that involves mammoth requirements.

**Sprint Backlog**—Each team has its own regular Sprint Backlog.

**Potentially Shippable Product Increment**—One perfection challenge in Scrum is that the output of each iteration is a potentially shippable product increment. This is not a difficult goal in a small product group, but requires a multi-year journey of improvement in a gargantuan group that has institutionalized weaknesses. Note that the product increment is not per team. Rather, all teams need to integrate their output into one potentially shippable increment. This means the teams need to continuously integrate their code and coordinate in any other way required. These issues are explored in the companion book's *Continuous Integration* and *Coordination* chapters.

---

3. In an ideal organization with few impediments and all participants understanding Scrum, most ScrumMasters would or should disappear. We have seen a few groups that were good enough so that one ScrumMaster could serve three teams.

### Events

- Sprint Planning
- Daily Scrum
- Product Backlog Refinement
- Sprint Review
- Sprint Retrospectives
- Joint Retrospective

**Sprint Planning**—As usual, consists of two timeboxed steps:

*Part One*—One participant is the Product Owner. If there are only a few teams and they can all fit comfortably together in one room, the second 'participant' could be *all* team members. Otherwise, the second 'participant' is one or two representatives from each team; we prefer two so that each team has more than one perspective. As usual, the ScrumMaster should not represent the team in meetings, including this one. What happens in Part One? The usual goals and activities, but now involving several teams in one room. For example, backlog items are now offered to a set of teams, and any one of them may volunteer for an item. Note that when groups consistently do the **Product Backlog Refinement** (PBR) meeting each iteration, then Part One will be simple and quick, because almost all questions will have been previously resolved in the PBR meeting. If Part One is filled with questions and clarifications, or takes too much time, the PBR meetings are not being done skillfully. The companion book's *Planning* chapter has more tips.

*Part Two*—At the end of Part One, the representatives or teams return to their room and, in parallel, each team holds a normal Sprint Planning Part Two and creates their own Sprint Backlog. The companion book's *Planning, Design,* and *Requirements* chapters offers some relevant tips.

**Daily Scrum**—This is the usual Scrum event. In a multiteam context, it is sometimes useful to know what one or two other particular teams are doing. If these teams hold their Daily Scrum at different times, then it is possible to send scouts to observe other meetings as a *Chicken*. The companion book's *Coordination* chapter has other tips.

**Product Backlog Refinement**—This is the usual Scrum activity of continuously grooming[4] the Product Backlog. Scrum recommends that five or ten percent of each iteration be dedicated to this refinement but does not say how to do it. However, in the context of multiple teams, we suggest it be done as a focused workshop—such as a four-hour meeting once per iteration—so that all teams or team representatives can come together with the Product Owner. The companion book's *Planning, Requirements*, and *Multisite* chapters have related tips.

**Sprint Review**—Once again, the normal Scrum event. Participants include either all members of all teams or representatives. Because a ScrumMaster has a special responsibility in the Sprint Review to alert the Product Owner to any items that did not meet the Definition of Done, ScrumMasters will need to attend if there are any violations. The companion book's *Inspect & Adapt* chapter has a few relevant tips.

**Sprint Retrospectives**—Each team has its own individual retrospective. The companion book's *Inspect & Adapt* chapter has a few relevant tips.

**Joint Retrospective** (optional)—To improve the system as a whole, a Joint Retrospective is useful. We observe that these work best with only a few representatives from each team. In contrast to the usual guideline to avoid including a ScrumMaster as a team representative at meetings, in this case consider including the ScrumMaster (along with other team representatives) because the retrospective is a place to learn more about systemic impediments to effective Scrum—an issue directly related to ScrumMaster responsibilities. This meeting is held after the individual team retrospectives. Since individual retrospectives are routinely held at the very end of the iteration, we see that groups are likely to hold a Joint Retrospective early during the first week of the *subsequent* iteration. The companion book's *Inspect & Adapt* chapter has some relevant tips.

---

4. 'Grooming' is a popular term for this activity, but it is an English word often not understood by non-native speakers.

## Other Elements

**Definition of Done** (DoD)—The DoD applies to all items for all teams. Therefore, the DoD reflects what *all* teams are capable of achieving. We usually see large product groups write the product-level DoD on a wiki page that all teams refer to, perhaps during Sprint Planning Part One. The Joint Retrospective is a good place to explore changes to the DoD. The companion book's *Planning* chapter has a few relevant tips.

**Continuous Integration** (CI)—CI takes on special prominence in multiteam development. As explored in the *Feature Teams* chapter, feature teams shift the focus of coordination away from planning and toward code. Rock-solid CI for all developers—whether 20 or 200—is an absolute foundation for successful large-scale Scrum. The companion book's *Continuous Integration* chapter has some tips.

## TRY…LARGE-SCALE SCRUM FW-2 FOR 'MANY' TEAMS

Large-scale Scrum framework-2 builds on—rather than replaces—framework-1.

Beyond ten teams (or even less), the Product Owner cannot effectively work with all the teams or all the details in the Product Backlog. At this point it is useful to identify the major **requirement areas** and then divide the Product Backlog into separate **Area Backlogs**, each with its own **Area Product Owner** (APO) and its own dedicated Scrum Feature Teams. This is explored in the *Requirement Areas* chapter.

Consequently, framework-2 of large-scale Scrum introduces two new roles, **Area Product Owner** and **Product Owner Team** (all APOs and the Product Owner), and one more artifact, **Area Backlog**. To be precise, the Area Backlog is not a separate backlog; it is simply a view onto the Product Backlog for one area.

Note that there may also be a Product Owner Team in framework-1, but in that case, the helpers are not APOs.

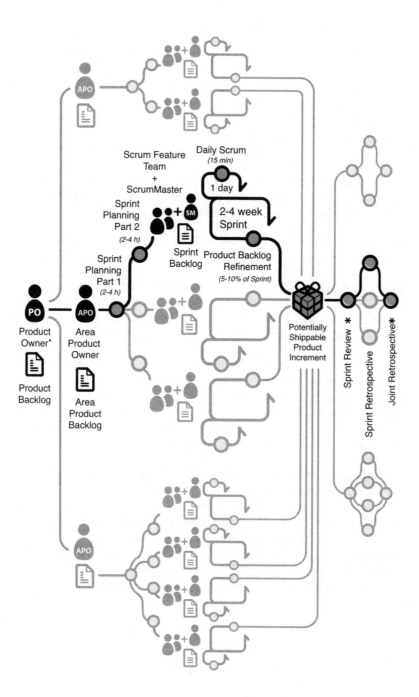

Figure 11.2 large-scale Scrum FW-2

There are some changes to events in framework-2:

**Pre-Sprint Planning**—Before Sprint Planning, usually in the last week of the prior iteration, the Product Owner Team needs to coordinate the overall prioritization of the Product Backlog. The Product Owner usually wants to discuss priorities in each Area Backlog, and the members want feedback from each other on their ideas. More broadly, this team wants to meet each iteration to consider where they are and where they want to go as a whole product.

**Sprint Planning**—There is separate Sprint Planning for each requirement area. Each involves an Area Product Owner and the teams of that area. It is otherwise the same as framework-1.

**Product Backlog Refinement**—There is a separate refinement activity for each area, with the Area Product Owner and teams.

**Sprint Review**—There is a separate Sprint Review for each area. Each involves the Area Product Owner and teams. The Product Owner may attend particular reviews that he or she is especially interested in. It is otherwise the same as framework-1.

**Joint Review** (optional)—There are times when the Product Owner Team (plus representatives from various Scrum Feature Teams) wants to hold a product-level joint review. They discuss issues, improvements, and features of interest to the majority of the Product Owner Team. Not surprisingly, they demo items that are of broad interest or that are critical to the next release.

**Joint Retrospectives** (optional)—As in framework-1, representatives from multiple teams may want to hold a retrospective for systems-level learning and improvement. This may happen at the area level and/or at the overall product level, with representatives from different areas. As mentioned in the *Multisite* chapter of the companion book, a (physical) site-level Joint Retrospective is also common, because improvement issues are often related to the physical or cultural environment of one site... "We need more whiteboards in this building."

## SCALING SOME ISSUES

When adopting large-scale Scrum, certain issues, dysfunctions, or misconceptions are highlighted. These include the following...

*Fake ScrumMasters*—In large groups there is usually an existing cadre of established project or first-level team managers. It is not uncommon that these assign themselves the title of ScrumMasters or are assigned this title by higher management.

*fake ScrumMaster p. 250*

*Coordination Meetings* and *Scrum of Scrums* (SoS)—The SoS is one mechanism proposed in Scrum for multiteam coordination. There are alternatives. Comments:

❑ One coordination and/or SoS dysfunction is that the coordination activity is co-opted by an existing management layer rather than handled by regular team members. As discussed in the *Teams* chapter (and the *Coordination* chapter of the companion book), healthy self-managing teams are *themselves* responsible for their coordination and communication with other groups.

❑ A variant dysfunction is that a coordination meeting (such as a SoS) is attended by ScrumMasters—fake or real. This inhibits real self-managing teams that can function independently of ScrumMasters. We suggest rotating representatives from teams to attend coordination meetings.

❑ Another potential misconception and/or dysfunction—perhaps surprising—is the assumption that the group *needs* a multi-team coordination meeting such as an SoS. Why is coordination needed? It may be a sign that there are not real cross-functional, cross-component feature teams that can work independently on a complete feature, or a sign that there is not a focus on coordination at the code level through continuous integration.

❑ There are cases for which a coordination meeting is important. However, a misconception is that the meeting must involve the whole product group. In fact, it may be sufficient for one requirement area or some other subset of teams.

❏ Arguably the most common misconception regarding the SoS is the assumption that it is the best or only way to hold a coordination meeting in Scrum. The SoS seemed a reasonable idea when first proposed (based on limited experiments), but there are alternatives that people now realize may work better, such as Open Space Technology meetings or Town Hall meetings. The *Coordination* chapter in the companion book elaborates.

## CONCLUSION

Cornerstones for effective large-scale Scrum are the thinking tools and organizational tools explored in this book. The companion *Practices* book explores many concrete action tools.

# Miscellany

## Chapter

## Book

# SCRUM PRIMER

*by Pete Deemer & Gabrielle Benefield[1]*
*(see www.scrumprimer.com for more)*

A note to readers: There are many concise descriptions of Scrum available online, and this primer aims to provide the next level of detail on the practices. It is not intended as the final step in a Scrum education; teams that are considering adopting Scrum are advised to equip themselves with Ken Schwaber's *Agile Project Management with Scrum* or *Agile Software Development with Scrum*, and take advantage of the many excellent Scrum training and coaching options that are available; full details are at scrumalliance.org. Our thanks go to Ken Schwaber, Dr. Jeff Sutherland, Mike Cohn, Craig Larman, and Bas Vodde for their generous input.

## TRADITIONAL SOFTWARE DEVELOPMENT

The traditional way to build software, used by companies big and small, was a sequential life cycle commonly known as "the waterfall." There are many variants (such as the V-Model), but it typically begins with a detailed planning phase, where the end product is carefully thought through, designed, and documented in great detail. The tasks necessary to execute the design are determined, and the work is organized using tools such as Gantt charts and applications such as Microsoft Project. The team arrives at an estimate of how long the development will take by adding up detailed estimates of the individual steps involved. Once stakeholders have thoroughly reviewed the plan and provided their approvals, the team starts to work. Team members complete their specialized portion of the work, and then hand it off to others in production-line fashion. Once the work is complete, it is delivered to a testing organization (some call this Quality Assurance), which completes testing prior to the product reaching the customer. Throughout the process, strict controls are placed on deviations from the plan to ensure that what is produced is actually what was designed.

---

1. This chapter is in slightly smaller font, reflecting the original primer, and signaling this chapter is a copy from another source.

This approach has strengths and weaknesses. Its great strength is that it is supremely logical – think before you build, write it all down, follow a plan, and keep everything as organized as possible. It has just one great weakness: humans are involved.

For example, this approach requires that the good ideas all come at the beginning of the release cycle, where they can be incorporated into the plan. But as we all know, good ideas appear throughout the process – in the beginning, the middle, and sometimes even the day before launch, and a process that does not permit change will stifle this innovation. With the waterfall, a great idea late in the release cycle is not a gift, it's a threat.

The waterfall approach also places a great emphasis on writing things down as a primary method for communicating critical information. The very reasonable assumption is that if I can write down on paper as much as possible of what's in my head, it will more reliably make it into the head of everyone else on the team; plus, if it's on paper, there is tangible proof that I've done my job. The reality, though, is that most of the time these highly detailed 50-page requirements documents just do not get read. When they do get read, the misunderstandings are often compounded. A written document is an incomplete picture of my ideas; when you read it, you create another abstraction, which is now two steps away from what I think I meant to say at that time. It is no surprise that serious misunderstandings occur.

Something else that happens when you have humans involved is the hands-on "aha" moment – the first time that you actually use the working product. You immediately think of 20 ways you could have made it better. Unfortunately, these very valuable insights often come at the end of the release cycle, when changes are most difficult and disruptive – in other words, when doing the right thing is most expensive, at least when using a traditional method.

Humans are not able to predict the future. For example, your competition makes an announcement that was not expected. Unanticipated technical problems crop up that force a change in direction. Furthermore, people are particularly bad at planning uncertain things far into the future – guessing today how you will be spending your week eight months from now is something of a fantasy. It has been the downfall of many a carefully constructed Gantt chart.

In addition, a sequential life cycle tends to foster an adversarial relationship between the people that are handing work off from one to the next. "He's asking me to build something that's not in the specification." "She's changing her mind." "I can't be held responsible for something I don't control." And this gets us to another observation about sequential development – it is not much fun. The waterfall model is a cause of great misery for the people who build products. The resulting products fall well short of expressing the creativity, skill, and passion of their creators. People are not robots, and a process that requires them to act like robots results in unhappiness.

A rigid, change-resistant process produces mediocre products. Customers may get what they first ask for (at least two translation steps removed), but is it what they really want once they see the product? By gathering all the requirements up front and having them set in stone, the product is condemned to be only as good as the initial idea, instead of being the best once people have learned or discovered new things.

Many practitioners of a sequential life cycle experience these shortcomings again and again. But, it seems so supremely logical that the common reaction is to turn inward: "If only we did it better, it would work" – if we just planned more, documented more, resisted change more, everything would work smoothly. Unfortunately, many teams find just the opposite: the harder they try, the worse it gets! There are also management teams that have invested their reputation – and many resources – in a waterfall model; changing to a fundamentally different model is an apparent admission of having made a mistake. And Scrum is fundamentally different...

## AGILE DEVELOPMENT AND SCRUM

The agile family of development methods evolved from the old and well-known iterative and incremental life cycle approaches. They were born out of a belief that an approach more grounded in human reality – and the product development reality of learning, innovation, and change – would yield better results. Agile principles emphasize building working software that people can get hands on quickly, versus spending a lot of time writing specifications up front. Agile development focuses on cross-functional teams empowered to make decisions, versus big hierarchies and compartmentalization by function. And it focuses on rapid iteration, with continuous customer input along the way. Often when people learn about agile development or Scrum, there's a glimmer of recognition – it sounds a lot like back in the start-up days, when we "just did it."

By far the most popular agile method is Scrum. It was strongly influenced by a 1986 *Harvard Business Review* article on the practices associated with successful product development groups; in this paper the term "Scrum" was introduced, relating successful development to the game of Rugby in which a self-organizing (self-managing) team moves together down the field of product development. It was then formalized in 1993 by Ken Schwaber and Dr. Jeff Sutherland. Scrum is now used by companies large and small, including Yahoo!, Microsoft, Google, Lockheed Martin, Motorola, SAP, Cisco, GE, CapitalOne and the US Federal Reserve. Many teams using Scrum report significant improvements, and in some cases complete transformations, in both productivity and morale. For product developers – many of whom have been burned by the "management fad of the month club" – this is significant. Scrum is simple and powerful.

# SCRUM SUMMARY

## Try...Learn and do standard Scrum

Scrum is an iterative, incremental framework for projects and product or application development. It structures development in cycles of work called Sprints. These iterations are 1-4 weeks in length, and take place one after the other. The Sprints are of fixed duration – they end on a specific date whether the work has been completed or not, and are never extended. They are timeboxed. At the beginning of each Sprint, a cross-functional team selects items (customer requirements) from a prioritized list. They commit to complete the items by the end of the Sprint. During the Sprint, the chosen items do not change. Every day the team gathers briefly to report to each other on progress, and update simple charts that orient them to the work remaining. At the end of the Sprint, the team reviews the Sprint with stakeholders, and demonstrates what they have built. People obtain feedback that can be incorporated in the next Sprint. Scrum emphasizes working product at the end of the Sprint that is really "done"; in the case of software, this means code that is integrated, fully tested and potentially shippable. Key roles, artifacts, and events are summarized in Figure 12.1.

A major theme in Scrum is "inspect and adapt." Since development inevitably involves learning, innovation, and surprises, Scrum emphasizes taking a short step of development, inspecting both the resulting product and the efficacy of current practices, and then adapting the product goals and process practices. Repeat forever.

Figure 12.1 Scrum roles, artifacts, and events

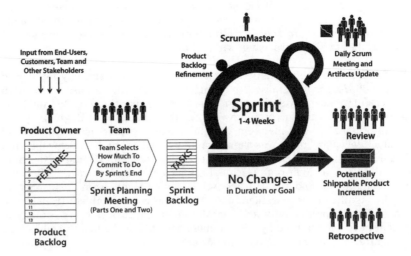

# SCRUM ROLES

In Scrum, there are three primary roles: The Product Owner, The Team, and The ScrumMaster. The **Product Owner** is responsible for maximizing return on investment (ROI) by identifying product features, translating these into a prioritized feature list, selecting the features for the next Sprint, and continually re-prioritizing and refining the list. The Product Owner has profit and loss responsibility for the product, assuming it is a commercial product. In the case of an internal application, the Product Owner is not responsible for ROI in the sense of a commercial product (that will generate revenue), but they are still responsible for maximizing ROI in the sense of choosing – each Sprint – the highest-business-value lowest-cost items. In some cases, the Product Owner and the customer are the same person; this is common for internal applications. In others, the customer might be millions of people with a variety of needs, in which case the Product Owner role is similar to the Product Manager or Product Marketing Manager position in many product organizations. However, the Product Owner is somewhat different than a traditional Product Manager because they actively and frequently interact with the team, personally offering the priorities and reviewing the results each two- or four-week iteration, rather than delegating development decisions to a project manager. It is important to note that in Scrum there is one and only one person who serves as – and has the final authority of – Product Owner.

The **Team** builds the product that the customer is going to use: the application or website, for example. The team in Scrum is "cross-functional" – it includes all the expertise necessary to deliver the potentially shippable product each Sprint – and it is "self-organizing" (self-managing), with a very high degree of autonomy and accountability. In Scrum, teams are self-organizing rather than being led by a team manager or project manager. The team decides what to commit to, and how best to accomplish that commitment; in Scrum lore, the team are known as "Pigs" and everyone else in the organization are "Chickens" (which comes from a joke about a pig and a chicken deciding to open a restaurant called "Ham and Eggs," and the pig having second thoughts because "he would be truly committed, but the chicken would only be involved").

The team in Scrum is seven plus or minus two people, and for a software product the team might include analysts, developers, interface designers, and testers. The team develops the product and provides ideas to the Product Owner about how to make the product great. In Scrum, the team should be 100 percent dedicated to the work for one product during the Sprint; avoid multitasking across multiple products or projects. Stable teams are associated with higher productivity, so avoid changing team members. Application groups with many people are organized into multiple Scrum teams, each focused on different features for the product, with close coordination of their efforts. Since one team does all the work (planning, analysis, programming, and test) for a complete customer-centric feature, Scrum teams are also known as *feature teams*.

The **ScrumMaster** helps the product group learn and apply Scrum to achieve business value. The ScrumMaster does whatever is in their power to help the team be successful. The ScrumMaster is not the manager of the team or a project manager; instead, the ScrumMaster serves the team, protects them from outside interference, and educates and guides the Product Owner and the team in the skillful use of Scrum. The ScrumMaster makes sure everyone on the team (including the Product Owner, and those in management) understands and follows the practices of Scrum, and they help lead the organization through the often difficult change required to achieve success with agile development. Since Scrum makes visible many impediments and threats to the team's and Product Owner's effectiveness, it is important to have an engaged ScrumMaster working energetically to help resolve those issues, or the team or Product Owner will find it difficult to succeed. Scrum teams should have a dedicated full-time ScrumMaster, although a smaller team might have a team member play this role (carrying a lighter load of regular work when they do so). Great ScrumMasters can come from any background or discipline: Engineering, Design, Testing, Product Management, Project Management, or Quality Management.

The ScrumMaster and the Product Owner cannot be the same individual; at times, the ScrumMaster may be called upon to push back on the Product Owner (for example, if they try to introduce new deliverables in the middle of a Sprint). And unlike a project manager, the ScrumMaster does not tell people what to do or assign tasks – they facilitate the process, supporting the team as it organizes and manages itself. If the ScrumMaster was previously in a position managing the team, they will need to significantly change their mindset and style of interaction for the team to be successful with Scrum. In the case that an ex-manager transitions to the role of ScrumMaster, it is best to serve a team other than the one that previously reported to the manager, otherwise the social or power dynamics are in potential conflict.

Note there is no role of project manager in Scrum. Sometimes an (ex-)project manager can step into the role of ScrumMaster, but this has a mixed record of success – there is a fundamental difference between the two roles, both in day-to-day responsibilities and in the mindset required to be successful. A good way to understand thoroughly the role of the ScrumMaster, and start to develop the core skills needed for success, is the Scrum Alliance's Certified ScrumMaster training.

In addition to these three roles, there are other contributors to the success of the product, including **managers**. While their role changes in Scrum, they remain valuable. For example:

- they support the team by respecting the rules and spirit of Scrum
- they help remove impediments that the team identifies
- they make their expertise and experience available to the team

In Scrum, these individuals replace the time they previously spent playing the role of "nanny" (assigning tasks, getting status reports, and other forms of micromanagement) with time as "guru" and "servant" of the team (mentoring, coaching, helping remove obstacles, helping problem-solve, providing creative input, and guiding the skills development of team members). In this shift, managers may need to change their management style; for example, using Socratic questioning to help the team discover the solution to a problem, rather than simply deciding a solution and assigning it to the team.

# STARTING SCRUM

The first step in Scrum is for the Product Owner to articulate the product vision. Eventually, this evolves into a refined and prioritized list of features called the **Product Backlog**. This backlog exists (and evolves) over the lifetime of the product; it is the product road map (Figure 12.2). At any point, the Product Backlog is the single, definitive view of "everything that could be done by the team ever, in order of priority". Only a single Product Backlog exists; this means the Product Owner is required to make prioritization decisions across the entire spectrum.

Figure 12.2  Product Backlog

| Item | Details (wiki URL) | Priority | Estimate of Value | Initial Estimate of Effort | New Estimates of Effort Remaining at end of Sprint... | | | | | |
|------|------|------|------|------|---|---|---|---|---|---|
| | | | | | 1 | 2 | 3 | 4 | 5 | 6 |
| As a buyer, I want to place a book in a shopping cart (see UI sketches on wiki page) | ... | 1 | 7 | 5 | | | | | | |
| As a buyer, I want to remove a book in a shopping cart | ... | 2 | 6 | 2 | | | | | | |
| Improve transaction processing performance (see target performance metrics on wiki) | ... | 3 | 6 | 13 | | | | | | |
| Investigate solutions for speeding up credit card validation (see target performance metrics on wiki) | ... | 4 | 6 | 20 | | | | | | |
| Upgrade all servers to Apache 2.2.3 | ... | 5 | 5 | 13 | | | | | | |
| Diagnose and fix the order processing script errors (bugzilla ID 14823) | ... | 6 | 2 | 3 | | | | | | |
| As a shopper, I want to create and save a wish list | ... | 7 | 7 | 40 | | | | | | |
| As a shopper, I want to to add or delete items on my wish list | ... | 8 | 4 | 20 | | | | | | |

The Product Backlog includes a variety of **items**, primarily new customer features ("enable all users to place book in shopping cart"), but also engineering improvement goals ("rework the transaction processing module to make it scalable"), exploratory or research work ("investigate solutions for speeding up credit card validation"), and, possibly, known defects ("diagnose and fix the order processing script errors"), if there are only a few problems. (A system with many defects usually has a separate defect tracking system.) Many people like to articulate the requirements in terms of "user stories" concise, clear descriptions of the functionality in terms of its value to the end user of the product.

The subset of the Product Backlog that is intended for the current release is known as the **Release Backlog**, and in general, this portion is the primary focus of the Product Owner.

The Product Backlog is continuously updated by the Product Owner to reflect changes in the needs of the customer, new ideas or insights, moves by the competition, technical hurdles that appear, and so forth. The team provides the Product Owner with estimates of the effort required for each item on the Product Backlog. In addition, the Product Owner is responsible for assigning a *business value estimate* to each individual item. This is usually an unfamiliar practice for a Product Owner. As such, it is something a ScrumMaster may help the Product Owner learn to do. With these two estimates (effort and value) and perhaps with additional risk estimates, the Product Owner prioritizes the backlog (actually, usually just the Release Backlog subset) to maximize ROI (choosing items of high value with low effort) or secondarily, to reduce some major risk. As will be seen, these effort and value estimates may be refreshed each Sprint as people learn; consequently, this is a continuous re-prioritization activity the Product Backlog is ever-evolving.

Scrum does not mandate the form of estimates in the Product Backlog, but it is common to use *relative estimates* expressed as "points" rather than absolute units of effort such as person-weeks.

Over time, a team tracks how many relative points they implement each Sprint; for example, averaging 26 points per Sprint. With this information they can project a release date to complete all features, or how many features can be completed by a fixed date.

The items in the Product Backlog can vary significantly in size or effort. Larger ones are broken into smaller items during the Product Backlog Refinement workshop or the Sprint Planning Meeting, and smaller ones may be consolidated.

One of the myths about Scrum is that it prevents you from writing detailed specifications; in reality, it is up to the Product Owner and Team to decide how much detail is required, and this will vary from one backlog item to the next, depending on the insight of the team, and other factors. State what is important in the least amount of space necessary – in other words, do not describe every possible detail of an item, just make clear what is necessary for it to be understood. Low priority items, far from being implemented and usually "coarse grained" or large, have less requirements details. High priority and fine-grained items that will soon be implemented tend to have more detail.

## SPRINT PLANNING

At the beginning of each Sprint, the **Sprint Planning Meeting** takes place. It is divided into two distinct sub-meetings, the first of which is called **Sprint Planning Part One**.

In Sprint Planning Part One, the Product Owner and Team (with facilitation from the ScrumMaster) review the high-priority items in the Product Backlog that the Product Owner is interested in implementing this Sprint. They discuss the goals and context for these high-priority items on the Product Backlog, providing the Team with insight into the Product Owner's thinking. The Product Owner and Team also review the "Definition of Done" that all items must meet, such as, "Done means coded to standards, reviewed, implemented with unit test-driven development (TDD), tested with 100 percent test automation, integrated, and documented." Part One focuses on understanding *what* the Product Owner wants. According to the rules of Scrum, at the end of Part One the (always busy) Product Owner may leave although they *must* be available (for example, by phone) during the next meeting. However, they are welcome to attend Part Two...

**Sprint Planning Part Two** focuses on detailed task planning for *how* to implement the items that the team decides to take on. The Team selects the items from the Product Backlog they commit to complete by the end of the Sprint, starting at the top of the Product Backlog (in others words, starting with the items that are the highest priority for the Product Owner) and working down the list in order. This is a key practice in Scrum: The team decides how much work they will commit to complete, rather than having it assigned to them by the Product Owner. This makes for a more reliable commitment because the team is making it based on their own analysis and planning, rather than having it "made" for them by someone else. While the Product Owner does not have control over how much the team commits to, he or she knows that the items the team is committing to are drawn from the top of the Product Backlog – in other words, the items that he or she has rated as most important. The team has the authority to also select items from further down the list; this usually happens when the team and Product Owner realize that something of lower priority fits easily and appropriately with the high priority items.

The Sprint Planning Meeting will often last a number of hours – the team is making a serious commitment to complete the work, and this commitment requires careful thought to be successful. The team will probably begin the Sprint Planning Part Two by estimating how much time each member has for Sprint-related work – in other words, their average workday minus the time they spend attending meetings, doing email, taking lunch breaks, and so on. For most people this works out to 4-6 hours of time per day available for Sprint-related work. See Figure 12.3.

Figure 12.3 hours
available calculation

| Sprint Length | 2 weeks |
|---|---|
| Workdays during Sprint | 8 days |

| Team Member | Available Days During Sprint* | Available Hours per Day | Total Available Hours |
|---|---|---|---|
| Tracy | 8 | 4 | 32 |
| Sanjay | 7 | 5 | 35 |
| Phillip | 8 | 4 | 32 |
| Jing | 6 | 5 | 30 |

\* Net of vacation and other days out of office

Once the time available is determined, the team starts with the first item on the Product Backlog – in other words, the Product Owner's highest priority item – and working together, breaks it down into individual tasks, which are recorded in a document called the **Sprint Backlog** (Figure 12.4). As mentioned, the Product Owner must be available during Part Two (such as via the phone) so that clarification is possible. The team will move sequentially down the Product Backlog in this way, until it's used up all its available hours. At the end of the meeting, the team will have produced a list of all the tasks with estimates (typically in hours or fractions of a day).

Scrum encourages multi-skilled workers, rather than only "working to job title" such as a "tester" only doing testing. In other words, team members "go to where the work is" and help out as possible. If there are many testing tasks, then all team members may help. This does not imply that everyone is a generalist; no doubt some people are especially skilled in testing (and so on) but team members work together and learn new skills from each other. Consequently, during task generation and estimation in Sprint Planning, it is not necessary – nor appropriate – for people to volunteer for all the tasks "they can do best." Rather, it is better to only volunteer for one task at a time, when it is time to pick up a new task, and to consider choosing tasks that will on purpose involve learning (perhaps by pair work with a specialist).

All that said, there are rare times when John may do a particular task because it would take far too long or be impossible for others to learn – perhaps John is the only person with any artistic skill to draw pictures. Other team members could not draw a "stick man" if their life depended on it. In this rare case – and if it is not rare and not getting rarer as the team learns, there is something wrong – it may be necessary to ask if the total planned drawing tasks that must be done by John are feasible within the short Sprint.

Many teams also make use of a visual task-tracking tool, in the form of a wall-sized task board where tasks (written on Post-It Notes) migrate during the Sprint across columns labeled "Not Yet Started," "In Progress," and "Completed." See Figure 12.5.

Figure 12.4 Sprint Backlog

| Product Backlog Item | Sprint Task | Volunteer | Initial Estimate of Effort | New Estimates of Effort Remaining at end of Day... | | | | | |
|---|---|---|---|---|---|---|---|---|---|
| | | | | 1 | 2 | 3 | 4 | 5 | 6 |
| As a buyer, I want to place a book in a shopping cart | modify database | | 5 | | | | | | |
| | create webpage (UI) | | 8 | | | | | | |
| | create webpage (Javascript logic) | | 13 | | | | | | |
| | write automated acceptance tests | | 13 | | | | | | |
| | update buyer help webpage | | 3 | | | | | | |
| | . . . | | | | | | | | |
| Improve transaction processing performance | merge DCP code and complete layer-level tests | | 5 | | | | | | |
| | complete machine order for pRank | | 8 | | | | | | |
| | change DCP and reader to use pRank http API | | 13 | | | | | | |

Figure 12.5 visual management with Sprint Backlog on cards; Daily Scrum

One of the pillars of Scrum is that once the Team makes its commitment, any additions or changes must be deferred until the next Sprint. This means that if halfway through the Sprint the Product Owner decides there is a new item he would like the team to work on, he cannot make the change until the start of the next Sprint. If an external circumstance appears that significantly changes priorities, and means the team would be wasting its time if it continued working, the Product Owner or the team can terminate the Sprint. The team stops, and a new Sprint Planning meeting initiates a new Sprint. The disruption of doing this is usually great; this serves as a disincentive for the Product Owner or team to resort to this dramatic decision.

There is a powerful, positive influence that comes from the team being protected from changing goals during the Sprint. First, the team gets to work knowing with absolute certainty that its commitments will not change, that reinforces the team's focus on ensuring completion. Second, it disciplines the Product Owner into really thinking through the items he or she prioritizes on the Product Backlog and offers to the team for the Sprint.

By following these Scrum rules the Product Owner gains two things. First, he or she has the confidence of knowing the team has made a commitment to complete a realistic and clear set of work they have chosen. Over time a team can become quite skilled at choosing and delivering on a realistic commitment. Second, the Product Owner gets to make whatever changes he or she likes to the Product Backlog before the start of the next Sprint. At that point, additions, deletions, modifications, and re-prioritizations are all possible and acceptable. While the Product Owner is not able to make changes to the selected items under development during the current Sprint, he or she is only one Sprint's duration or less away from making any changes they wish. Gone is the stigma around change – change of direction, change of requirements, or just plain changing your mind – and it may be for this reason that Product Owners are usually as enthusiastic about Scrum as anyone.

## DAILY SCRUM

Once the Sprint has started, the Team engages in another of the key Scrum practices: The **Daily Scrum**. This is a short (15 minutes or less) meeting that happens every workday at an appointed time. Everyone on the Team attends. To keep it brief, it is recommended that everyone remain standing. It is the team's opportunity to report to each other on progress and obstacles. In the Daily Scrum, one by one, each member of the team reports three (and only three) things *to the other members of the team*: (1) What they were able to get done since the last meeting; (2) what they are planning to finish by the next meeting; and (3) any blocks or impediments that are in their way. Note that the Daily Scrum is not a status meeting to report to a manager; it is a time for a self-organizing team to share with each other what is going on, to help them coordinate. Someone makes note of the blocks, and the ScrumMaster is responsible to help team members resolve them. There is no discussion during the Daily Scrum, only reporting answers to the three questions; if discussion is required it takes place immediately after the Daily Scrum in a follow-up meeting, although in Scrum no one is required to attend this. This follow-up meeting is a common event where the team adapts to the information they heard in the Daily Scrum: in other words, another inspect and adapt cycle. It is generally recommended not to have managers or others in positions of perceived authority attend the Daily Scrum. This risks making the team feel "monitored" – under pressure to report major progress every day (an unrealistic expectation), and inhibited about reporting problems – and it tends to undermine the team's self-management, and invite micromanagement. It would be more useful for a stakeholder to instead reach out to the team following the meeting, and offer to help remove any blocks that are slowing the team's progress.

# UPDATING SPRINT BACKLOG & SPRINT BURNDOWN CHART

Every day, the team members update their estimate of the amount of time remaining to complete their current task in the **Sprint Backlog** (Figure 12.6). Following this update, someone adds up the hours remaining for the team as a whole, and plots it on the **Sprint Burndown Chart** (Figure 12.7). This graph shows, each day, a new estimate of how much work (measured in person hours) remains until the team's tasks are finished. Ideally, this is a *downward* sloping graph that is on a trajectory to reach "zero effort remaining" by the last day of the Sprint. Hence it is called a *burndown* chart. And while sometimes it looks good, often it does not; this is the reality of product development. The important thing is that it shows the team their progress towards their goal, not in terms of how much time was *spent* in the past (an irrelevant fact in terms of *progress*), but in terms of how much work *remains in the future* – what separates the team from their goal. If the burndown line is not tracking downwards towards completion near the end of the Sprint, then the team needs to adjust, such as to reduce the scope of the work or to find a way to work more efficiently while still maintaining a sustainable pace.

While the Sprint Burndown chart can be created and displayed using a spreadsheet, many teams find it is more effective to show it on paper on a wall in their workspace, with updates in pen; this "low-tech/high-touch" solution is fast, simple, and often more visible than a computer chart.

Figure 12.6 new estimated remaining

| Product Backlog Item | Sprint Task | Volunteer | Initial Estimate of Effort | New Estimates of Effort Remaining at end of Day... | | | | | |
|---|---|---|---|---|---|---|---|---|---|
| | | | | 1 | 2 | 3 | 4 | 5 | 6 |
| As a buyer, I want to place a book in a shopping cart | modify database | Sanjay | 5 | 4 | 3 | 0 | 0 | 0 | |
| | create webpage (UI) | Jing | 3 | 3 | 3 | 2 | 0 | 0 | |
| | create webpage (Javascript logic) | Tracy & Sam | 2 | 2 | 2 | 2 | 1 | 0 | |
| | write automated acceptance tests | Sarah | 5 | 5 | 5 | 5 | 5 | 0 | |
| | update buyer help webpage | Sanjay & Jing | 3 | 3 | 3 | 3 | 3 | 0 | |
| | . . . | | | | | | | | |
| Improve transaction processing performance | merge DCP code and complete layer-level tests | | 5 | 5 | 5 | 5 | 5 | | |
| | complete machine order for pRank | | 3 | 3 | 8 | 8 | 8 | 8 | |
| | change DCP and reader to use pRank http API | | 5 | 5 | 5 | 5 | 5 | 5 | |
| . . . | . . . | . . . | | | | | | | |

Total (person hours)    50    49   48   44   43   34

Figure 12.7 Sprint
Burndown chart

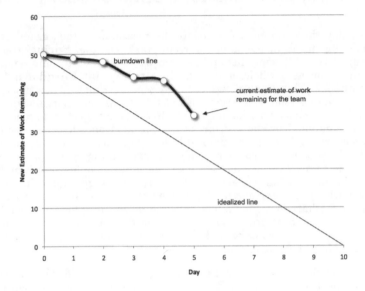

## PRODUCT BACKLOG REFINEMENT

One of the lesser known, but valuable, guidelines in Scrum is that five or ten percent of each Sprint must be dedicated by the team to refining (or "grooming") the Product Backlog. This includes detailed requirements analysis, splitting large items into smaller ones, estimation of new items, and re-estimation of existing items. Scrum is silent on how this work is done, but we suggest a focused workshop near the end of the Sprint, so that the team and Product Owner can dedicate themselves to this work without interruption. For a two-week Sprint, five percent of the duration implies that each Sprint there is a half-day Product Backlog Refinement workshop. This refinement activity is not for items selected for the current Sprint; it is for items for the future, most likely in the next one or two Sprints. With this practice, Sprint Planning becomes relatively simple because the Product Owner and Scrum Team start the planning with a clear, well-analyzed and carefully estimated set of items. A sign that this refinement workshop is not being done (or not being done well) is that Sprint Planning involves significant questions, discovery, or confusion.

## ENDING THE SPRINT

One of the core tenets of Scrum is that the duration of the Sprint is never extended – it ends on the assigned date regardless of whether the team has completed the work it committed to. Teams typically over-commit in their first few Sprints and fail to meet their objectives. They might then overcompensate and under-commit, and finish early. But by the third or fourth Sprint, teams typically have figured out what they are capable of delivering (most of the time), and they will meet their Sprint goals more reliably after that. Teams are encouraged to pick one duration for their Sprints (say, two weeks) and not change it. A consistent duration helps the team learn how much it can accomplish, which helps in both estimation and longer-term release planning. It also helps the team achieve a rhythm for their work; this is often referred to as the "heartbeat" of the team in Scrum.

## SPRINT REVIEW

After the Sprint ends, there is the **Sprint Review**, where the team reviews the Sprint with the Product Owner. This is often mislabeled the "demo" but that does not capture the real intent of this meeting. A key idea in Scrum is *inspect and adapt*. To see and learn what is going on and then evolve based on feedback, in repeating cycles. The Sprint Review is an inspect and adapt activity for the *product*. It is a time for the Product Owner to learn what is going on with the product and with the team (that is, a review of the Sprint); and for the team to learn what is going on with the Product Owner and the market. Consequently, the most important element of the Review is an in-depth *conversation* between the team and Product Owner to learn the situation, to get advice, and so forth. The review includes a demo of what the team built during the Sprint, but if the focus of the review is a demo rather than conversation, there is an imbalance.

A useful – but often overlooked – Scrum guideline is that the ScrumMaster is responsible for knowing the "Definition of Done" that was defined during Sprint Planning, and then during this meeting is responsible for telling the Product Owner if any of the items implemented by the team did not meet the definition. In this way, there is increased visibility regarding the quality of the work; teams cannot fake the quality by presenting software that appears to work well, but may be implemented with a messy pile of poor quality and untested code.

Present at this meeting are the Product Owner, Team members, and ScrumMaster, plus customers, stakeholders, experts, executives, and anyone else interested. The demo portion of the Sprint Review is not a "presentation" the team gives – there is no slideware. A guideline in Scrum is that no more than 30 minutes should be spent preparing for the demo, otherwise it suggests something is wrong with the work of the team. It is simply a demo of what has been built. Anyone present is free to ask questions and give input.

## SPRINT RETROSPECTIVE

The Sprint Review involves inspect and adapt regarding the *product*. The **Sprint Retrospective**, which follows the Review, involves inspect and adapt regarding the *process*. This is a practice that some teams skip, and that's unfortunate, because it's the main mechanism for taking the visibility that Scrum provides into areas of potential improvement, and turning it into results. It's an opportunity for the team to discuss what's working and what's not working, and agree on changes to try. The Team and ScrumMaster will attend, and the Product Owner is welcome but not required to attend. Sometimes the ScrumMaster can act as an effective facilitator for the retrospective, but it may be better to find a neutral outsider to facilitate the meeting; a good approach is for ScrumMasters to facilitate each others' retrospectives, which enables cross-pollination among teams.

A simple way to structure the Sprint Retrospective is to draw two columns on a whiteboard, labeled "What's Working Well" and "What Could Work Better" – and then go around the room, with each person adding one or more items to either list. As items are repeated, check marks are added next to them, so the common items become clear. Then the team looks for underlying causes, and agrees on a small number of changes to try in the upcoming Sprint, along with a commitment to review the results at the next Sprint Retrospective.

A useful practice at the end of the Retrospective is for the team to label each of the items in each column with either a "C" if it is *caused* by Scrum (in other words, without Scrum it would not be happening), or an "E" if it is *exposed* by Scrum (in other words, it would be happening with or without Scrum, but Scrum makes it known to the team), or a "U" if it's unrelated to Scrum (such as the weather). The team may find a lot of C's on the "What's Working Well" side of the board, and a lot of E's on the "What Could Work Better"; this is good news, even if the "What Could Work Better" list is a long one, because the first step to solving underlying issues is making them visible, and Scrum is a powerful catalyst for that.

## UPDATING RELEASE BACKLOG & BURNDOWN CHART

At this point, some items have been finished, some have been added, some have new estimates, and some have been dropped from the release goal. The Product Owner is responsible for ensuring that these changes are reflecting in the Release Backlog (and more broadly, the Product Backlog). See Figure 12.8. In addition, Scrum includes a **Release Burndown** chart that shows progress towards the release date (Figure 12.9). It is analogous to the Sprint Burndown chart, but is at the higher level of items (requirements) rather than fine-grained tasks. Since a new Product Owner is unlikely to know why or how to create this chart, this is another opportunity for a ScrumMaster to help the Product Owner.

Figure 12.8 new estimated remaining

| Item | Details (wiki URL) | Priority | Estimate of Value | Initial Estimate of Effort | New Estimates of Effort Remaining at end of Sprint... | | | | |
|---|---|---|---|---|---|---|---|---|---|
| | | | | | 1 | 2 | 3 | 4 | 5 |
| As a buyer, I want to place a book in a shopping cart (see UI sketches on wiki page) | ... | 1 | 7 | 5 | 0 | 0 | 0 | | |
| As a buyer, I want to remove a book in a shopping cart | ... | 2 | 6 | 2 | 0 | 0 | 0 | | |
| Improve transaction processing performance (see target performance metrics on wiki) | ... | 3 | 6 | 13 | 13 | 0 | 0 | | |
| Investigate solutions for speeding up credit card validation (see target performance metrics on wiki) | ... | 4 | 6 | 20 | 20 | 20 | 0 | | |
| Upgrade all servers to Apache 2.2.3 | ... | 5 | 5 | 13 | 13 | 13 | 13 | | |
| Diagnose and fix the order processing script errors (bugzilla ID 14823) | ... | 6 | 2 | 3 | 3 | 3 | 3 | | |
| As a shopper, I want to create and save a wish list | ... | 7 | 7 | 40 | 40 | 40 | 40 | | |
| As a shopper, I want to to add or delete items on my wish list | ... | 8 | 4 | 20 | 20 | 20 | 20 | | |
| ... | | | | | ... | ... | | | |
| | | | Total | 537 | 580 | 570 | 500 | | |

Figure 12.9 a Release Burndown chart

## STARTING THE NEXT SPRINT

Following the Sprint Review, the Product Owner may update the Product Backlog with any new insight. At this point, the Product Owner and team are ready to begin another Sprint cycle. There is no down time between Sprints – teams normally go from a Sprint Retrospective one afternoon into the next Sprint Planning the following morning (or after the weekend).

One of the principles of agile development is "sustainable pace," and only by working regular hours at a reasonable level can teams continue this cycle indefinitely.

## RELEASE SPRINT

The perfection vision of Scrum is that the product is potentially shippable at the end of each Sprint, which implies there is no wrap up work required, such as testing or documentation. Rather, the implication is that *everything* is completely *finished* every Sprint; that you could actually ship it or deploy it immediately after the Sprint Review.

However, many organizations have weak development practices and cannot achieve this perfection vision, or there are other extenuating circumstances (such as, "the machine broke"). In this case, there will be some remaining work, such as final production environment integration testing, and so there will be the need for a "Release Sprint" to handle this remaining work.

Note that the need for a Release Sprint is a sign of some weakness; the ideal is that it is not required. When necessary, Sprints continue until the Product Owner decides the product is almost ready for release, at which point there will be a Release Sprint to prepare for launch. If the team has followed good development practices, with continuous refactoring and integration, and effective testing during each Sprint, there should be little pre-release stabilization or other wrap-up work required.

## RELEASE PLANNING & INITIAL PRODUCT BACKLOG REFINEMENT

A question that is sometimes asked is how, in an iterative model, can long-term release planning be done. There are two cases to consider: (1) a new product in its first release, and (2) an existing product in a later release.

In the case of a new product, or *an existing product just adopting Scrum*, there is the need to do initial Product Backlog refinement before the first Sprint, where the Product Owner and team shape a proper Scrum Product Backlog. This could take a few days or a week, and involves a vision workshop, some detailed requirements analysis, and estimation of all the items identified for the first release.

Surprisingly in Scrum, in the case of an established product with an established Product Backlog, there should not be the need for any special or extensive release planning for the next release. Why? Because the Product Owner and team should be doing Product Backlog refinement every Sprint (five or ten percent of each Sprint), continuously preparing for the future. This *continuous product development mode* obviates the need for the dramatic punctuated prepare-execute-conclude stages one sees in traditional sequential life cycle development.

During an initial Product Backlog refinement workshop and during the continuous backlog refinement each Sprint, the Team and Product Owner will do release planning, refining the estimates, priorities, and content as they learn.

Some releases are date-driven; for example: "We will release version 2.0 of our project at a trade-show on November 10." In this situation, the team will complete as many Sprints (and build as many features) as is possible in the time available. Other products require certain features to be built before they can be called complete and the product will not launch until these requirements are satisfied, however long that takes. Since Scrum emphasizes producing potentially shippable code each Sprint, the Product Owner may choose to start doing interim releases, to allow the customer to reap the benefits of completed work sooner.

Since they cannot possibly know everything up front, the focus is on creating and refining a plan to give the release broad direction, and clarify how trade-off decisions will be made (scope versus schedule, for example). Think of this as the road map guiding you towards your final destination; which exact roads you take and the decisions you make during the journey may be determined en route.

Most Product Owners choose one release approach. For example, they will decide a release date, and will work with the team to estimate the Release Backlog items that can be completed by that date. In situations where a "fixed price / fixed date / fixed deliverable" commitment is required – for example, contract development – one or more of those parameters must have a built-in buffer to allow for uncertainty and change; in this respect, Scrum is no different from other approaches.

## APPLICATION OR PRODUCT FOCUS

For applications or products – either for the market or for internal use within an organization – Scrum moves groups away from the older *project-centric* model toward a *continuous application/product development* model. There is no longer a project with a beginning, middle, and end. And hence no traditional project manager. Rather, there is simply a stable Product Owner and a long-lived self-managing team that collaborate in an "endless" series of two- or four-week Sprints, until the product or application is retired. All necessary "project" management work is handled by the team and the business owner – who is an internal business customer or from Product Management. It is not managed by an IT manager or someone from a Project Management Office.

Scrum can also be used for true *projects* that are one-time initiatives (rather than work to create or evolve long-lived applications); still, in this case the team and Product Owner do the project management.

What if there is insufficient new work from one or more existing applications to warrant a dedicated long-lived team for each application? In this case, a stable long-lived team may take on items from one application in one Sprint, and then items from another in the next Sprint; in this situation the Sprints are often quite short, such as one week.

Occasionally, there is insufficient new work even for the prior solution, and the team may take on items from several applications during the same Sprint; however, beware this solution as it may devolve into unproductive multitasking across multiple applications. A basic productivity theme in Scrum is for the team to be *focused* on one product or application for one Sprint.

## COMMON CHALLENGES

Scrum is not only a concrete set of practices – rather, and more importantly, it is a framework that provides visibility to the team, and a mechanism that allows them to "inspect and adapt" accordingly. Scrum works by making visible the dysfunction and impediments that are impacting the Product Owner and the team's effectiveness, so that they can be addressed. For example, the Product Owner may not really know the market, the features, or how to estimate their relative business value. Or the team may be unskillful in effort estimation or development work.

The Scrum framework will quickly reveal these weaknesses. Scrum does not solve the problems of development; it makes them painfully visible, and provides a framework for people to explore ways to resolve problems in short cycles and with small improvement experiments.

Suppose the team fails to deliver what they committed to in the first Sprint due to poor task analysis and estimation skill. To the team, this feels like failure. But in reality, this experience is the necessary first step toward becoming more realistic and thoughtful about their commitments. This pattern – of Scrum helping make visible dysfunction, enabling the team to do something about it – is the basic mechanism that produces the most significant benefits that teams using Scrum experience.

One common mistake teams make, when presented with a Scrum practice that challenges them, is to change Scrum, not change themselves. For example, teams that have trouble delivering on their Sprint commitment might decide to make the Sprint duration extendable, so they never run out of time – and in the process, ensure they never have to learn how to do a better job of estimating and managing their time. In this way, without coaching and the support of an experienced ScrumMaster, organizations can mutate Scrum into just a mirror image of its own weaknesses and dysfunction, and undermine the real benefit that Scrum offers: Making visible the good and the bad, and giving the organization the choice of elevating itself to a higher level.

Another common mistake is to assume that a practice is discouraged or prohibited just because Scrum does not specifically require it. For example, Scrum does not require the Product Owner to set a long-term strategy for his or her product; nor does it require engineers to seek advice from more experienced engineers about complex technical problems. Scrum leaves it to the individuals involved to make the right decision; and in most cases, both of these practices (along with many others) are well advised.

Something else to be wary of is managers imposing Scrum on their teams; Scrum is about giving a team space and tools to manage themselves, and having this dictated from above is not a recipe for success. A better approach might begin with a team learning about Scrum from a peer or manager, getting comprehensively educated in professional training, and then making a decision as a team to follow the practices faithfully for a defined period; at the end of that period, the team will evaluate its experience, and decide whether to continue.

The good news is that while the first Sprint is usually very challenging to the team, the benefits of Scrum tend to be visible by the end of it, leading many new Scrum teams to exclaim: "Scrum is hard, but it sure is a whole lot better than what we were doing before!"

## RESULTS FROM SCRUM

The benefits of Scrum reported by teams come in various aspects of their experience. At Yahoo!, we migrated nearly 200 teams to Scrum over three years, totaling over 2000 people. These have ranged from consumer-facing, design-heavy websites such as Yahoo! Photos, to the mission-critical back-end infrastructure of services such as Yahoo! Mail, which serves hundreds of millions of customers.

Several times each year we surveyed everyone at Yahoo! using Scrum (including Product Owners, Team Members, ScrumMasters, and the functional managers of those individuals) and ask them to compare Scrum to the approach they were using previously. Some summary data is presented here:

- **Productivity**: 68% of respondents reported Scrum is better or much better (4 or 5 on a 5-point scale); 5% reported Scrum is worse or much worse (1 or 2 on a 5-point scale); 27% reported Scrum is about the same (3 on a 5-point scale).

- **Team Morale**: 52% of respondents reported Scrum is better or much better; 9% reported Scrum is worse or much worse; 39% reported Scrum is about the same.

- **Adaptability**: 63% of respondents reported Scrum is better or much better; 4% reported Scrum is worse or much worse; 33% reported Scrum is about the same.

- **Accountability**: 62% of respondents reported Scrum is better or much better; 6% reported Scrum is worse or much worse; 32% reported Scrum is about the same.

- **Collaboration and Cooperation**: 81% of respondents reported Scrum is better or much better; 1% reported Scrum is worse or much worse; 18% reported Scrum about the same.

- Team productivity increased an average of 36%, based on the estimates of the Product Owners.

- 85% of team-members stated that they would continue using Scrum if the decision were solely up to them (15% said either "No" or "Undecided").

## RECOMMENDED READINGS

- The first book on Scrum was *Agile Software Development with Scrum* (Schwaber and Beedle) and this is well worth study. It highlights aspects of Scrum—such as the relationship to complex adaptive systems—that are not always emphasized but are important.

- *Agile Project Management with Scrum* (Schwaber) is valuable; it includes significant discussion on the role of a ScrumMaster.

# RECOMMENDED READINGS

## Systems Thinking

•W. Edwards Deming's *Out of the Crisis* is a master work by arguably the most well-known systems thinker and quality expert. It opens with the modest goal, "The aim of this book is transformation of the style of American management… It requires a whole new structure, from foundation upward." Deming also advocates the *System of Profound Knowledge* in which managers (1) appreciate there is a *system*, (2) understand common-cause and special-cause variation (queueing theory is related to variation), (3) understand limitations of knowledge and reasoning mistakes, and (4) know credible psychology and social research results so that behavior- or motivation-related policies are *not* based on "common sense." The core of the book centers around his famous *14 Points for Management*, including (for example), "*Eliminate management by objective. Eliminate management by numbers, numerical goals. Substitute leadership.*"

•Jay Forrester's *Industrial Dynamics* is the classic text on system dynamics—well written and insightful. Although written in the early 1960s, it is as relevant today as when published. It goes beyond cause-effect modeling to also model the flow and inventories of information, money, and material in systems. The book includes formal mathematical modeling but this is not obligatory to appreciate system dynamics.

•Weinberg's *Quality Software Management: Systems Thinking* and *An Introduction to General Systems Thinking* are worthwhile. Written from the perspective of an experienced consultant in systems development.

•Senge's *The Fifth Discipline* is a classic that advocates the need for leadership to apply systems thinking (it is the *fifth* discipline) and other key disciplines for a great, sustainable enterpise. The others include leaders with (1) personal mastery and (2) reflection on their beliefs and faulty reasoning, the (3) definition and communication of a meaningful shared vision, and (4) the ability of teams to learn. We recommend ignoring—at least during the first few years of practice—the 'archetypes' notion presented in the book. It was well meant as a learning aid but has been observed to distract and intimidate people from learning and applying basic system dynamics modeling. The 'archetypes' are not part of original system dynamics.

•*The Fifth Discipline Fieldbook* is an in-depth resource, written from the viewpoint of many practitioners and consultants.

•The organizational-learning writings from Argyris, Putnam, McLain, and Schön. Important concepts include d*ouble-loop learning* and *high-advocacy/high-inquiry dialogue*. Classic works include *Action Science* and *Organizational Learning*.

•The publications and resources available through the *Society for Organizational Learning* (www.solonline.org).

## Lean Thinking

•Dr. Jeffrey Liker's *The Toyota Way* is a thorough cogent summary from a researcher who has spent decades studying Toyota and their principles and practices.

•*Inside the Mind of Toyota* by Professor Satoshi Hino. Hino spent many years working in product development, followed by an academic career. Hino has "spent more than 20 years researching the subject of this book." This is a data-driven book that looks at the evolution and principles of the original lean thinking management system.

•*Extreme Toyota* by Osono, Shimizu, and Takeuchi is a well-researched analysis of the Toyota Way values, contradictions, and culture, based on six years of research and 220 interviews. It includes an in-depth analysis of Toyota's strong business performance. Hirotaka Takeuchi was also co-author of the famous 1986 Harvard Business Review article "The New New Product Development Game" that introduced key ideas of Scrum.

•*Lean Product and Process Development* by Allen Ward and *The Toyota Product Development System* by Liker and Morgan are useful for insights into development from a lean perspective.

•*Toyota Culture* by Liker and Michael Hoseus. Hoseus has worked both as a plant manager and HR manager at Toyota, bringing an insider's in-depth understanding to this book on the heart of what makes a lean enterprise work.

•*Lean Thinking* by Drs. Womack and Jones is an entertaining and well-written summary of some lean principles by authors who know their subject well. As cautioned earlier in this chapter it presents an anecdotal and condensed view that may give the casual reader the wrong impression that the essential key of lean is waste reduction rather than a culture of manager-teachers who understand lean thinking and help build the pillars of respect for people and continuous improvement with Go See and other behaviors.

•*The Machine That Changed the World: The Story of Lean Production* by Womack, Jones, and Roos was based on a five-year study at MIT into lean and the Toyota system.

•*Workplace Management* by Taichii Ohno is a short book by the creator of the Toyota Production System. It was out-of-print but has been recently re-translated by Jon Miller and is now available. The book does not talk much about TPS but it contains a series of short chapters that show well how Taichii Ohno thought about management and lean systems.

•Mary and Tom Poppendieck's books *Lean Software Development* and *Implementing Lean Software Development* are well-written books that make important connections between lean thinking, systems thinking, and agile development.

## Queueing Theory

•*Managing the Design Factory* by Don Reinertsen is a classic introduction on queueing theory and development. Reinertsen has a broad and deep grasp of both product development and business economics and weaves these insights together into one of our favorite books on product development. This is the book that popularized the model of *thinking tools* for process improvement and organizational change.

•*Flexible Product Development* by Preston Smith was the first widely-popular general product development book that introduced agile software development concepts—including Scrum and Extreme Programming—to a broader audience. This text includes an analysis of queueing theory and variability, and their relationship to development.

## False Dichotomies

### *Be* Agile

•*Agile Software Development* by Alistair Cockburn. Emphasizes the principles and theory underlying agile methods, with a special focus on communication.

•*Agile Software Development with Scrum* (Schwaber and Beedle) and *Agile Project Manage-*

*ment with Scrum* (Schwaber) both explore how to *be* agile.

•*Agile & Iterative Development: A Manager's Guide* (Larman) summarizes the key ideas and introduces Scrum, Extreme Programming, and older iterative methods such as Evo.

•*Extreme Programming Explained: Embrace Change* (2E) by Kent Beck with Cynthia Andres. Although both Scrum and the DSDM agile methods predate XP, this is the book and Beck is the person that really kicked off the widespread popularity of agile development. Beck credits his 1980s co-worker Ward Cunningham with making seminal agile contributions. Beck and Cunningham are also noteworthy for having introduced the idea of *design patterns* to the software community [BC88], and Cunningham created the widely popular *wiki* concept and technology that is used for Wikipedia (www.wikipedia.org) and within many companies applying agile methods.

## Feature Teams

•*Dynamics of Software Development* by Jim McCarthy. Originally published in 1995 but republished in 2008. Jim's book is a true classic on software development. Already in 1995 it emphasized feature teams. The rest of the book is stuffed with insightful tips related to software development.

•"XP and Large Distributed Software Projects" by Karlsson and Andersson. This early large-scale agile development article is published in *Extreme Programming Perspectives*. It is a insightful and much under-appreciated article describing the strong relationship between feature teams and continuous integration.

•"How Do Committees Invent?" by Mel Conway. This 40-year article is as insightful today as it was 40 years ago. It is available via the authors website at www.melconway.com.

•*Agile Software Development in the Large* by Jutta Eckstein. This is the first book published on the topic of scaling agile development. It describes the experience of a medium-sized (around 100 people) project and stresses the importance of feature teams in large-scale development.

•"Promiscuous Pairing and Beginner's Mind" by Arlo Belshee. This article is not directly related to feature teams or large-scale development but it does contain some fascinating experiments that question some of the assumptions behind specialization.

## Teams

•*Leading Teams*, by Richard Hackman. Harvard professor Richard Hackman is a long-time team researcher. His book is currently our favorite team-related book. It has a strong focus on helping management in their change to team-based work.

•*Leading Self-Directed Work Teams*, by Kimball Fisher. This book has a strong focus on the change in role when one becomes a team leader of a self-directed team.

•*The Project Manager's Bridge to Agility*, by Michele Sliger and Stacia Broderick. Michele and Stacia are two Scrum Trainers and also PMI-certified PMPs. Traditional project managers will find here an explanation of the difference in thinking from a PMI PMBOK perspective. When reading it, please read their "agile project manager" as ScrumMaster.

•*The Wisdom of Teams*, by Jon Katzenbach and Douglas Smith. This is probably the most popular team reference and certainly worth reading.

•*The Five Dysfunctions of a Team*, by Patrick Lencioni. Written like a novel, it covers well the need for conflict in teams.

•*Fast Cycle Time*, by Chris Meyer. Recently republished (2007), this is a true classic on product development and talks about cross-functional (multifunctional) teams in detail.

•*Revolutionizing Product Development*, by Steven Wheelwright and Kim Clark. Another classic in product development literature; has one chapter on cross-functional integration.

•*Software for Your Head*, by Jim and Michele McCarthy. Jim and Michele spent years in 'boot camps' to find the most efficient ways for teams to work. They documented this as a set of protocols in this book.

•*Peopleware*, by Tom DeMarco and Tim Lister. This classic on the importance of people in software development also has a couple of chapters focusing on teams.

# Requirement Areas

## Organization

•*Work Redesign*, by Richard Hackman. A book written in 1980s and mainly focused on administration and factory work. But the ideas in this book are as insightful today as they were thirty years ago. In the last part, Hackman made predictions about the future of work that are surprisingly accurate.

•*One More Time: How Do You Motivate Employees?* by Frederick Herzberg. The first part of this classic article is about motivation and the hygiene/motivator theory. The last part looks at work redesign from a slightly different angle than that of Hackman.

•*Communities of Practice: The Organizational Frontier*, by Etienne Wenger and William Snyder. This is a *Harvard Business Review* article and is a short and easy-to-read introduction to the concept of CoP.

•*Cultivating Communities of Practice* by Etienne Wenger, Richard Dermott, and William Snyder. What, why, and how? These questions are answered with lots of practical examples.

•*Six Dangerous Myths About Pay*, by Jeffrey Pfeffer. This short article not only covers the pay-per-performance myth, but also several other pay-related myths.

•*Punished by Rewards*, by Alfie Kohn. Are incentive systems the only reward-related problem or is more going on? Kohn takes a deep dive in the subject of rewarding at work and in the classroom. This analysis challenges some fundamental assumptions behind rewarding.

•*Abolishing Performance Appraisals*, by Tom Coens and Mary Jenkins. Are performance appraisals rooted in good insight, credible organizational research, and evidence? This analysis concludes that no evidence exists that they work and that the assumptions behind performance appraisals are shaky at best.

•*Measuring and Managing Performance in Organizations*, by Rob Austin. What happens if you give incentives but are not able to measure all the workers' output? This is one of the questions Rob Austin tries to answer in his book. His model shows that *measurement dysfunctions* are the outcome, ironically resulting in *poorer* performance.

•*Maverick*, by Richardo Semler. Semco, a Brazilian company from São Paolo has gradually *freed* its employees. Once a fairly traditional company, Semco went through a major change and became one the most studied companies in the world because of their innovative HR practices. *Maverick* describes this change.

•*Birth of the Chaordic Age*, by Dee Hock. "Self-management cannot happen in traditional industries such as banking." Not so. Dee Hock is the founder of Visa and describes how it was build on the principles of self-organization.

•*Business Without Bosses*, by Charles Manz and Henry Sims. What would happen without managers? Would there be total chaos? Not at W. L. Gore. They practice 'unmanagement' and do not have an organization chart at all. Chapter 6 of *Business Without Bosses* describes how W. L. Gore operates.

•*The Google Story*, by David Vise. One of the most successful companies of the last decade: Google. This book describes the history of Google and some of the interesting practices within Google. It is a little superficial, but still worth reading.

•*The Future of Management*, by Gary Hamel. "What will be the future role of management?" is the key question in Hamel's book. Chapters 4–6 study three companies with innovative organizational practices: Whole Foods Market, W. L. Gore, and Google.

## Large-Scale Scrum

## Scrum Primer

•The first book on Scrum was *Agile Software Development with Scrum* (Schwaber and Beedle) and this is well worth study. It highlights aspects of Scrum—such as the relationship to complex adaptive systems—that are not always emphasized but are important.

•*Agile Project Management with Scrum* (Schwaber) is valuable; it includes significant discussion on the role of a ScrumMaster.

# BIBLIOGRAPHY

AB07  Ancona, D., Bresman, H. 2007. *X-Teams: How to Build Teams That Lead, Innovate and Succeed*. Harvard Business School Press

Ambler03  Ambler, S., 2003. "Isn't That Special?" *Dr. Dobbs Journal*, Jan. 2003

AMNS96  Adler, P., Mandelbaum, A., Nguyen, V., Schwerer, E., 1996. "Getting the Most Out of Your Product Development Process," *Harvard Business Review*, Mar–Apr 1996

Ancona05  Ancona, D., 2005. *Leadership in an Age of Uncertainty*, at http://sloanleadership.mit.edu/pdf/LeadershipinanAgeofUncertainty-researchbrief.pdf

Anderson07  Anderson, D., 2007. "Kanban in Action," *Agile Management Blog*, at http://www.agilemanagement.net/Articles/Weblog/KanbaninAction.html

APS85  Argyris, C., Putnam, R., Smith, D. 1985. *Action Science*. Jossey-Bass

AS95  Argyris, C., Schon, D. 1995. *Organizational Learning II: Theory, Method, and Practice*. Prentice Hall

Austin96  Austin, R., 1996. *Measuring and Managing Performance in Organizations*, Dorset House

BA03  Berczuk, S., Appleton, B., 2003. *Software Configuration Management Patterns*, Addison-Wesley

Baker95  Baker, B., 1995. "On Finding Duplication and Near-Duplication in Large Software Systems," *Proceedings of the Working Conference on Reverse Engineering*, 1995

BC88  Beck, K., Cunningham, W., 1988. "Using Pattern Languages for Object-Oriented Programs," *Conference Proceedings: OOPSLA 1987*, ACM

BC04  Beer, M., Cannon, M., 2004. *Promise and Peril in Implementing Pay for Performance*, HBR Working paper, at http://www.hbs.edu/research/facpubs/workingpapers/abstracts/0102/02-064.html

BCHW94  Bowen, K., Clark, K., Holloway, C., Wheelwright, S., 1994. "Development Projects: The Engine of Renewal," *Harvard Business Review*, Sep 1, 1994, also in [CW95]

Beck99  Beck, K., 1999. *Extreme Programming Explained: Embrace Change (1st edition)*, Addison-Wesley

Beck04  Beck, K., with Andres, C., 2004. *Extreme Programming Explained: Embrace Change (2nd edition)*, Addison-Wesley

Belshee05a  Belshee, A., 2005. "Promiscuous Pairing and Beginner's Mind," *Proceedings of Agile 2005 Conference*

Belshee05b | Belshee A., 2005. "Promiscuous Pairing and the Least Qualified Implementer," *Agile Toolkit Podcast*, at http://agiletoolkit.libsyn.com/index.php?post_id=15636

BF00 | Beck, K., Fowler, M., 2000. *Planning Extreme Programming*, Addison-Wesley

Blaumer64 | Blaumer, R., 1964. *Alienation and Freedom*, University of Chicago Press

Boehm00 | Boehm, B., 2000. *Software Cost Estimation with Cocomo II*, Prentice Hall

Bogsnes09 | Bogsnes, B., 2009. *Implementing Beyond Budgeting*, John Wiley

Brooks75 | Brooks, F., 1975. *The Mythical Man-Month*. Addison-Wesley

Brooks95 | Brooks, F., 1995. *The Mythical Man-Month: Essays on Software Engineering (2nd Edition)*, Addison-Wesley

BT03 | Boehm, B., Turner, R., 2003. *Balancing Agility and Discipline: A Guide for the Perplexed*, Addison-Wesley

CEK01 | Cooper, R., Edgett, S., Kleinschmidt, E., *Portfolio Management for New Products*, Basic Books

CF91 | Clark, K., Fujimoto, T. 1991. *Product Development Performance*, Harvard Business School Press

Christensen03 | Christensen, C., 2003. *The Innovators Dilemma*, Collins Business

CJ02 | Coens, T., Jenkins, M., 2002. *Abolishing Performance Appraisals*, Berrett-Koehler

Cockburn01 | Cockburn, A., 2001. *Agile Software Development*, Addison-Wesley

Cockburn04 | Cockburn, A., 2004. *Crystal Clear: A Human-Powered Methodology for Small Teams*, Addison-Wesley

CK08 | Cohn, M., Keith, C., 2008. "How to Fail with Agile: 20 Tips to Help You Avoid Success," *Better Software Magazine*. Jul–Aug 2008

Conway68 | Conway, M., 1968. "How Do Committees Invent?" *Datamation Magazine*, Apr 1968

Cooper01 | Cooper, R., 2001. *Winning at New Products: Accelerating the Process from Idea to Launch*, Basic Books

Cooper07 | Cooper, R., "Winning at New Products: Pathways to Profitable Innovation," *Stage-gate Product Innovation Papers Reference #22*, at http://www.stage-gate.com/knowledge.php

Cooper08 | Cooper, R., "The Stage-Gate Idea-to-Launch Process — Update, What's New and NexGen Systems," *Stage-gate Product Innovation Papers Reference #30*, at http://www.stage-gate.com/knowledge.php

Covey04 | Covey, S., 2004. *The 8th Habit: From Effectiveness to Greatness*, Free Press

Crosby84 | Crosby, P., 1984. *Quality Without Tears*, McGraw-Hill

CS95 | Cusumano, M., Selby, W., 1995. *Microsoft Secrets*, Simon & Schuster

CW92 | Clark, K., Wheelright S., 1992. *Revolutionizing Product Development*, Harvard Business School Press

CW95    Clark, K., Wheelwright, S., 1995. *The Product Development Challenge*, Harvard Business School Press

Davis97    Davis, M., 1997. *Game Theory: A Nontechnical Introduction*, Dover Publications

Deming67    Deming, W. E., 1967. "Walter A. Shewhart, 1891-1967," *The American Statistician*, Apr 1967

Deming82    Deming E. W., 1982. *Out of the Crisis*, MIT Press

Deming94    Deming, E. W., 1994. *The New Economics*, MIT Press

DeMarco01    DeMarco, T., 2001. *Slack*. Random House

DeMarco08    DeMarco, T., 2008. *Adrenaline Junkies and Template Zombies: Understanding Patterns of Project Behavior*, Dorset House

Derby07a    Derby, E., 2007. "Should a ScrumMaster Give Performance Appraisals?" *Scrum Alliance Articles*, at http://www.scrumalliance.org/articles/8-should-a-scrummaster-give-performance-appraisals

Derby07b    Derby, E., 2007. "Performance Without Appraisal," *Scrum Alliance Articles*, at http://www.scrumalliance.org/articles/50-performance-without-appraisal

DL77    Davis, S., Lawrence, P., 1977. *Matrix*, Addison-Wesley

DL99    DeMarco, T., Lister, T., 1999. *Peopleware: Productive Projects and Teams*, Dorset House

Drucker92    Drucker, P., 1992. "Planning for Uncertainty," *The Wall Street Journal*, Jul 22 1992

Eckstein04    Eckstein, J., 2004. *Agile Software Development in the Large*, Dorset House

Eckstein09    Eckstein, J., 2009. *Agile in the Face of Global Software Development*, Draft

Fisher99    Fisher, K., 1999. *Leading Self-Directed Work Teams*, McGraw-Hill

Forrester58    Forrester, J. W., 1958. "Industrial Dynamics—A Major Breakthrough for Decision Makers," *Harvard Business Review*, Volume 36, Number 4

Forrester61    Forrester J. W., 1961. *Industrial Dynamics*, Pegasus Communications

Fowler03    Fowler, M., 2003. "Cannot Measure Productivity," at http://martinfowler.com/bliki/CannotMeasureProductivity.html

FPE05    Franklin, G., Powell, J. D., Emami-Naeini, A., 2005. *Feedback Control of Dynamic Systems*, Prentice Hall

Friedman06    Friedman, T., 2006, *The World is Flat*, Farrar, Straus and Giroux

Fujimoto99    Fujimoto, T., 1999. *The Evolution of a Manufacturing System at Toyota*, Productivity Press

Galbraith93    Galbraith, J., 1993. *Competing with Flexible Lateral Organizations*, Addison-Wesley

George02    George, M., 2002. *Lean Six Sigma: Combining Six Sigma Quality with Lean Production Speed*, McGraw-Hill

GH98    Gross, D., Harris, C. M., 1998. *Fundamentals of Queueing Theory*, Wiley-Interscience

Goldratt84    Goldratt, E. M., 1985. *The Goal*, North River Press

Goldratt97    Goldratt, E. M., 1997. *Critical Chain*, Gower

Hackman02    Hackman, R., 2002. *Leading Teams*, Harvard Business School Press

Hamel06    Hamel, G., 2006, "The Why, What and How of Management Innovation," *Harvard Business Review*, Feb 2006

Hamel07    Hamel, G., 2007. *The Future of Management*, Harvard Business School Press

Hayashi08    Hayashi, N., 2008. "Top Engineer Explains How Toyota Develops People," *Nikkei Business Online*, Translated at http://www.gembapantarei.com/2008/08/toyotas_top_engineer_on_how_to_develop_thinking_pe.html

Herzberg87    Herzberg, F., 1987. "One More Time: How Do You Motivate Employees?" *Harvard Business Review*, Sep–Oct 1987

HF03    Hope, J., and Fraser, R., 2003. *Beyond Budgeting: How Managers Can Break Free from the Annual Performance Trap*, Harvard Business School Press

HGG00    Holland, S., Gaston, K., Gomes, J. 2000. "Critical Success Factors for Cross-Functional Teamwork in New Product Development," *International Journal of Management Reviews*, Volume 2, Issue 3, 2000

Highsmith02    Highsmith, J. 2002. *Agile Software Development Ecosystems*. Addison-Wesley

Highsmith04    Highsmith, J. 2004. *Agile Project Management: Creating Innovative Products*, Addison-Wesley

Hino06    Hino, S., 2006. *Inside the Mind of Toyota: Management Principles for Enduring Growth*, Productivity Press

Hirenabe07    Hirenabe, K., 2008. "Visualizing Agile Projects using Kanban Boards," InfoQ Articles, at http://www.infoq.com/articles/agile-kanban-boards

Hirenabe08    Hirenabe, K., 2008. "Kanban Applied to Software Development: from Agile to Lean," *InfoQ Articles*, at http://www.infoq.com/articles/hiranabe-lean-agile-kanban

HKL93    Henke, J., Krachenberg, R., Lyons, T., 1993. "Cross-Functional Teams: Good Concept, Poor Implementation!" *Journal of Product Innovation Management*, Volume 10

HLC85    Hayes, R., Lorenz, C., Clark, K., 1985. *The Uneasy Alliance: Managing the Productivity-Technology Dilemma*, Harvard Business School Press

HO80    Hackman, R., Oldman, G., 1980. *Work Redesign*, Prentice Hall

Hock99    Hock, D., 1999. *The Birth of the Chaordic Age*, Berrett-Koehler Publishers

HS08    Hopp, W., Spearman, M., 2008. *Factory Physics*, McGraw-Hill

Imai86    Imai, M., 1986. *Kaizen: The Key To Japan's Competitive Success*, McGraw-Hill

| Ishikawa85 | Ishikawa, K., 1985. *What Is Total Quality Control? The Japanese Way*, Prentice Hall |

Ishikawa85   Ishikawa, K., 1985. *What Is Total Quality Control? The Japanese Way*, Prentice Hall

Ishikawa86   Ishikawa, K., 1986. *Guide to Quality Control*, Asian Productivity Organization

JAH00   Jeffries, R., Anderson, A., Hendrickson, C., 2000. *Extreme Programming Installed*, Addison-Wesley

Jensen96   Jensen, R., 1996. "Management Impact on Software Cost and Schedule," *CrossTalk The Journal of Defense Software Engineering*, July 1996

Johnson02   Johnson, J., 2002. "Keynote speech," *Extreme Programming 2002 Conference*

Jones01   Jones, C., 2001. *Software Assessments, Benchmarks, and Best Practices*, Addison-Wesley

Jones08   Jones, C., 2008. *Applied Software Measurement*, McGraw-Hill

KAL00   Karlsson, E., Andersson, L., Leion, P., 2000. "Daily Build and Feature Development in Large Distributed Projects," *Proceedings of the 2000 International Conference on Software Engineering*

KA01   Karlsson, E., Andersson, L., 2001. "XP and Large Distributed Software Projects," *Extreme Programming Examined*, Addison-Wesley

Kahn05   Kahn, K., 2005. *The PDMA Handbook of New Product Development*, John Wiley

Kato06   Kato, I., 2006. *Summary Notes from Art Smalley Interview with Mr. Isao Kato*, at http://artoflean.com/documents/pdfs/Mr_Kato_Interview_on_TWI_and_TPS.pdf

Katz82   Katz, R., 1982. "The Effects of Group Longevity on Project Communication and Performance," *Administrative Science Quarterly*, Volume 27, Mar 1982

Katzenbach98   Katzenback, J., 1998. *Teams At the Top*, Harvard Business School Press

Keith08   Keith, C., 2008, "Agile Game Development," *Agile 2008 Conference Talk*

Kerth01   Kerth, N., 2001. *Project Retrospectives: A Handbook for Team Reviews*, Dorset House

KLTFB07   Kaner, S., Lind, L., Toldi, C., Fisk, S., Berger, D., 2007. *Facilitator's Guide to Participatory Decision-Making*, Jossey-Bass

Kohn93   Kohn, A., 1993. *Punished by Rewards*, Houghton Mifflin

Krebs08   Krebs, J., 2008. *Agile Portfolio Management*, Microsoft Press

KS93   Katzenbach, J., Smith, D., 1993. *The Wisdom of Teams*, Harper Collins

KS01   Katzenback, J., Smith, D., 2001. *The Discipline of Teams*, John Wiley & Sons

Lacey06   Lacey, M., 2006. "Adventures in Promiscuous Pairing: Seeking Beginner's Mind," *Proceedings of Agile 2006 Conference*

Larman03   Larman, C., 2003. *Agile and Iterative Development: A Manager's Guide*, Addison-Wesley

| | |
|---|---|
| Laukkanen06 | Laukkanen, P., 2006. *Data-Driven and Keyword-Driven Test Automation Frameworks*. Helsinki University of Technology, Master's Thesis, at http://code.google.com/p/robotframework/ |
| LB03 | Larman, C., Basili, V., 2003. "Iterative and Incremental Development: A Brief History," *IEEE Computer*, June 2003 |
| Leffingwell07 | Leffingwell, D. 2007. *Scaling Software Agility*, Addison-Wesley |
| Lencioni02 | Lencioni, P., 2002. *The Five Dysfunctions of a Team: A Leadership Fable*, Jossey-Bass |
| Levitt60 | Levitt, T., 1960. "Marketing Myopia," *Harvard Business Review*, July– Aug 1960 |
| LH08 | Liker, J., Hoseus, M., 2008. *Toyota Culture: The Heart and Soul of the Toyota Way*, McGraw-Hill |
| Liker04 | Liker, J., 2004. *The Toyota Way*, McGraw-Hill |
| LM06a | Liker, J., Meier, D., 2006. *The Toyota Way Fieldbook*, McGraw-Hill |
| LM06b | Liker, J., Morgan J., 2006. *The Toyota Product Development System*, Productivity Press |
| LM07 | Liker, J., Meier, D., 2007. *Toyota Talent*, McGraw Hill |
| Lopp07 | Lopp, M., 2007, *Managing Humans*, Apress |
| Malone05 | Malone, T., 2005. *The Future of Work*, Harvard Business School Press, |
| Mason05 | Mason, M., 2005. *Pragmatic Version Control with Subversion*, The Pragmatic Programmers |
| McCarthy95 | McCarthy, J., 1995. *Dynamics of Software Development*, Microsoft Press |
| McGrath96 | McGrath, M., 1996. *Setting the PACE in Product Development*, Butterworth-Heinemann |
| McGrath04 | McGrath, M., 2004. *Next Generation Product Development: How to Increase Productivity, Cut Costs, and Reduce Cycle Times*, McGraw-Hill |
| MCM95 | Mohrman, S., Cohen, S., Mohrman, A., 1995. *Designing Team-Based Organizations*, Jossey-Bass |
| Meyer93 | Meyer, C., 1993. *Fast Cycle Time: How to Align Purpose, Strategy, and Structure for Speed*, Free Press |
| MJ05 | Moløkken-Østvold, K., and Jørgensen, M., 2005. "A Comparison of Software Project Overruns—Flexible versus Sequential Development Models". *IEEE Transactions on Software Engineering*. Volume 31, Number 9, Sept |
| MM02 | McCarthy, J., McCarthy, M., 2002. *Software For Your Head: Core Protocols for Creating and Maintaining Shared Vision*, Addison-Wesley |
| MS95 | Manz, C., Sims, H., 1995. *Business Without Bosses*, Wiley |

Mugge04     Mugge, P., 2004. *Integrated Product Development: IBM's model for managing innovation*, presentation at Program Manager Forum, at http://www.pmi-portland.org/DocumentLibrary/events/meetings/meeting_pdfs/mugge.pdf

NT86        Nonaka, I., Takeuchi, H., 1986. "The New New Product Development Game," *Harvard Business Review*, Jan 1986, also in [CW95]

NT95        Nonaka, I., Takeuchi, H., 1995. *The Knowledge-Creating Company*, Oxford University Press

NTI84       Nonaka, I., Takeuchi, H., Imai, H., 1984. "Managing the New Product Development Process: How Japanese Companies Learn and Unlearn," *Harvard Business School 75th Anniversary Colloquium*, also in [HLC85]

Ohno07      Ohno, T., 2007, *Workplace Management*, Gemba Press

Ohno88      Ohno, T., 1988. *The Toyota Production System: Beyond Large-scale Production*, Productivity Press

OK99        Olsson, K., Karlsson E., 1999. *Daily Build. Rapid Development and Control.*,Swedish Engineering Industries

OO00        Olson, G., Olson, J., 2000. "Distance Matters," *Human-Computer Interaction*, Volume 15, September 2000

OST08       Osono, E., Shimizu, N., Takeuchi, H., 2008. *Extreme Toyota: Radical Contradictions That Drive Success at the World's Best Manufacturer*, Wiley

O'Toole77   O'Toole, J., 1977. *Work, Learning, and the American Future*, Jossey-Bass

Owen97      Owen, H., 1997. *Open Space Technology: A User's Guide*, Berrett-Koehler Publishers

Parker02    Parker G. M., 2002. *Cross- Functional Teams: Working with Allies, Enemies, and Other Strangers*, Jossey-Bass

Parkinson57 Parkinson, C., 1957. *Parkinson's Law,* Buccaneer Books

Pfeffer98   Pheffer, J., 1998. "Six Dangerous Myths about Pay," *Harvard Business Review*, May-June 1998

Pfeffer07   Pheffer, J., 2007. *Testimony to Congress about Evidence-Based Practices*, at http://www.evidence-basedmanagement.com/

PMBOK04     Project Management Institute, 2004. *A Guide to the Project Management Body of Knowledge*, Project Management Institute

PMI06       Project Management Institute, 2006. *The Standard for Portfolio Management*, Project Management Institute

Poppendieck03   Poppendieck, M., Poppendieck, T., 2003. *Lean Software Development: An Agile Toolkit for Software Development Managers*, Addison-Wesley

Poppendieck04   Poppendieck, M., 2004. "Unjust Deserts," *Better Software Magazine*, Jul–Aug 2004

Poppendieck06   Poppendieck, M., Poppendieck, T., 2006. *Implementing Lean Software Development: From Concept to Cash*, Addison-Wesley

Prechelt00    Prechelt, L., 2000. draft. "An empirical study of working speed differences between software engineers for various kinds of task," submission to *IEEE Transactions on Software Engineering*, 2000

PS06a    Pfeffer, J., Sutton, R., 2006. "A Matter of Fact," *People Management*, Sep 2006

PS06b    Pfeffer, J., Sutton, R., 2006. "Act on Fact, Not Faith," *Stanford Social Innovation Review,* Spring 2006

PS06c    Pfeffer, J., Sutton, R., 2006. *Hard Facts, Dangerous Half-Truths And Total Nonsense*, Harvard Business School Press

Raymond    Raymond, E. *The Jargon File*. www.catb.org/jargon

Reeves92    Reeves, J., 1992. "What is Software Design?" *C++ Journal*, Fall 1992

Reinertsen83    Reinertsen, D., 1983. "Whodunit? The search for new-product killers," *Electronic Business*, Volume 9, Number 8

Reinertsen97    Reinertsen, D., 1997. *Managing the Design Factory*, Free Press

Robot08    Robot Framework, at http://code.google.com/p/robotframework/

Royce70    Royce, W., 1970. "Managing the Development of Large Software Systems," *Proceedings of IEEE Westcon*

RS99    Rother, M., Shook, J., 1999. *Learning to See: Value Stream Mapping to Add Value and Eliminate Muda*, Lean Enterprise Institute

SB01    Schwaber, K., Beedle, M., 2001. *Agile Software Development with Scrum*, Addison-Wesley

SB08    Sliger, M., Broderick, S., 2008. *The Project Manager's Bridge To Agility*, Addison-Wesley

Schwaber04    Schwaber, K., 2004. *Agile Project Management with Scrum*, Microsoft Press

Schwaber05    Schwaber, K., 2005. *Certified ScrumMaster Course*, version 6.3

Schwaber07    Schwaber, K., 2007. "Scrum Release 2.0?" *Scrum Alliance Articles*, at http://www.scrumalliance.org/articles/12-scrum-release-

Semler95    Semler, R., 1995. *Maverick*, Grand Central Publishing

Semler03    Semler, R., 2003. *The Seven-Day Weekend*, Penguin Books

Senge94    Senge, P., 1994. *The Fifth Discipline*, Doubleday Business

Sherman93    Sherman, S., 1993. "A Brave New Darwinian Workplace," *Fortune Magazine*, Jan 1993

SJS03    Streibel, B., Joiner, B., Scholtes, P., 2003. *The Team Handbook*, Joiner/Oriel Inc

SKRRS94    Senge, P., Kleiner, A., Roberts, C., Ross, R., Smith, B., 1994. *The Fifth Discipline Fieldbook*, Doubleday Business

Smeets07    Smeets, M., 2007. Personal communications and mail to Dutch Agile User Group

| | |
|---|---|
| Smith05 | Smith, P., 2005. "Accelerated Product Development: Techniques and Traps," in [Kahn05] |
| Smith07 | Smith, P., 2007. *Flexible Product Development: Building Agility for Changing Markets*, Jossey-Bass |
| Spolsky04 | Spolsky, J., 2004. *Joel on Software*, Apress |
| Spolsky07 | Spolsky, J., 2007. *Smart and Gets Things Done*, Apress |
| Spolsky08 | Spolsky, J., 2008. *More Joel on Software*, Apress |
| SR98 | Smith, P., Reinertsen, D., 1998. *Developing Products in Half the Time: New Rules, New Tools*, Wiley |
| Stacey07 | Stacey, R., 2007. *Strategic Management and Organisational Dynamics*, Prentice Hall |
| Steinbock02 | Steinbock, D., 2002. *The Nokia Revolution*, AMACOM |
| Sterman00 | Sterman, J., 2000. *Business Dynamics*, McGraw-Hill |
| Sutherland07 | Sutherland, J., 2007. Mail to ScrumTrainer list |
| Sutherland08 | Sutherland, J., 2008. Mail to ScrumTrainer list |
| Taylor11 | Taylor, F. 1911., *The Principle of Scientific Management*, Harper and Brothers Publishers |
| TCKO00 | Teasley, S., Covi, L., Krishnan, M., Olson, J., 2000. "How does Radical Collocation Help a Team Succeed?" *Proceedings of the 2000 ACM Conference on Computer Supported Cooperative Work* |
| TN07 | Tengshe, A., Noble, S., "Establishing the Agile PMO: Managing Variability Across Projects and Portfolios," *Proceedings of Agile 2007 Conference* |
| Toyota01 | Toyota, 2001. *Toyota Way 2001*, Toyota Motor Company |
| Toyota08 | Toyota, 2008. http://www.toyota.co.jp/en/vision/message/ Accessed on 21 Sep 2008 |
| VersionOne08 | VersionOne, 2008. (3rd annual) *The State of Agile Development*, VersionOne, Inc. |
| Vise06 | Vise, D., 2006. *The Google Story*, Delta |
| Vodde07 | Vodde, B., 2007. "Plan of Action: A Technique for Creating Retrospective Actions Tied to Long-term Goals," *Scrum Alliance Articles*, at http://www.scrumalliance.org/articles/61-plan-of-action |
| Ward06 | Ward, A., 2006. *Lean Product and Process Development*, Lean Enterprise Institute |
| WBW91 | Wellins, R., Byham, W., Wilson, J., 1991. *Empowered Teams*, Jossey-Bass |
| Weinberg75 | Weinberg, G., 1975. *An Introduction to General Systems Thinking*, Dorset House |
| Weinberg92 | Weinberg, G., 1992. *Quality Software Management: Systems Thinking*, Dorset House |

Wenger98   Wenger, E., 1998. *Communities of Practice: Learning, Meaning and Identity*, Cambridge University Press

WJR90   Womack, J., Jones, D. T., Roos, D., 1990. *The Machine That Changed the World*, Harper Perennial

WJ96   Womack, J., Jones, D. T., 1996. *Lean Thinking*, Free Press

WS00   Wenger, E., Snyder, W., 2000. "Communities of Practice: The Organizational Frontier," *Harvard Business Review*, Jan 2000

WMS02   Wenger, E., McDermott, R., Snyder, W., 2002. *Cultivating Communities of Practice*, Harvard Business School Press

# INDEX